IN SEARCH OF A SPORRAN

A spirited woman's journey across the world to find it

by

Cynny Sharp

Published 2006 by arima publishing

www.arimapublishing.com

ISBN 1-84549-100-9

Printed and bound in the United Kingdom

Typeset in Garamond 11/16

Swirl is an imprint of arima publishing

arima publishing
ASK House, Northgate Avenue
Bury St Edmunds, Suffolk IP32 6BB
t: (+44) 01284 700321

www.arimapublishing.com

*For my wonderful family, my many old friends and those new ones I made on my way;
for Lilias Bell and her aunt Lady Jean Fforde who introduced us, and for
Saxton Bampfylde Hever.*

Together they changed my life.

To Stephen,
    for giving me
the Chance of a new
beginning.

Cyy my

7th April 2006
Long Framlington

Introduction

At forty-nine years of age, after twenty-three years and seventeen homes as an army wife, I am now on my own.

Some time ago I said to myself that if nothing startling had happened in my life within five years, I would go forth and travel in my fiftieth year. And yet, reaching the end of each month with ingenuity and a clutch of different jobs, from working in an art gallery and taking a lodger to weekend babysitting, editing wartime memoirs, and even life modelling, it remained only a dream.

But dreams can come true - if you make them possible. A small final sum of money from my divorce settlement, a quest for a lost kilt, and a much respected friend saying 'Go for it, girl!' made up my mind . . .

What now follows is my travel journal, and the dream that changed my life.

May 1996, Stockbridge, Hampshire

CONTENTS

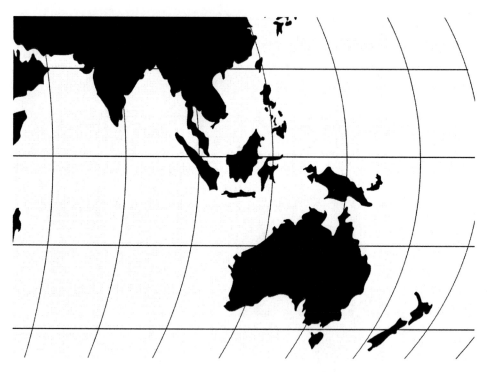

Outgoing journey - Nepal to New Zealand

A FISTFUL OF TICKETS

CARPE DIEM - Seize the day! This has been my motto for seven long months now, having decided, in October 1995 to do something about my life. I mapped out an itinerary, wrote to friends and contacts around the world, let my house, organised inoculations, malaria tablets, Power of Attorney, international driving licence, visas and post restante addresses (sparse email then) . . . and bought . . . a short-wave radio, my favourite scent and a decent umbrella. My many friends were tolerant and disbelieving, but wonderfully generous, when they finally realised I meant business. The Geriatric Backpacker with Style was almost there. And yet, Kathmandu, the River Kwai, Milford Sound, all seemed like distant jewels; would they really be part of my life to come?

The day I left England

Startlingly, the end of May 1996 brought the realisation that my familiar life was being gently shed, like a flower heavy with petals. Giving up the keys to my home, Goose Cottage, was a relief, as without a tenant my plans would never work. Next my gallery key was handed over and a major part of my life, my job, was relinquished - hopefully just for a while. My mother cared for me with tremendous support, disorientated as I was, as the day of departure drew near. My car was left with a friend while other kind souls ferried me up to London, to my twenty-three year old daughter, Gemma. There I slept surrounded by rucksacks and the paraphernalia of the traveller, uncertain as to whether I was elated or sad.

Seven months apart is a long time for a mother and for a daughter. Jasper, my son, flew down from university in Edinburgh and two wonderfully happy days followed. We walked in sunshine across Battersea Park and all ate Sunday brunch together. My children were full of apprehension (whilst trying on my larger rucksack I had fallen over!) and a little sad, but bravely excited for me. Driving to Gatwick I was still disbelieving, following weeks and months of planning this adventure. The young had given me a stout blank journal, some socks, a cassette of haunting music, a bath plug, and a hand-written book of poems. How fortunate I am.

Sunday 2nd June, Gatwick and the moment I parted from Jasper was hard. He hugged me to him tightly, crumpled, and walked swiftly away.

Out of nowhere friends appeared to surprise me, including Bert my Chelsea pensioner friend resplendent in his scarlet uniform - and then I had to go. Hugs for my darling daughter, smiles and kisses all round and I was on my own. On my own with a fistful of round-the-world tickets, a pair of rucksacks, and a plane to catch to Kathmandu. Only then, on the plane, as we raced down the runway towards the Himalayas, did I shed an incredulous tear - and thanked the heavens for this moment . . . my dream begins.

We took off at 8pm, tea was served an hour later and we landed at Frankfurt for a stopover where I brushed my teeth and changed into bed mode, ready for a lengthy sleep; no chance - dinner arrived at half past midnight. During the meal, a Nepalese OAP across the aisle from me had flown into a rage on being presented with his chicken dish and yelled for every stewardess and eventually the Captain, before dumping his supper on the floor. We never discovered his problem, but he was wonderfully theatrical and caused much amusement. Suddenly, dinner over, a kind of musical seats began as seasoned Himalayan travellers made a dash for rows of three adjacent empty seats, lifted the arm rests and lay along the length, making use of the small blue pillows provided. I reclined my seat, but jammed as I was between a monosyllabic couple of uncertain nationality, it wasn't to be a luxurious night. Lights dimmed at last, and I slept fitfully for a couple of hours.

At two-thirty in the morning up went the lights and 'Namaste! Namaste!' cried the pretty Nepalese hostesses - (change of crew at Frankfurt - they were fresh as a daisy). We were told it was now 9am (oriental brain-washing?) as we flew high above the desert to Dubai. It was stunningly beautiful: the sun rose and below lay vast arid plains and mountainous sand dunes with rivers meandering like ribbons between them. Dubai, an expensive city surrounded by wild desert and ugly tanker berths, sported a Harrods-like Duty Free shop; even the departure lounge clock was a highly ornate Omega. Off again, and you could feel the excited anticipation as the last leg of the journey began; later I would come to understand why.

Wednesday 5th June 1996 - Hotel Potala, Kathmandu Nepal; never in my life did I imagine I would have the opportunity and experience of visiting a country so beloved by the British, indeed fabled for her dramatic beauty and gentle people. Kathmandu was twenty-six degrees and sultry but not stifling we were informed, and the crew were applauded with much clapping as we landed. I found my luggage, including a huge black plastic bin liner full of second-hand jumpers and T-shirts to which a blind eye had been turned. My large rucksack alone weighed in at over 30lbs, and my day sack or bergen at 20lbs. I emerged.

Jagdish Rai, an ex-Gurkha and leader of my trek, was there to meet me. A small brown man, beautifully neat and with a smile as broad as a melon - a new friend. Off we drove in a taxi to my hotel, hopefully the one recommended by a friend at home. The room was dark and dingy but had a bathroom and loo, though airless and with no fan. I had arrived. Jagdish had invited me to supper with his family that evening and his son collected me. I only saw his sitting room, comfortable with plush sofas and chairs, and as is the custom we all took off our shoes as we entered. We ate a wonderful Nepalese curry with dhal, spicy hot pickles and lots of jasmine tea. Later that evening they put me in a taxi back to my hotel. The driver had some sort of a nervous twitch, spitting out of the window in unison with his honking horn, about every hundred yards.

During my short walkabout on arrival I had been captivated by the tiny shops lining dirt paths, the fragrance of incense and the many heady spices. Despite the relentless commotion of bicycle bells, hooded three-wheeled scooters looking like motorised sewing machines, taxi horns and porters (carrying sacks, chests-of-drawers or canaries on their heads) there was no annoyance whatsoever; everyone was good-natured and patient. I had also spied another hotel, and on investigation it proved to be the one I had originally meant to stay in - the two names were similar – Potala Guesthouse and Hotel Potala. So next day, rucksacks on front and back again, I moved. My new room was bright with windows on two sides and a view of the roof garden next to my room - a jumble of pots, bamboo, flowers and ferns - and beyond, a magnificent view of the distant mountains surrounding Kathmandu. Showers and loo were shared and basins lined the corridor, dormitory style, but at £1.70 per night I minded not a bit.

Oh! Where do I start? The city is like a medieval film set. The dirt paths criss-cross each other in rabbit warrens of shops, markets, ancient temples, squares and old houses. Cattle, being sacred, lie about here and there, and canaries, chicks and cockerels are safely kept beside the paths under bamboo globes. Everywhere there is noise and merchants shouting their trade. Jagdish took me round the ancient part of the city, where I saw temples to the Monkey God and the Elephant God, some hundreds of years old and cleaned daily by the same families for generations.

Jagdish led me through a very low stone doorway and into a tiny, sunny courtyard shaded by the fern-like canopy of a jasmine tree. Here, in a stone building around the courtyard, lived a young girl; this was the Temple of the Living God. Tradition decrees that a small girl of only four or five is chosen from a particular tribe for this role; she is supposedly possessed of holy powers from birth. A selection test is arranged, whereby the little girl is shut in a room for a while with blood-smeared walls and severed animal heads on the floor. The stench and sight is appalling, and if the girl is not moved and does not cry, she is the chosen one. She is then taken from her family (for whom it is a great honour) and remains in the Temple of the Living God until she is ten or eleven years old, seeing no one but a few servants; very occasionally other children are brought in to play with her. When, at puberty, she is free to go, no one will marry her, as it is bad luck to do so - and the family must care for her thereafter.

Back on the street, different castes sold different wares; on a bridge I saw ten men and women standing by their sewing machines. There were five on each side of the road as if preparing for the start of a race. They were waiting for customers to bring them cloth, which they would then whizz up into garments in the space of six or seven minutes. The Nepalese women and girls are very beautiful, their brilliant saris carefully secured and shown off with jewelled bracelets and they often wore tiny glittering stones in their noses or on their foreheads.

I always felt safe, using common sense, such as never counting my money in public, and wearing my money belt everywhere. I was constantly confronted by merchants keen for me to visit their shops, change money, and buy khukris, Tiger balm or to go to a movie, but I was never touched, and a firm 'no' was enough. The monsoon had just started and when the rain came it poured, but only once or twice a day, and life went on as normal but with hundreds of bobbing black umbrellas atop rickshaws and saris. I went to Pumpernickels, much frequented by back-packers, for breakfast, where grapefruit trees shaded an open area set with bamboo tables. There, for under a pound, I enjoyed banana whole-wheat porridge, freshly whizzed mango juice, and apple strudel. A feast!

One morning I set off to track down a friend, Ava - a cousin of the Queen of Nepal - with whom, when I was married, I had become friendly some years ago in America. Her husband had been the Nepalese Attaché there, and she had replied to my letter from England and looked forward to seeing me. She worked in the Lufthansa office, but was away that day. A friend and colleague of hers, Mrs Bishnu Rana, led me to a nearby restaurant for my lunch, sat down with me and told me much about Nepal. On leaving, after the delicious local fare I had chosen, I found that she had settled my bill. As I returned to my hostel along the Kantipath, the main road leading to the Royal Palace, fox bats hung in rows high up in the trees like dead leaves clinging by a thread and swinging in the breeze over the traffic below. What a humming, happy place, colourful, noisy and utterly fascinating.

NEPALESE FLAT

On Trek

It is Thursday 6th June and Jagdish collected me and my rucksacks by taxi en route to Kathmandu's domestic airport. There, our bags were checked in and he asked me if I'd like to go through a curtain marked 'Ladies' - 'Yes please' I said (always make use of a loo stop). Instead, behind the curtain I found an air hostess, smart but stern in her sari, who asked if I was carrying any Nepalese knives, and if I wanted a smoking or non-smoking seat. I emerged but Jagdish was ages; I have no idea what they asked him. A short wait, and we climbed aboard a marvellous old Avro twin prop plane, which reminded me of old Pathé News film clips. A great throaty noise arose as the propellers started up and we were away. The plane was full of Nepalese families returning home to the hills - groups of shy berry-brown children and wizened grandparents. From my window I could see the high mountains way above the rice paddies, and the straw-roofed houses clinging to the slopes of the foothills. At twenty-two thousand feet the snowy peaks dazzled blindingly in the sun and we were served delicious fizzy lemonade and shortbread biscuits. Twenty minutes later we were in Pokhara, standing around in twenty-eight degrees of sun awaiting our bags. Porters pushed the baggage trolley to the shade of the tree under which we waited, and after Jagdish had checked our trekking permit in a nearby office, we drove off in a taxi.

Trekking is carefully controlled, and there are police checkpoints along the trails so that, hopefully, anyone who gets lost can be tracked. I didn't see much of Pokhara, which has sprung up round a large lake, as we drove up into the hills. On the way, in a wide, stony riverbed, I noticed rickety old buses and cars in the middle of the shallow water. 'Car wash' said Jagdish simply, and indeed it was, the owners sloshing water over the bodywork in a merry fashion. We saw girls in bright saris planting rice - the whole village will lend a hand in turn to each farmer, planting rice in his particular paddy field. This takes on a rather festive air, the girls wearing new dresses and singing; rich farmers might even lay on a band and despite being up to their calves in mud all day, Jagdish told me no one minded.

We reached our destination and met up with our head porter, Gan, who was to carry my large rucksack and generally look after me. The porters are superb; they complain if they have to walk for too long on flat land, preferring a slope and the steeper the better. 'Nepalese flat' according to Jagdish, is about forty-five degrees to us. They carried all our luggage, fuel, food and bedding etc. for eight days. There were six of them and they have been known to carry incredible loads. When a bank was built in a remote hill town, a porter was required to deliver the bank's safe weighing 163kg. One man volunteered, and, asking for extra pay, was readily employed - for £18.00. With a normal load it would have been a three-day trek, whereas he did it in five days.

Our trek began. We started up the hill and were immediately in lush forest up above the rice paddies. It was very easy going, with wide stone steps made of rough-hewn rock. We passed local women collecting firewood with huge cornet-shaped woven baskets on their backs, supported with headbands. There were many butterflies, often yellow and black, and a wonderful arrangement fluttered by, a twin-propeller affair in fluffy, feathery, glossy black plumage with a black and white fan-shaped tail. Jagdish told me they called this one Madam Butterfly. We walked for an hour or so, ever higher, before stopping for an excellent packed lunch of chicken drumsticks, fish paste sandwiches, mango juice and fruit. On again, through sweet chestnut and walnut trees many, many metres high. Along their shady branches were festooned beautiful white orchids with buttery yellow centres, some reaching up along the mossy branches to catch the rain water, others swaying downwards in delicate fronds like tiny butterflies. An enchanting sight, and one we saw constantly for the next few days. Some orchids were wee, some larger in big clumps and often very high up, garlanding the trees. Jagdish had seen these particular ones on sale in England for £5 a root; here they are fed to the cattle!

Jagdish was a wonderfully informative and amusing guide. He told me stories of past treks; of the hugely fat Australian woman who gave up on foot, and when a horse was procured for her, it turned out to be skin and bones. One particular cook was excellent at his job but a useless planner, and had come to Jagdish on the penultimate day of a trek to say there was no more food. Porters were despatched in four or five different directions to walk all night to villages many hours away, to procure sugar and eggs etc. Later on he showed me a fern beside the path, which was extremely strong when dried, and used by the local people as pens, hence the fern's name of Lord Rana's Pen. Up and down we walked, into vast, deep valleys and up, through small villages of mud houses with roofs of slate tiles or thatch. Men ploughed strips eight feet wide with pairs of oxen in tiered paddy-fields ranged up the hillside, the oxen having to turn on a sixpence.

We had half a dozen porters altogether, and after lunch two of them, whom we were due to meet further up the hill, came hurrying down the path towards us. Gan, on instructions from Jagdish, gave them twenty rupees - about thirty pence - and they disappeared past us down the hill. Early that evening they reappeared, having walked for five hours - to buy a kilo of carrots as they had left the original ones behind by mistake in Kathmandu!

The trek was almost indescribable, exceeding anything I had previously dreamed of. As the monsoon was just beginning we stayed in simple teahouses along the trail, rather than under canvas. The teahouses consisted of low wooden or mud-walled buildings, often with a narrow dining area up on stilts to the side. I slept in the most enchanting rooms; one was a tiny, dark room, with mud walls and floor, two beds opposite the door and between them, set into the thick walls, a wooden shuttered unglazed window. I was provided with a thick down sleeping bag, a cotton sleep sheet to put inside it and a little kapok pillow. Very cosy.

As I awoke about five o'clock one morning, I could hear the deep throaty croak of the water buffalo in his stall outside and chickens scuffling below my window, whilst a cuckoo was calling in the valley. We had watched in wonder the previous evening, as the sun set over the snowy peaks far away, beyond us. We could see

Annapurna 2, 3 and 4 - huge, towering mountains, though between them the Fishtail - the Machapuchre - was in cloud. As I opened the shutters early that morning a stunningly breathtaking sight lay before me. The sacred, unconquered Fishtail mountain stood clear and majestic, the rising sun brilliant on its glistening silver slopes. All around me, tier upon tier of paddy-fields rising to a dense forest of walnut and sweet chestnut trees, basked in the early sun. A veil of morning mist lay in the valley below, and the women of the family were drawing water from the tap beneath my window on the flat stones and washing themselves. It was a most moving and peaceful sight, and I sat by my window gazing in silence.

At six o'clock every morning, my porter, Gan (meaning 'wisdom' in Nepalese), brought me a mug of steaming tea and a plate of biscuits. A quarter of an hour later, a bowl of hot water arrived for me to wash in. Shortly afterwards, Jagdish and I were served breakfast, either in an elevated dining area with wonderful views, in a courtyard or at a table on the grass. Honey and marmalade were laid out on a tablecloth, and bowls of porridge and brown sugar were brought, followed by fried eggs, tomatoes and lots of toast and butter, pineapple juice and tea - a feast. Then a quick loo stop (a porcelain bowl set into the ground in a stone shed with two porcelain squares each side, to stand on). Then tooth-brushing (next door to the shed was the 'bathroom' - again, a rough stone floor and a tap and a shower - all cold - and a hole in the floor for drainage) and we were off.

Jagdish walked in front with me following him, and Gan brought up the rear. The other porters would catch us up after clearing breakfast, packing and loading up. They would then go on ahead and prepare a lunch stop. The birds we saw were, for me, the stuff of dreams. Mynah birds, which nest near houses and imitate human voices, and the scarlet Minvet - a little bird the size of a sparrow, a brilliant geranium red, his wife as yellow as a canary. The sight of these pairs, swooping together against the glossy dark green jungle leaves was a glorious sight. High in a tree amongst the orchids I saw a bright blue bird the colour of a summer delphinium - wonderful to see - a verditer flycatcher, flitting hither and thither chasing flies, and then darting back to his favoured perch. The laughing thrush did just that, high in the treetops, and I saw kingfisher-blue Indian rollers, drongos, and a pretty red sunbird. I was in heaven!

Jagdish told me a charming story; his grandmother always planted her seeds according to the migrating birds as, high up in the Everest region where they lived, there were no calendars. Whenever she heard the geese flying over the house from India, on their way to Siberia, sometimes in the middle of the night, she would promptly get up and plant her pumpkin and cucumber seeds which never failed. Jagdish showed me so many plants including nettles for making cloth and a variety of leaf the hillsmen fed to the pigs, called gogglydoo.

Beginning our trek each day at half past seven, we would stop for a break at about ten o'clock and Gan would produce tea from an enormous thermos he carried everywhere, and scrumptious biscuits, and we would rest for a while. As we often climbed two to three thousand feet and six or seven miles in that time, down into huge gorges and valleys, and then high, high up into hilltop villages, the break was very welcome. Once, rounding a bend on a narrow rocky path beside a steep gorge, we came upon two travelling salesmen sitting on enormous boulders, with one giving the other a cut-throat shave! 'Himalayan barber' said Jagdish.

By the time we reached our lunch stop, the porters had laid out a large blue tarpaulin with a karrimat on top - for memsahib (me) - on one occasion beside a river, at the bottom of a deep and very beautiful valley. Jagdish would sit by me, though never on the karrimat. I would loosen or remove my walking boots, and once found a leech had struck on my ankle, inside a bloodstained sock. I hadn't felt a thing and it didn't hurt, but bled for a while. Lunch consisted of tuna and cucumber sandwiches, coleslaw or grated carrot with orange, apple and mayonnaise and chips, all prepared on site by our porters. Afterwards oh joy! - a juicy fresh mango, and Jagdish to cut it for me with his kukri.

Our lunchtime picnics were wonderful, and I feel sure the intrepid Victorian traveller, Lady Hester Stanhope, would have approved. I would then write this journal for a while and we would talk, then on and up again. Jagdish was such a gentle man; finding a small beetle on the path he would turn it over very tenderly with his stick to show me, and then turn it back again to continue on its way. We found several flowering orchid fronds had fallen on the path, complete with leaves and bulbous roots, and Jagdish would pick them up and find a suitable cleft in a tree in which to give them a new home. He showed me huge kapok trees, and magnolia trees from which canoes were fashioned.

Other delicious things were served for lunch: yak cheese sandwiches - very tasty - and chapatis, freshly baked by the porters when the bread ran out. We usually reached our night stop by mid to late afternoon, prices were negotiated, a room was found for me, and water produced. All meals were preceded by my being given a small bowl of warm water in which to wash my hands. Tea and biscuits followed, once I had taken off my boots and put on a dry shirt. Most days I was wringing wet with the exertion.

CEDRIC WITH SAUCE

We climbed over three thousand feet on one day - it was very, very hard work, but wonderfully exhilarating to look back at our lunch stop, now a tiny speck far below us. After my tea, Jagdish would ask the owner of the teahouse for hot water, in order for me to have a 'bath'. 'Cold shower' meant just that, in a shed, whilst 'hot bath' - don't get excited - meant a bucket of hot water and a jug; quite wonderful, and better than any five-star hotel on those high hill tops. Marijuana grew everywhere, often in huge clumps outside the loos for some reason. It's a weed that grows wild in Nepal, the farmers are supposed to dig it up, but don't ever seem to get round to it. Then I would write my journal. Supper, at about half past seven, was always delicious and how the porters magically produced what they did, on a kerosene stove, I have no idea. Chicken joints in spicy sauce, roast potatoes, chicken curry, fern stew (we picked them as we walked and very good they were), banana and apple fritters, rice pudding and banana bread - all made from scratch.

A lunch stop on trek, Nepal

On one occasion we had bright orange 'blackberries' - again picked beside our path - with custard, yum. After supper I would drink a little whisky with Jagdish and one night he shared the bottle I had given him with a nice old ex-Gurkha soldier in the remote teahouse where we were staying; they swapped war stories for hours. The porters were aged between twenty and forty. One of them had nine children; beginning one every time he returned home from a trek. Jagdish said his wife now had 'the pills'. Another had fought off a bear single-handed near Everest, knifed it across the face, and survived.

The tiny Nepalese houses were very basic indeed. Made of wood, bamboo and sometimes brick, they were single storied, devoid of furniture and with mud walls and floors. The families sat on rush matting and laid thick homespun woollen blankets down to sleep under. They made everything themselves and were totally self-sufficient, cut off as they were high up in the hills. Travelling salesmen ('travelling businessmen' as Jagdish called them) walked in flip-flops from village to village, selling food and provisions, but many of the hill people didn't use money, so never bought anything. And yet, a peep inside the almost completely dark interior of the little houses would reveal shelves of immaculately shiny metal mugs, plates and cutlery. I took photographs of one house outside which rush 'umbrellas' were being woven, as well as mats for roofing and for drying corn on. I gave the six village children a balloon each and they had wonderful fun blowing them up. A chicken roosting in the eaves above where Jagdish, Gan and I were having a tea break, laid an egg and made a hell of a celebratory din. Only then did we discover an ailing grandmother lying on a rush mat behind a curtain right beside us. She called from her sickbed to the children to ask us if there was anything we needed - water, or cushions. What touching kindness.

Another time, in the middle of the path, we found a witch doctor's offering, to spirit away evil demons from a sick person in a nearby house. A little cotton flag secured on a stick and beside it, nestling in overlapping banana leaves, a clay effigy sprouting feathers, and the fresh entrails and heart of a chicken. I had to pinch myself to remember it was 1996. I saw more wonderful birds: a beautiful glossy black and white shrike, and a long-beaked sunbird – orange, red and brilliant emerald green. Huge crested serpent eagles soared effortlessly thousands of feet above the valley floor, so called as snakes literally freeze in terror when they swoop down, enabling an easy catch.

We often passed groups of children in the mountains, all impossibly dressed in smart school uniform, with little bags, flip-flops, and umbrellas. Children attend school from the age of five until they are seven or eight. They are by then quite often the most learned members of the village, but, needed for work in the fields or house, they are discouraged from continuing school - there seems no point in their being educated further, and one can understand why. Once, a small boy in a giggling group on their way to school, handed me a beautiful pink crocus-like flower, with a cheery 'Hello!' in English.

We passed under clouds of wild roses, covering the treetops; Chinese roses, creamy white with pink centres and so pretty - while the butterflies...! Either huge and brilliant or exquisitely tiny they soared past us in all manner of shapes, yellow and black or bright blue, some beautifully delicate, the palest blue and pink, floating like bubbles of chiffon in the breeze. Butterflies in Nepal don't flutter by, but drift and float, amazingly high in the warm air, above gorges, forests and hillsides. I gasped with joy, every time I saw one. As my family know, I am given to heart-stopping shrieks and yells, if I spy a wonderful bird, flower or tree; I am not sure

Jagdish and Gan would have lasted much longer if I had been on an extended trek - although we were usually very Gurkha-like and stealthy if we saw something of particular interest.

Umbrellas! These bastions of our civilisation are a part of every Nepali's wardrobe, be he a poor peasant or a businessman. When the monsoon rains come it is often not cold at all, thus an umbrella is all that is needed. I was continually bemused by coming across very simple people, literally scratching a living from a tiny rice paddy, marching off down a path in rags, barefoot and carrying an umbrella. Few umbrellas were coloured, most were black and the only time they were not employed in the rain was while farmers worked in the fields, when an ingenious, woven, half moon shaped rush contraption was used over the head, leaving both hands free to plant and weed.

I asked Jagdish all about provisioning for trekking and the oddest thing I learnt was that on a long trek with many people, walking at high altitude, the porters would buy a few live chickens before setting out, and then kill one for the table every few days. The last one was left until the high peaks, when it developed altitude sickness, then this one too met its doom; this system was the best way to keep meat fresh.

Day 5 – Monday 10th June.

Up to now I have been frantically trying to catch up with this journal, recording the kaleidoscope of things I have seen and done since arriving in Kathmandu. Today at last I am back in step. I awoke this morning to find the Fishtail Mountain briefly visible in the mist, at about half past five. We breakfasted in a small lookout bower, up some steep steps - a wooden, glass-sided structure for viewing Annapurna South and the sacred Fishtail. Porridge and honey, boiled eggs, chapatis and tea were brought by the porters. After breakfast, Jagdish took me into the family kitchen in the teahouse to show me an ancient brass and wooden tube some three feet high, in which yak butter tea was made. Water, milk, yak butter, salt and tea are placed in the deep container, mashed with a wooden plunger until thick, and then heated over the fire. The kitchen was small and very dark, and, with her permission I photographed the woman of the house at her open mud oven, stirring pans.

Off we went that morning, at half past seven. I have found, interestingly enough, that the most comfortable thing in which to trek is a flimsy mid-length cotton skirt bought for a pound in Kathmandu. My expensive and highly recommended trekking trousers bought in England were most uncomfortable, and walking uphill at an angle of fifty-five degrees in ninety-degree heat they stuck to my legs giving little freedom of movement. My thin blue zipped thermal top is super; you perspire like mad and yet it keeps you completely dry. I didn't bother with a hat, whilst short, thick socks and stout walking boots completed the picture.

That morning we saw beautiful little pink orchids growing straight out of mossy green tree trunks, white anemones and the delicate pink flowers of wild ginger. At nine thousand feet it began to rain and Gan put a huge transparent plastic bag over most of himself and my rucksack, which he was carrying, whilst Jagdish and I put up our umbrellas. We climbed up through low cloud and rhododendron forests making for a ridge, and crossed many tree trunk and plank bridges over rivers and streams.

We had tea by a river at mid-morning and I saw several water birds - river chats, and on the rocks pretty, curtseying dippers. Jagdish was a star, producing excellent flower and bird books on numerous occasions, from which we would identify a particular bird or an orchid. Suddenly we all stopped; he had spied a pika, a little animal looking like a furry brown hamster, which lives in the rocks. Tail-less and with rabbit ears, it sat eating grass and preening its long whiskers - 'Yeti Food' the Nepalese call it - they say the Yeti eats them.

We had to be rather careful not to slip on water buffalo droppings - very loose at this time of year, due to a lot of water in the grass I was told; I did manage to step in one or two. After a mammoth climb up a very steep path with tree roots acting as steps, we clambered over a ledge and there was lunch and my mat spread out for me. I would take the opportunity to dry my washed clothes in the midday sun taking care to hang my underwear out of sight of the porters. We had excellent fried potato cakes that day, with chilli sauce, salad, very good Malaysian baked beans and huge fresh mangoes. I sat in the shade with Jagdish and felt very spoilt. On again, and at last, about an hour and a half later, in mist, we reached the ridge at eleven thousand feet. It rained a bit but it was warm and fresh. All around us grew tiny yellow, mauve and white alpine blooms, flowering viburnum and late, brilliant pink rhododendrons. It was so beautiful. Here there were fir trees, lime green on one side of the needle and silver on the other and very pretty.

In a thick bamboo grove, Gan collected and peeled bamboo shoots for our supper. We planned to have fern curry, bamboo shoots with fenugreek and other delicious things. Later that afternoon we reached Ghorepani, the highest point, quite a big village with a large school, many lodges and even an international telephone line, although it only worked spasmodically, oh, and electricity. I was found a bedroom in a mud and wooden house (no electricity here) directly facing vast hills below, now in cloud, and the eighth highest mountain in the world called Dhaulagiri, at eight thousand metres. Fleetingly seeing the mountains, which in the next second would disappear, was just like attending an extraordinary theatre. The cloud obscured them (Jagdish said they were being painted for me!) and then suddenly, at the crack of dawn before the sun rose, there they were. The misty morning cloud evaporated and the peaks towered majestically, awe-inspiring, vast and snowy, right there in front of me. It was absolutely breathtaking.

Day 6 – Tuesday 11th June

I was awoken at four o'clock as planned, but our hoped for walk up nearby Poon Hill to watch the sun rise over the huge mountain range before us was not to be. Jagdish, Gan and I had a discussion in the thick, damp fog, and all went back to bed. After a supper of bamboo shoots, which we had picked, mustard greens (a species of kale) rice, dhal and a fermented cabbage pickle, I had had fireworks on the loo at two o'clock in the morning. My loo was right next door to the porters' quarters - most embarrassing - and they all seemed to be smiling at me next morning! After a late breakfast of porridge, fried egg, tomato and a pancake, I wrote my journal at a table outside, high above the village; we planned to stay until lunch time hoping the cloud would clear. Sadly it didn't, but much made up for it that day.

We began our journey down the mountain through jungle thick with vast oak trees, mahonia, daphne (from which writing paper is made) and chestnut. I saw the most beautifully colourful bird - out with the book to identify an orange-bellied leaf bird. I so loved all the birds. A golden-breasted tit babbler swooped down and early that morning I had again been woken by a laughing thrush, cackling away to greet the dawn. Rounding a corner, in a thick bamboo grove, we came upon a very large monkey. He sat up a tree and watched us watching him. He had wonderfully thick cocoa brown fur with a creamy ruff round his face, a pale tummy and a very long tail. They are very destructive animals, and will sometimes attack a lone walker. I was told that women on their own have been raped by monkeys in the jungle - a horrific thought.

We saw mule trains on our path far, far below (we descended over five thousand feet that day) and Jagdish told me the down trains travel in the morning and the up trains in the afternoon, carrying grain and other provisions to and from Tibet. At a resting place in a small village, we found a chicken seller with a pair of tiered bamboo cages full of white chickens for sale. After some bartering, poor unfortunate Cedric (for that is what I christened him) was weighed and the deal was struck. Thus began a lively and at times noisy descent of the mountain by way of the well-known thousand steps from the village of Ulleri. (It is said there are over three and a half thousand stone steps down the mountain but I am afraid I neglected to count them all.) We were on the main Pokhara - Tibet route, and for the first time passed a few European trekkers ascending the path.

As we walked we discussed sauces and methods of producing tasty chicken dishes while poor Cedric became more and more voluble. In truth, Jagdish said, it was because as we descended from the relative cool of the mountain where we had purchased our supper, so it became warmer, and Cedric livelier. Gan carried him tenderly under one arm, the chicken's legs tied together with string. Later we passed through dense green jungle and from our mysteriously dark path I suddenly caught the most wonderfully fragrant perfume. Glancing round, I spied several very tall stems of white Madonna lilies, growing just above the path. Virginal and elegant, we came across many more, perfuming the deep, green jungle as if it were a heavenly garden.

As we walked, Jagdish would talk to me about all sorts of things. Occasionally I would correct his excellent English, at his request, but one word he often used and which I found most endearing (and unwilling to correct!) was 'fliming' rather than filming. He often took BBC camera crews to the area we'd been in and told me of their exploits. We descended five thousand feet down steps that afternoon, and definitely needed our lunch of bamboo shoots, spicy samosas, puffy pouri - deep fried puffy balls - and potato curry. It was exhausting, and the thermos of tea brought to us by the porters on our arrival at the little village of Tirkhedhunga, was nectar. Soon afterwards I had a real hot shower: 'Solar Power Shower' read the sign, which was almost true, less the 'power'.

The villages were now quite different to the tiny homesteads we had seen on our way up. They were literally built around these long, long steps, which wound in zigzags for miles down the mountainside. We could see into family kitchens, chicken runs, buffalo stalls and dark little bars as we passed. There were frequent resting places, called chautara, built as a large oblong block of stones, perhaps six or seven feet long with a smaller block on top, so that you could rest your pack on the higher ledge and sit on the lower one. I dug in my rucksack for balloons to give to a few children and quite suddenly, as Jagdish had warned me, many more came tumbling out of their houses and running up the steps to where we rested (with Cedric lying on the ground, legs tied and asleep) to plead for them, tiny hands clasped together and fingertips touching in the Nepalese greeting 'Namaste'. My balloons were soon gone and much enjoyed.

Day 7 – Wednesday 12th June

Poor Cedric was delicious, with sauce and lots of wonderful vegetables and rice. And for pudding, a chocolate cake for me as a surprise, with a delicate flower on top, traced in egg white - what an amazing culinary achievement! As I write, it is ten to one local time and I am sitting in hot sunshine beside a wide and rocky river. The hills rise hundreds of feet from both banks, and we are having a last picnic on a flat, grassy patch just above the rushing water. I have paddled and thanked the stars for all this; it is so utterly glorious, and I really don't feel I deserve it. Five porters are cooking my lunch and I have just been brought water to wash my hands in. We have had such a happy and fascinating last morning.

After a noisy night in a little wooden room high above the jungle in the teeth of the monsoon - a row of rooms on stilts with a verandah - the air was fresh and everything in sight was dripping and steaming. The monsoon had shown its full force last night with deafening, torrential rain and lightning - it was pretty exciting. The banana trees and bamboo below my room swayed and bowed in the downpour - oh, and my bedroom roof was made of corrugated iron! When I awoke at half past five in the morning, I found every ant in the Himalayas was sheltering in my bedroom.

We enjoyed an excellent breakfast of eggs and tomatoes, sausages and pancakes, in full view of the whole village. The dining area was rather like a public open-sided beach bar, which I found rather embarrassing. The porters laid a cloth as usual, brought me a bowl of water to wash my hands in and waited on Jagdish and me lovingly, under the intense gaze of a few local villagers. Afterwards, the millions of cicadas began their chorus as we started downhill on our final leg. We trekked down through a wonderfully lush river valley and once again I saw so much; cardamom growing beneath the mandarin trees, a lemon grove, turmeric bushes, small lime trees, flowering coffee bushes covered in tiny, white sweet-smelling stars, and pineapples growing under guava trees. It was really exciting to see all these fruits and spices - familiar in their packaging at the grocers at home - growing naturally in that wet and sunny valley in Nepal. On a corner above our stony path, I noticed an immensely tall tree perched on a ledge overhanging the river below. Swinging from the branches were strings of beautiful heart-shaped leaves, fresh green on one side and ruby red on the other. Like some wonderful glass necklace they swayed in the air above the valley, translucent against the bright sun.

And so, these magical days came to an end. I had learned much about Nepal from Jagdish, the last fascinating fact being that above nine thousand feet, the women have to use pressure cookers otherwise nothing boils properly. Our route: Pokhara, Dhampus, Landrung, Chomrong, Tadapani, Ghorepani, Ulleri, Tirkhedhunga, Birethanti, Lumle, Ndudanda and back to Pokhara.

PRAYERS FOR A SON

<u>Day 8 – Thursday 13th June</u>

We spent one last day en route back to Kathmandu. Jagdish and I took a taxi back to Pokhara, while the porters went ahead by bus. Our journey proved to be the hairiest imaginable, forty kilometres down a road built by the Chinese, with wide, smooth tarmac. If our driver overtook another vehicle and the road ran out width-wise, he just accelerated into the ditch and out again. Windows with handles missing were opened by means of a spanner in the glove box. We made it, praise be to God, Buddha, Allah et al and spent the night in a Pokhara hotel owned by a friend of Jagdish's, a kindly ex-Gurkha sergeant. All went well as he tripped over his many 'memsahibs' to me and informed me I was 'The most upper class lady I've ever had to stay'! I was given a comfortable room with views of the now distant mountains and a proper loo and bath. I was interested to learn that he had sent his two daughters, aged eight and ten, to stay in a nearby hostel and that they went to school from there, only returning home once a month. There was too much disruption in the hotel, he explained.

To produce only daughters is a disappointment in Nepal, and while we were in the hotel, the local Lama arrived with his retinue and proceeded to transform one of the hotel reception rooms into the most extraordinary shrine. Symbolic and brilliantly colourful, a row of tables displayed a mass of flowers, icons, and effigies, many with rupee notes stuck into them as offerings. The Lama was well fed and watered for three days; all this was in order to pray for a son. If, at a later date, none appeared, the hotel owner would be expected to take a second wife and either keep both, or divorce the first. I discussed this at length - sensitively I hope - with Jagdish; it is the custom here, and we must respect that. We had curried goat (castrated, I was told) for supper that evening, bony but tasting excellent.

The next morning we flew back to Kathmandu into thirty-four degree heat. Jagdish and I drove to his home and his family welcomed me so warmly. I sent faxes from Jagdish's office (little email then) to my mother and to the trekking company in England, praising it to the skies. Half an hour later my mother sent me one. How lovely, and there were letters from my son and a friend awaiting me; I had such a happy evening, reading them.

Jagdish and I became good friends. He commended me on my fitness and said I could quite easily manage a trek to ABC - Annapurna Base Camp or to the Everest Base Camp. We'll see. . I SHALL RETURN TO THESE MOUNTAINS ONE DAY, I PROMISE MYSELF.

OLD FRIENDS, NEW FRIENDS

<u>Friday 14th June</u>
Jagdish collected me from my hotel and we drove for miles through Kathmandu in a taxi to meet his 'Uncle' the celebrated Nepalese painter, Lain Bangdel. His house was large and cool and he was a charming man in his seventies, with a very beautiful wife. I liked his figurative oil paintings very much; they sold for many thousands of dollars in America. He also wrote and taught. Awarded a KCVO (Knight Commander of the Royal Victorian Order) in 1986, Prince Charles comes to as many of his exhibitions as he can - perhaps we could entice Mr Bangdel over to the gallery in Stockbridge.

Mr Bangdel was a fascinating man, reminding me very much of another wise and gentle man, Laurens Van der Post who was very close to Prince Charles, and who I had met a few times in my twenties. After we left, we negotiated the main Post Office - seething was the word, with all human life - where I went to the 'Mail Cancellation' counter. You had to personally witness your letters being franked to be sure they would reach their destinations. Then I checked 'S' in the Post Restante office; there were over three hundred letters from all over the world, to travellers with surnames beginning with 'S'. It proved very interesting indeed, sifting through addressees' names such as 'Suki light of me live Kashawa' and 'Andy sex-job Gray' . . . under 'S' for some reason.

I then walked to the Royal Palace in Durbar Square, no longer used but a most impressive building. The various rooms gave 'Intimate glimpses of Royal Life', and included weapons and photographs of royal visits to foreign towns. Some of the written English was amusing; pinned next to a portrait of the last King aged nine in an impossibly smart suit, was a sign 'The look of innocence and deep sense betokens the Royal career'. Photographic records of overseas forays (depicting hunting parties etc) were entitled 'Scenes from his multi-faceted life' and a poem commemorating the King's birthday began 'Our beloved King Mahendra, whose message flush around . . .'. His watches were exquisite, saddles and howdahs sumptuous, the shirts worn at his Coronation made by Tootal and his monogrammed bicycle, a Raleigh, made in England.

On the way back to my hostel I bought three pounds of huge mangoes for less than a pound, for breakfasts in my room. I went to bed very early as the heat (it was ninety four degrees that day) had sapped my energy.

<u>Saturday 15th June</u>
Well, I have been on this adventure for just two weeks, and yet it seems far longer. How do I feel? Very happy, very grateful and very relaxed. I suppose keeping healthy is my top priority. Feeling well, energetic and bubbly is paramount, the more so as I am on my own. I buy bottled water, avoid salads and eat at the many recommended cafés and restaurants. The small, loving presents, given to me by my

very many friends on departing, and often used, bring to mind the encouragement and incredulous enthusiasm with which I was launched by them all. I am very confident, never over-confident though, I do enjoy being on my own and I never seem to feel lonely. At the moment, there are two lots of people asking me to visit them here, and I shall do so when I am fully rested; the trek was physically demanding, and I am so pleased that my feet, my back and my head worked well together.

The knowledge of the life I shall return to is constantly with me. My happy home, wonderful family and galaxy of friends are priceless, but life is in a way, a gilded cage. There are restrictions on my time away, due to the demands of my job and limitations that lack of money obviously imposes. So, there are very, very strong reasons for me to soak up, bask in and experience totally, everyone and everything that comes my way. This is a chance of a lifetime, perhaps never to be repeated and I am so aware of this. Peculiarly I don't feel as far away as my family feel I am, and loving letters and poems given to me by my children on my departure, full of encouragement and admiration - hardly deserved, but welcome - help to ease the pain. I miss my family very much. My responsibilities here are very few, so surely I cannot fail to soar happily across the world.

<u>Sunday 16th June</u>

I was quietly sewing a Nepalese badge on to my rucksack at about half past seven last night, when there was a knock at my door. I had planned an early night, having eaten a mango in my room after a chicken lunch in mid-afternoon. There was Jagdish, who had come to check up that I 'was okay' and also to check that I had received my cleaned walking boots and two faxes, from my brother Hugh and from Jasper (it's wonderful hearing from everyone) via his sons earlier that day. He hovered, and so I asked if he would like a drink, and in the end we walked down to Rum Doodles, the mountaineers' haunt nearby. After a large bottle (shared) of Carlsberg, he treated me to a splendid steak - and shared another beer. I asked him about one or two sensitive subjects, about the many men you see in Kathmandu holding hands (nothing in it, it is just a friendly gesture he told me) and about arranged marriages. We heard a crowd roaring in another bar down the street, and later found out they were watching England v Scotland in the World Cup; England won, two nil.

This morning, I joined a tour of the city laid on by Jagdish for a team of regular and Territorial Army soldiers who had arrived from England the previous night for a trek. They are rather coarse and disrespectful, but very funny. Our guide, Sunil, introduced himself, 'Two nil, two nil' they chanted, at the only Scotsman in the group. Sunil then told us we would first visit the largest Stupa (Buddhist tomb) in the world 'yeah, telling me he was in a stupor!' someone shouted; it got worse. They weren't madly interested in anything until we reached the riverside Shiva Hindu temple some time later, the site of all cremations in Kathmandu. A corpse was prepared by the water, rhesus monkeys splashed about and logs were being piled up.

Words such as 'barbecue' were bandied about. I found the cremation fascinating; it somehow seemed quite natural and didn't worry me. Hindus believe we are made up of five elements: earth, wind, fire, sky and water and though our bodies die, our souls do not and they are reborn many times.

Tomorrow I am off to a school in Bhaktapur, the medieval city where 'The Little Buddha' was filmed, to meet a friend of a friend.

<u>Monday 17th June</u>

Last night in a small restaurant, I fell into conversation with two English girls who had been to school in Salisbury, and lived near me in Hampshire. They were very helpful, having done the reverse trip to me, and told me much about Thailand, Bali and New Zealand. Information like this is invaluable, being current and first-hand.

Today I rang Gemma and Jasper, for three minutes each, which cost twelve pounds and well worth it. I would rather save money in some other way, as we all need to talk to each other. Later, I took a taxi to the Kathmandu bus station from where I caught a trolley bus to Bhaktapur. What an experience. Three quarters of an hour on a high voltage vibrator. I had been warned by Nepalese friends about the discomfort, smell and pickpockets, but Biju the school headmaster's son whom I was to visit, had said it would be fine and it was. The other passengers smiled and seemed interested but soon got used to me sitting there. The trick is to look quite confident and not to make eye contact, but just to smile benignly. It was filthy, fumy and smelly but at only four rupees as against three hundred for a taxi, well worth it. Biju, a young, good-looking man, met me and we walked up dingy side streets to Springdale English Secondary Boarding School.

Springdale English Secondary Boarding School, Bhaktapur, Nepal

Housed in earth-floored buildings, three hundred pupils aged from three to eight were schooled in every subject. The pupils included over twenty handicapped children, who would have had to have been disregarded by their families, if they had stayed at home. The staff of eight were totally dedicated, working a six and a half day week. The children's manners were charming, and I read and talked to them for a short while. They needed more large floor puzzles and picture blocks and simple story books, so I promised to try and muster some when I returned to England. They were awaiting more English girls who were coming out to teach through the GAP organisation and were desperately needed. What a wonderful school!

Later, Biju took me into the old part of the city. It is even more breathtaking than Kathmandu, with stupendously beautiful twelfth to seventeenth century palaces, courtyards and temples. Pagodas originated in Nepal in the thirteenth century and the designs were then taken to China and Thailand. The streets were extremely narrow, with intricate wooden carvings on many of the buildings. Everywhere you turned there were bells, spice markets, beautiful twelfth century tiled houses, ancient artefacts, wells, and gold spires atop the roofs. A camera was almost useless. Biju bought me a Sprite and remarked 'Sorry, no pipes' (straws) and we sat up inside a temple at one of the carved windows and watched the square below. The spectacular Five-Tiered Temple is world famous and I took many photographs. On our way back to his house, Biju treated me to a tiny terracotta potful of 'Bhaktapur curd', which was absolutely scrumptious. Rather like sweetish, lemony, spiced yoghurt, it was one of the most delicious local delicacies I had tasted.

His family asked me to stay for supper in their very old, narrow, seven storied house. Just as we sat on cushions arranged in a circle on the floor to eat, the monsoon raged again, and all the lights went out. We then proceeded with a happy candlelit supper consisting of several different curries and that gorgeous curd again. Afterwards, in pitch darkness, Biju escorted me on a hair-raising half-hour walk with a weak torch through the monsoon, avoiding a river, potholes, animal mess and fleets of rickshaws. We waved the last trolley bus back to Kathmandu to a halt in the middle of the road and on I jumped. Wow! It vibrated so much that my teeth chattered and I couldn't read any of the road signs. Most of the (all male) passengers were asleep, and those that weren't soon ignored me. The journey was very hairy as we skidded throughout the monsoon downpour, with the bus's hydraulic doors on the blink, opening and shutting every thirty seconds as the bus lurched onwards, trapping the occasional unwary passenger.

Tuesday 18th June

This morning I decided to take a rickshaw to Mike's Breakfast, some distance away. I bartered like mad with the bicycle rickshaw man which he loved, and I am getting quite good at it. I had a delicious breakfast at the American-owned café, of scrambled egg with mushrooms, cheese and spinach mixed into it and two huge muffins spread liberally with mango jam and butter. This feast lasted me until seven o'clock in the evening. Mike's Breakfast is well known amongst visitors and a very colourful place, with tables set round a pond in the garden of a pretty house amongst beautiful trees and flowers. I ordered iced coffee, because it looked so good, and, with Mozart playing gently through speakers in the trees it seemed impossibly peaceful for Kathmandu.

Once finished and back into the din of traffic I made my way to the Post Office once more. This is housed in a large dark building and I have now got the hang of what you do. To merely post letters, you approach a special counter and watch them being franked; to send large envelopes, you go to one counter to have them weighed, another for stamps and back to the franking dept; then you tackle the Post Restante. There are usually about two hundred and fifty 'S' letters to sort through. There is an ancient overhead fan and I grab the only stool, so it is not too bad. Yesterday I found two letters addressed to a name I recognised so I wrote a message on the back of one them saying 'I think your parents know...' (and the names of friends of mine) 'Please send them my love' and signed my name. The names and the stamps are fascinating, with letters arriving from every country imaginable. 'Andy Sex king Sutherland' this time and 'Steven Ra Ra Saska' and 'Jo Angel Beloved Sutton'.

A restful morning followed, writing more letters in the roof garden next to my room. I have got the laundry sorted out. I wash undies each evening in the shower and they dry overnight in my room, under the fan. My shoes are all excellent - the Sebago deck shoes for every day and the ungainly but wonderful Terradactyl sandals for the shower and the monsoon. I will take my walking boots to Chitwan for the jungle treks and elephant rides - dear Jagdish has washed them for me. Skirts I wash in the shower too, and larger things are laundered by the hotel very well and cheaply.

Wednesday 19th June

Most of today was taken up with postcard writing and with having another superb curry lunch with Jagdish, Joymit and Philemon Rai. What a spread they laid on for me; I felt very spoilt. I showed them all my photos which they thought were good, and Jagdish loved the one of me and my high altitude lunch. They offered to send a fax home for me, too good an opportunity to miss, so I scribbled one out. Later in my hostel I had a briefing from the Tiger Temple tour man and I was given my air tickets for my jungle adventure, which sounds wonderful.

Thursday 20th June

Realising I hadn't taken many photos of Kathmandu, I ate a hearty breakfast - iced coffee, cheese and tomato omelette, toast and jam - which lasted me the entire day. I then set off with camera and brolly to the Old Quarter. It is an amazing city . . . the photos will tell all. One of the many painted Holy Men hailed me - our paths keep crossing - the idea is that you take his photo in exchange for money – ten rupees is the going rate. I offered him three rupees, which we both laughed about, but when he realised I was deadly serious, he relented and is now on film. The heart of Kathmandu is such a small place and you begin to recognise faces after a while. I took a rickshaw to the Yak and Yeti Hotel, just to see how the other half live. Very smart, air-conditioned and full of bejewelled, roly-poly Indians; the rounder you are, the wealthier you are in this part of the world. I ordered iced tea and sat on a huge sofa, watching - rather longingly, I must admit - more rotund Indians wallowing about in a gorgeous pool. It was extremely hot outside. After drinking a revolting concoction somewhat akin to orange juice and marmite, I attempted to pay. This took fifteen minutes and I was not impressed.

I walked about two miles back to my dear little Hotel Potala, refreshed and happy I was not rich enough to be a Yak and Yeti guest. Philemon was there (Jagdish's younger son) with faxes for me from my mother and brother, Hugh, oh, how lovely! I showered and tried to look smart for a supper invitation to my friends, the Shah's. Difficult. It is so hot, and ten minutes after you have changed and made yourself look beautiful (relative term) you end up shiny and sticky again. Sadip Shah's brother collected me in a Land Rover, which madly impressed the local night hawkers.

My friends live in an enormous house, and it was an excellent evening. Their son Dipta at nineteen and a half, looked very much the same as he had at nine, when we had first met the family ten years before while all living in Washington DC. I met several Jesuit Fathers, also supper guests, who teach at St Xavier's School here in Kathmandu and arrange further education for their pupils all over the globe at United World Colleges. UWC is a global education movement bringing together students selected on merit from across the world. The Fathers were most interesting and two of them, Father Brooks and Father Francis had lived in Nepal for twenty-three and forty-seven years respectively. I learn so much at these gatherings. There were also ten of Dipta's Nepalese classmates there, now studying as far afield as Italy and Hong Kong. Sadip, his father, commands the 10th Brigade, a crack Commando Brigade, and Ava his pretty wife, told me he had been called away on urgent business. He returned in due course. Ava gave me such an affectionate welcome and we chatted like very old, close friends. She produced photos of my son Jasper and Dipta in America playing together aged nine and eleven. Dipta was home from New Mexico where he is studying English, Physics and Music.

The problems with this distant education are twofold: firstly, only sixty per cent of these students finally return home to Nepal (it used to be eighty per cent) and secondly, if they do return, the resident businessmen can make life rather difficult for them. Many of these are wealthy Indians, some are Nepali-educated locals, and all are I suppose, envious and suspicious of the education the United World Colleges offer (although selection is very much on merit, not financial status) after the schooling at St Xavier's private school in Kathmandu. It was wonderful to see Ava again after so long, and we had a good talk. She was clearly upset that after only five weeks of his three month annual holiday, Dipta had decided to return to America. I assured her it was quite normal - he had seen his parents, his motorbike and his friends and now wanted to return to America and earn some money. Ava wants me to have lunch with her next week.

CHUMPUKALEE

<u>Friday 21st June</u>

It was a good thing I rose early - Jagdish knocked at my door at half past seven with a fax from Gemma. He joined me for breakfast and then we said our goodbyes. He asked me if I would send him a catalogue from the firm Cotswold Camping and details of coach tours round Europe, and of course I will oblige as soon as I get home.

Later that morning I was sitting in a small twenty-seater plane, being offered cotton wool and sweets by the stewardess. We had an easy flight to Bharatpur over the hills of Nepal. Below us, they looked like a jigsaw puzzle with tiny pieces, each wiggly join a deep river valley or gorge, and each piece a high hill. The Tiger Temple naturalist was there to meet me on arrival and we piled into a Harrison Ford jeep minus doors, and roared off. The heavens opened up, and it was an exciting drive, minus windscreen wipers, some twelve kilometres to a wide river. On the way, we passed sprawling villages alongside a good tarmac road, and I saw barrows piled high with pineapples, watermelons, cucumbers and children. We crossed two rivers and drove through a ford before turning off the main road. My naturalist friend was a rather uninspiring young man from Darjeeling called Jigmy. He was a fan of Gary Lineker's and we discussed his career, footwork and reputation for some time; my son would have been proud of me. Off the main road we were almost immediately on the outskirts of the jungle. Tiny huts with rough straw roofs were dotted here and there by the bumpy track and eventually we came to a very wide river.

Out of the jeep we leapt and into a saalwood dugout canoe; immediately I spotted a crocodile in the water . . . .The current was very strong indeed, but Footy Fan and I were ferried skilfully across, to where another old battered jeep, this time cut off all round at elbow level, was waiting. The river forms the boundary of the Royal Chitwan National Park and I was welcomed, as I stepped ashore, by some of the Park staff, with orange juice and a cool, damp towel. (Not a lot of initiative here, as it was raining hard and quite chilly). We drove for five miles through high elephant grass to the Tiger Temple Lodge itself where I was to stay. What an amazing place! A vast circular straw-roofed, open-sided hut, served as dining room, sitting room and meeting place. Surrounding it, beautifully sited in the jungle, were small, pretty wooden lodges on stilts, with bamboo walls and thatched roofs. After a scrumptious Nepalese lunch, I was taken to my lodge. It was tastefully furnished with twin beds, a small sofa and coffee table, a tiny verandah at the front, on which were a chair and table and, beyond my bedroom, a flush loo, decent basin and an excellent (cold) shower. It was gorgeous. The jungle grew all around and over each lodge.

A little later I was accompanied on an elephant ride. The two huge animals were backed up to a high platform from where Jigmy and I sprung aboard our separate chargers. Thus ensued a fascinating two hours swaying through twenty-foot high elephant grass, thick jungle and swamp. Much against my instincts, but on dear

Jagdish's advice, I slipped my elephant driver thirty rupees (about forty pence) and whispered 'tiger', into his left ear. If you do this at the beginning of your stay Jagdish told me, the driver will try a little bit harder to spot the elusive Bengal tiger.

We saw five groups of one-horned rhino that afternoon, eight in all, including a baby. It was wonderful to see them so close, only yards from the elephant's trunk, the proximity caused a lot of snorting and stamping from the rhinos and growling sounds from deep inside the elephant – all quite exciting. We saw many deer - red spotted, pretty creatures, and parakeets flying high over the trees and as the light faded we turned for our jungle home. Supper that evening was a lively affair, as a big, jolly Malaysian fellow called Benjamin joined me. He ran a similar jungle lodge in Sabah, Borneo and was on a fact-finding trip. He found it too hot here. It was very steamy and humid, but no worse than I remember Washington DC had been when the air-conditioning had broken down. I turned in early, about nine o'clock and listened to the BBC World Service news on my tiny radio (with the ear pieces in so as not to disturb the jungle night) as I lay on my bed in the heat, watching fireflies winking from every window like tiny, drifting stars. Immensely beautiful.

In the night it rained heavily, and everything was wonderfully drippy and steamy as I rose early in the morning. I had a cold shower, and two smart flunkies, dressed impossibly like doormen at the Ritz with colourful, fez-like hats, brought me tea at six o'clock. Breakfast was interesting - chips, an omelette, fried onions, peas, toast and butter and a good attempt at marmalade. Only Jagdish's wife, Joymit, has made me a really decent cup of tea so far. I gulped down my malaria tablet (no ill effects whatsoever so far, thank God) and then we were up and away, swaying through the bamboo, atop our elephants again. The large, upturned and well-upholstered stool on top of the elephant is meant for four people - two on each side - but as it is low season, I have the whole contraption to myself and can sit as I like.

After chips for breakfast, I found sitting astride the beast, with my legs either side of the driver's shoulders best. Crossing a small stream, I saw a kingfisher very close by. Suddenly, rounding a corner in dense jungle, we came upon a leopard on the path. He swiftly melted into the undergrowth - 'Leopard' hissed my driver, urging Freddie, our elephant to follow. What a commotion! We crashed blindly through bushes, trees and foliage, the driver very excited, and saw the leopard again briefly. What a thrill; there are very few left here I was told. Next, by a small river, hidden in long, long grass some fifteen feet high, we came across a huge rhino, half submerged having his early morning bath. Freddie was again urged, in grunts and prods down to the water's edge. Up onto the far bank, only twenty or so yards from us, the indignant rhino crashed, with much splashing and snorting. These are 'unicorn' rhinos sporting only one horn, unlike the two-horned African species. He was massive; they often weigh over two tons.

During the morning we swayed majestically down narrow paths, the driver reaching up with his stick to push high branches aside for me, or urging Freddie to find a way round a fallen tree or through thick bushes, and we saw all manner of life; wild peacocks high in the trees, herons, egrets, thickset wild boar ('live bullets', as they are called here as they can bolt or charge at incredible speed) and an impossibly tall termite mound. We came to the river Narayani, a holy river flowing from Tibet into the Ganges and the second largest river in Nepal. There Freddie obediently knelt on command, and I stepped gracefully on to the top of his rump, then down into his curled tail and thence to terra firma. A canoe awaited us and we drifted downriver in the sun in blissful silence.

I thought of my children, Gemma and Jasper, curled up asleep in Suffolk that weekend, and of how unselfish they had been over my trip. I thought of my mother, so supportive and enthusiastic and of my brother Hugh, living from day to day with his large family and all his responsibilities, mainly through his paint brush and canvas. And here am I, cares to the wind and sky. Look forward Cynny, not back . . . and so to the bank further downstream and the Land Rover home to my jungle lodge. As I write, I am on the edge of the jungle, overlooking vast grasslands, with trees and mountains beyond. I am sitting on a bench, under a little thatched roof perched on a tree trunk. All around me, the foliage moves - birds, some as tiny as butterflies - moths, creepers, insects . . . and the man from the Ritz has just brought me a cup of tea.

Later - I am afraid I have complained to Luck, the Temple Tiger manager, about my guide and naturalist, Jigmy. He is a bored, boring, totally unenthusiastic young Indian. When I exclaimed, for instance 'What's that, Jigmy?' he answered, 'termite mound' in a flat monotone - 'and what is it made of?' I asked brightly. 'Mud'. End of conversation. No explanation, no spark, nothing. Luck thanked me and said I wasn't the only one to have complained, and he thought Jigmy had been feeling unwell. Luck said he himself would come on the afternoon elephant safari with me.

Early in the afternoon Jigmy took me to see one of the young elephants named Chumpukalee ('chum-pook-alee') and proceeded to give me a good, if statistical, elephant 'briefing' - all very interesting stuff. I fed Chumpukalee with half a dozen of the three hundred elephant sandwiches she ate every day (corn, molasses and salt, wrapped in banana leaf strips and tied in a bundle) and watched her having a bath. She had a ball, lying down virtually submerged on her side in the muddy water. It was wonderful to be instructed entirely on my own as no one else is staying at Temple Tiger at present. The camp can accommodate up to seventy people, so I daresay it is like Butlins in high season. (Two extraordinary facts in particular remain with me, that elephants can suffer badly from elephant pox, and that they sweat through their toenails!)

Later on, all three of us boarded our noble beasts again, and swayed forth into the jungle - Luck rode with me and the dreary Jigmy followed on another elephant. We had a marvellous time. Luck had incredible eyesight, and we saw four species of beautiful kingfishers, tortoises in the muddy monsoon streams (the deer eat them, I learnt), turtles, many deer, and once a magnificent buck deep in the jungle. In the small sunny clearing you could see his pretty, spotted rump and elegant branching antlers. We surprised a mother and her fawn, who both turned small, startled heart-shaped faces towards us through the tall, waving elephant grass; a moment I shall long remember. Way up in a tree, impossibly perched on a branch, wobbled a fully-grown peacock, his crest up, balancing with his tail. Luck told me that when they are young they must be given (or must find) poisonous things to eat, such as scorpions or poisonous snakes, or they will not survive. I did not believe him at first and don't quite understand it now, but perhaps that is why my brother Hugh's young peacocks died - I don't think that a) he would have been too keen on that idea, and b) there aren't many scorpions in Warwickshire.

We saw more rhino, and Luck was definitely my sort of man. Instead of charging about after anything interesting, we would slowly approach the rhinos, and he was keen to leave them in peace, once I had taken my photographs. He is Nepali and was brought up in the jungle, very much respecting the trees and animals. I suspect Jigmy, from Darjeeling, was there for the beer. We also saw thick strangler vines, which slowly squeeze the life out of victim trees, both roots and trunk, until the tree collapses. I learnt that this vine grows up clockwise in the Northern hemisphere and anti-clockwise in the Southern hemisphere - fascinating. After supper I had an early night; I attempted to listen to the news, but all I could get was half an hour's transmission of the sudden death play-off between England and Spain. Gazza then hurt his leg, the whole thing hurt my brain, and I gave up. Instead I watched the flickering fireflies in the jungle outside, before I fell asleep.

Sunday 23rd June

I rose at half past five and, after a cold shower, went for a wonderful bird-watching walk with Jigmy and Luck. Apparently, according to Mr Misra, the owner of the Lodge, a tiger had been angrily circling the camp all night. We found fresh tiger tracks and heard the beast make a kill not far from us amongst a herd of spotted deer; most exciting. I saw orioles and rollers and many other birds. After breakfast it poured with rain and seemed set for the day.

I am writing this sitting in a steamer chair high up in a kind of tree house, which serves as the camp library overlooking the grasslands. With a pair of very powerful binoculars and a glorious view, I don't mind the rain a bit. However, I have learned a couple of very interesting facts, one of them about myself. Firstly, as I know my brother Hugh strongly believes, you have to be so careful not to see the wonders of other worlds merely through the eye of the camera (or video recorder). It is so easy to point and shoot and miss the second completely with the naked eye, and thus ones' reaction, and the sounds and scents and the wider picture. Secondly, although I am loving this visit into true (if partially inhabited by man) jungle, I really do prefer the hills. The bird and animal life here is rich and breathtaking, but I discover I am an open spaces person - hills, mountains, valleys, rivers are where I feel euphoric and glad to be alive. The dark, humid, eerie canopy of the forest, mysterious and exciting, but sometimes rather depressing, makes me reflective and somewhat withdrawn, a feeling I don't really care for.

Monday 24th June

The rains have well and truly arrived. I managed another wonderful two-hour elephant safari last night in the evening sun, spying many rhinos, deer and gorgeous birds. Then, after another cold shower, I discovered a most wonderful pastime - swinging gently in a huge hammock, overlooking the grasslands, but best of all, lying under the tall jungle trees, their vast leaves darkening in the dusk, listening to the beautiful taped music I have with me and watching the glittering fireflies – heaven. I wondered if I could string a hammock across my garden at Goose Cottage.

I was woken at five o'clock this morning, the intention being to take a canoe ride downriver for an hour or so and walk back. However, due to the monsoon the river was too swollen to navigate and my boat trip was cancelled. It was teeming with rain. After another strange breakfast of chips, fried onions, two boiled eggs and dry chilli beans, my lacklustre friend Jigmy suggested an elephant safari instead.

What a joke! Clad in my Gortex jacket and with a bamboo hat crammed on top of the hood, we squelched out into the jungle in rain so hard we could only see about twenty yards ahead. It was mad. We found a couple of rhino and some deer, but photos were impossible, and the binoculars poured water down my neck if I lifted them to my eyes. It was vastly uncomfortable. I am not sure that, had any of my friends been with me, they would have seen the funny side. I returned, poured the water out of my walking boots, wrung out my bra and pants and drank a cup of strong tea. Since then, sadly, it has poured all day, so perhaps they should think twice before offering holidays here in the monsoon. This afternoon I have written letters, slept and listened to my music. My clothes are not drying at all as it is so damp. Thank God for the British sense of humour!

That evening I mounted my elephant for another drippy but quite interesting safari. I was thrilled to see a paradise flycatcher - a black and white bird, most beautifully marked, with a long, long ribbony tail, which floated through the air as it flew past. We also saw a wild bison, grazing peacefully alongside a rhino - a memorable sight. Some of the birds here have such long names; by the time a 'grey-breasted, rufus headed, three-toed pied bulbul' has been pointed out it has probably flown. The elephants themselves are wonderful; they smell earthy and warm and, combined with the smell of the jungle and grasses after rain, make you feel very close to nature. The elephants' belching and farting sound exactly the same noise, you just have to guess which comes from which end!

Well, the ten Italians expected today have cancelled, and I don't blame them a bit. It is now dreary and dark beyond belief, and with twelve hours of rain today, rather a waste of my time and money. However, some you win, some you lose.

<u>Tuesday 25th June</u>

My last morning was brighter and at breakfast a somewhat embarrassed Luck waived my bar bill and gave me a lovely straw hat (the one I'd borrowed for my safaris) as a souvenir. And so I departed, by elephant down to the river, then across the swirling waters by canoe and then by car past a village of mud huts. Half the villagers were planting rice, a back-breaking job, whilst others sat around picking nits out of each other's hair, or staring into space. Babies slept in tiny cotton hammocks slung in front of the huts. I saw many things on the long journey to the airport in the jeep; amazingly smart school children sporting white shoes and socks, white shorts and shirts, walking to school - boys arm in arm, girls arm in arm while a group of small boys peed onto the road. Others, their parents not able to afford schooling (for which one pays here), sat around their smallholdings scuffing the dust. We overtook a rich man taking his wife shopping by tractor, her brilliant sari billowing out behind them.

We finally reached the airport where a ramshackle, dilapidated stone building served as the tiny terminal whilst goats and water buffalo grazed on the airstrip. Ear-piercing five minute, four minute, and two minute sirens warned of incoming aircraft, of which there were two a day.

Later. Well, events took an interesting turn in the middle of the last sentence. Jigmy called me aside, away from the handful of other passengers, to talk to me 'urgently and privately'. He had just been told that my flight was delayed by an hour at least, and that monsoon rain was expected at Bharatpur, where we were, very soon, possibly delaying me even further. Did I want a seat on the tiny Everest Airplane, which was landing as we spoke? The damage was to be fifty dollars in cash. The prospect of hours in a one-hole airport with my boring companion was too much, so, after various extremely hurried negotiations, my large rucksack was re-routed, my previous ticket cancelled and I asked for assurance that I would get a refund on my original ticket. Then a quick pose for a photo beside the smart little aircraft, and off we flew.

The whole procedure, from sitting peacefully writing my journal to lift off, had taken just eleven minutes. The twelve-seater Dornier 128 Everest Airplane was amazingly fast, and apart from seeing smoke puffing up from the floor ('vapour', the sari-clad hostess assured me) the flight was excellent - just over ten minutes back to Kathmandu, with peppermints, cotton wool, mango juice and peanuts proffered. These tiny Everest Airplanes are known as 'Himalayan Concordes' and, knocking ten minutes off my outward journey, I was not surprised.

So, eventually I arrived back at the Potala again, to be greeted by Raisa and her sister Rokeya (the pretty, young Tibetan girls who ran the hostel) with a fax from my son Jasper (via Jagdish, who had left on a trek) and my mother's letter addressed directly to the Potala. Letters addressed like this very rarely get through, as you really have to have a PO Box in Nepal, so both girls were surprised and delighted for me. That evening an unseen hand delivered a second letter from my mother; both had taken about eleven days to reach Nepal. How lovely it was sitting in the roof garden, reading of Jasper's and Mummy's news from England - everyone is wonderful in helping to make me feel so loved - God bless them all.

Wednesday 26th June

I faxed the trek organiser in England last night, with comments on my jungle trip - an expensive exercise, but he had wanted to know how I had got on. This morning I rang Jan Salter, a friend of a friend of mine in England. I had wanted to visit Patan, a historical suburb of Kathmandu, and it seems she's an artist and is exhibiting in the museum there — perfect. We arranged to meet there the next afternoon.

JAIL AND JAN

Thursday 27th June

How strange life is, and how often I find I am given opportunities and have found doors opened for me out of the blue, metaphorically speaking. This morning, sitting at The Northfield Café for my breakfast, I got into conversation with a woman called Jeanette from Manchester. She was staying at the fabled Kathmandu Guest House and asked me if I'd like to see inside it. I did, and it was really fun - at $6 per night, much more than my modest abode, but very nice, with a sort of après trek/ski feeling about it. In the lobby, various people were watching live coverage of Wimbledon; I couldn't believe it. On our way out, we looked at the noticeboard where travellers advertise kit for sale, and for people to join them on treks to Tibet etc and where they leave messages for one another. There was a notice giving information about two young Brits in jail. One was in a Kathmandu jail and the other some eight kilometres away at a place I had never heard of.

Relishing a challenge, and a much better way to spend part of a day than writing cards or marvelling at temples, I found a map of the valley and searched in vain for the name of the place. No luck - back to the Guest House, who told me the jail was in or near - Patan, where I was going anyway, that afternoon, to meet Jan. I am sure it was all meant to be, as the jail could have been anywhere. I bought soap, a toothbrush, toothpaste, 'English toffees', envelopes, paper and stamps and sellotape (none of the airletters/envelopes here stick down properly) and I bought a book in a second hand bookshop, of which there are many in Kathmandu. Difficult. Every book seemed to feature a 'courtroom drama' or 'high tension jail riot' or, worse still 'underworld trafficking excitement'! I played safe with grown-up Roahl Dahl stories 'a collection for insomniacs' which sounded about right.

Off I went in a taxi some nine kilometres into the countryside beyond Patan. The jail was very secure, built round a courtyard colourful with pots of flowers and everyone seemed friendly but efficient. Where was I from? Who was I coming to see? After a wait outside the bars and then inside the bars, Steve Jones from London appeared. Thin, and obviously not one hundred percent well, he seemed very grateful for the goodies - I had also bought some mangoes en route - but he wasn't allowed my last two inches of whisky left over from my trek; the guards looked longingly at it instead. He had served fourteen months of a five-year sentence for trying to smuggle hashish out of Nepal; he and a friend had been shopped by the dealer, and caught at the airport. My interest was not in the whys and wherefores, merely that he was someone's son, and possibly someone's brother. He could only remember part of his mother's telephone number in Bournemouth, so gave me her address instead; I'll ask my mother to ring her.

He talked and talked and at one point asked rather pathetically if I could return another day - but I was leaving on the Monday. His only hope of an early release was a change of Government in Nepal - the Communists would issue an amnesty. He was the only foreigner in his jail and I am so very glad I went. I told him I was not a do-gooder, but I had a son, and hoped someone would do the same for him in similar circumstances - God forbid that that should ever happen.

The taxi had waited for me, and drove me into Patan, another spectacularly beautiful city full of medieval temples. It was a separate kingdom until 1769 and was far less frenetic and touristy than Durbar Square in Kathmandu. I found the museum eventually and loved Jan's paintings. Mainly oils and drawings, they depicted the tremendous variety of Nepalese tribes and castes, girls in brilliantly colourful local costumes, children and old men. I longed to buy a poster, but could not lug it around with me. The museum was housed in a long, low temple, with ornately carved windows, and shutters made up of tiny square holes rather like waffles. There were five or six floors, and it was a perfect place in which to exhibit. In the courtyard outside was a Buddhist stupa, with huge white prayer flags fluttering at each corner, on the end of which was a tiny bell. I could have sat for hours at a window, of which there were very many, in deep, cool recesses, with large, square red cushions to sit on.

I would have watched the many happenings in the tiered temples ringing the square below, or peacefully contemplated the serene paintings around me in that beautiful building lit by the sunlit courtyard. Jan herself whom I hadn't met before, had lived in Nepal on and off for years and had even adopted a Nepali boy who was now married. She sat with me and we talked; occasionally she broke off to give an interview to a pressman. Oh! A lovely afternoon . . . and I returned to the Potala, a beaming Raziya and yet another letter for me. I sat in the roof garden with a coke and read it. A happy end to a God-given day; Carpe Diem in its real sense. How lucky I am.

My last two days in Nepal were overcast and it poured with rain, but this was also fun, rather like a cartoon show. Cyclists of all shapes and sizes balanced umbrellas of all descriptions as they careered through the traffic, the very smart policemen wore small transparent pale blue plastic bags over their hats and I saw men wearing the traditional small embroidered Nepalese hats, shiny white plastic macs (very 1960s) above bare hairy legs and little short wellies. There seemed to be more cows than usual lying around on the main roads - three on the busy roundabout by the Post Office - equating to cows on three lanes round Marble Arch. They are of course sacred, and just lie about contentedly, chewing, whilst scooters, taxis, rickshaws, and cyclists skid round them. I made my last visit to Kathmandu Post Office. I registered a packet of photos to my children and to my Chelsea Pensioner friend, Sergeant Bert. After the usual scouring through many hundreds of letters I found one from a great girlfriend, Susie - oh, how lovely!

I walked quite a distance back to the Potala, avoiding the usual pavement craters, begging mothers and babies (which I hate so much - my heart goes out to them) crippled children, men weeing by the road . . . and later, on my bed, lay entranced reading Susie's letter - of English and Irish gardens, people, smart parties, Western life. What a wonderful letter; the friends I have met here, over meals and in the hostel, have been so very different. That is of course, one of my reasons for coming away; I have been befriended by a Harvard student, Marta, who is researching a

'Let's Go - Nepal' travel guide and asked me to have supper with her one night; she is twenty two and from New York.

Another day two New Zealand girls said they had heard I had been to Chitwan and to a prison and could I tell them all - in return they gave me lots of ideas about New Zealand. Then at breakfast one day I sat at a big table in a nearby café and was immediately befriended by Mary and Jade from Australia. Mary was waif-like and pretty with a holey vest of uncertain colour draped off one shoulder and Jade - well, he looked just like George Best on a rather bad day. They were charming, giving me all sorts of addresses in Bali, Malaysia, Singapore and Thailand. Mary asked if I knew if she could have her baby in England; apparently, there was one due, somewhere below the vest.

Yesterday – Saturday 29th June, I had my palms read. Jagdish kept telling me about a really good man named Lalji, so I took the plunge. It was fascinating, with a proper consulting room and an efficient assistant. She took ink prints of my palms, thumbs and the sides of my hands. Lalji then set to work with an illuminated magnifying glass, a ruler, coloured pens and a cassette recorder, to tell me a few home truths about myself. He looked just like Yul Brynner in 'The King and I' with a huge, smooth, shaven head, wonderfully arched eyebrows and beautiful brown eyes. He wore a long sleeved, high-necked, full-length dark blue robe. His usual sessions ran for four to six hours but I could only afford one hour. I bet you would like to know what he said! He assessed my character accurately and pinpointed the years in which I had had good and bad major happenings and was spot on. I am now hopeful Mr Right is out there somewhere though the year in which he finally delivers the Cadbury's Milk Tray is my secret. It was riveting and Lalji a disturbingly mesmeric man.

I was invited out with the Shahs again last night, and collected by Sadip in his self-drive staff car (a jeep with stiff covered pennant on the bonnet) much to the gaping amazement of the band of Tiger Balm, khukri and rickshaw hawkers loitering outside the Potala. What a strange life I lead here - I relish the anonymity of the scruffy backpacking scene, actually not that scruffy as most people have very good kit, and yet the top echelon in Nepal live like kings and occasionally that is fun to savour too.

We went to an extremely smart Chinese restaurant. Ava's family owned the whole complex I gathered, and there was much clicking of heels on entering and leaving (I had never seen a Chinese restaurant owner salute before). I felt very underdressed beside Ava in her gorgeous peacock blue and gold sari - she is a pretty woman. Sadip explained fascinating politics and alarming corruption/Maoist/Communist problems to me and I wished I had had a tape recorder. Ava told me in very hushed tones, practically under the table, about the Third Prince who had left his wife after twenty or so years and now lives in London. This is quite unheard of, utterly unacceptable and certainly not understood here. Arranged marriages and subservience are still part of the accepted culture in Nepal.

Tuesday 2nd July

Well, having thought I would be really sad as we whizzed down the runway and left this marvellous country, just the opposite happened. Having waited almost four hours for our Thai Airways flight to depart from Kathmandu yesterday, the word 'cancelled' eventually appeared on the small television screen beside our flight number. Chaos ensued, as no announcements were made and no information whatsoever was given to the assembled passengers.

Eventually we were all bussed off to a five-star Holiday Inn hotel, where we ate ourselves to sleep, not me personally, but most of the goggle-eyed budget back-packers did. We were all treated to a sumptuous lunch, dinner and breakfast, hot baths, live Wimbledon on television, swimming pool and air-conditioning; a far cry from The Potala. We were some distance from the town, and as we reached the hotel at four in the afternoon, for lunch, I did not venture out again. Instead, I watched Wimbledon and wrote letters on my vast bed. We were called at half past five in the morning, eventually flying out at midmorning, but that is a long story.

NIGHT TRAIN TO CHIANG MAI

As I write this I am at Bangkok railway station - a seething mass of humanity swarming about in thirty-nine degree heat; I am travelling north up to Chiang Mai on the sleeper.

I arrived in Bangkok on Tuesday 2nd July and made my way by taxi to the Dusit Thani Hotel, where I had arranged to meet a friend of a friend, Kate Dufall. The traffic jams of which I had heard are quite indescribable; it usually takes an hour to travel a few miles. The heat and high humidity were stifling, but both taxi and hotel were air-conditioned. I was greeted by a pair of hotel doormen dressed like performing monkeys, with gold and purple hats sporting long earflaps and strange little skirts rather like those worn by Roman soldiers. They did not bat an eyelid, as I swept in with my sunhat, two rucksacks and great aplomb, T-shirted and baggy trousered.

The hotel was sumptuous, with gorgeous Thai girls floating about in long, tight silk skirts split to their thighs, carrying baskets of heavenly orchids whilst a pianist played by the indoor waterfall. I ordered afternoon tea and strudel, and for that, paid an entire day's food budget had I been back in Nepal! It was fun though. Later on, Kate arrived looking very glamorous and we took a taxi to her home.

Her husband David had been the Australian Defence Attaché in Bangkok and they have lived here on and off for twenty years. He now works as a consultant. He is also President of the Southerners' (Australia and New Zealand) rugby football team and runs the annual Bangkok Rugby Sevens tournament. Kate works for the Consular Section of the British Embassy, dealing with all Commonwealth citizens arrested in Thailand - a most interesting job. Their airy house in a Bangkok suburb was a lovely place to make camp for a while, and I was given a large bedroom with my own bathroom, air-conditioning and a maid, Sai Chon, to iron, wash, cook and hail taxis for me. On the first night we had a delicious Thai supper (Sai Chon was a wonderful cook). Next morning I laid out all my belongings putting aside a pile to post back home to England.

The next few days were filled with delicious 'namanow sodas' (fresh lime, sugar, salt and soda water - yummy) lazing at home and sightseeing. I learnt to say 'thank you' phonetically 'cop coon car' and 'hello' was 'sawadiika' and never to insult the royal family, which includes not licking stamps. You can be arrested for doing so. I was swiftly and pointedly passed a moistened rubber pad in the Post Office when I forgot. I sped (well, traffic jams allowing) to the Grand Palace and the Temple of the Emerald Buddha as a first stop on my sightseeing itinerary. It was astounding, and had it not been so authentic, ancient and holy, I might have expected to see Donald Duck waddling about amongst the opulent buildings! The whole area was very beautiful, with temples, spires and mosaic shrine, lots of gold leaf and brilliantly coloured tiled roofs; the porcelain mosaic came from China, the marble from Italy.

The Temple of the Emerald Buddha contained a solid jade Buddha several feet high, towering above the glass-like marble floor, on tier upon tier of gold daises. We were asked not to point our feet at the Buddha, which was considered a sin. The sight of the vast floor, peopled with cross-legged, kneeling or sitting men and women with legs bent prettily sideways and cooled by enormous fans blowing the wonderful scent of the frangipani and lotus flowers towards us all, was extremely peaceful. I then made my way to Wat Po, another complex of incredible temples, where Mary (Kathmandu, mother-to-be) had recommended I had a massage.

I found the Wat Po Traditional Massage School, where rows of beds arranged in pairs - just mattresses in rows along shelves - were awaiting their victims. The whole building was open-sided and fans played above each bed. I paid my five pounds for a massage, and also elected to pay an extra fifty pence for a 'clean bedsheet'. A man of about twenty-five beckoned me. For an hour in a pair of baggy Chinese trousers, which I slipped on to replace my skirt, he stretched, pummelled, pinched and contorted me, and I had a fit of the giggles which rather unnerved him. It was agony but surprisingly relaxing.

Later on, I visited Jim Thompson's house. He was an American who had worked for the OSS (forerunner of the CIA) before the war and then settled in Thailand in the 1950s, leaving his wife in America. He was instrumental in promoting and running the Thai silk industry, which then boomed. He owned four typical Thai houses built in different styles and in close proximity, together forming a wonderfully interesting home, full of character and set amidst huge palm trees and lush jungle flowers. He collected Chinese, Siamese and Burmese antiques and these can be seen today inside his house. In 1967 he disappeared whilst out for a walk in the Cameron Highlands in Malaya. Some suspected a CIA link (and his sister was murdered the following year, in America) but it seems more likely he was run over by a local lorry driver, who then hid his body.

I went to a very informal drinks party one night in a bar attached to the British Embassy, and was asked out the following evening by a couple of English businessmen. However, as Kate and I had had a very late night drinking cappuccinos in the red light district the night before, right opposite a pick-up bar (quite fascinating), I was shattered and declined. I was also exhausted after my massage. My whole body, including my facial muscles, toes and fingers were stretched, pulled and bent. Yes, the red light district was amazing, and we had such fun trying to guess which of the high-heeled, micro-skirted and very made up girls were male and which female and discussing the intricacies of walking off with a fat, unshaven German or drunken Englishman - riveting.

A fascinating fact about Thailand is that every single building, be it a home, hotel or office, has a spirit house built alongside it. This is usually in the form of a large bird table, with an elaborately spired and ornamented dolls' temple perched on top of it. If you enlarge or improve your house in any way then you have to do the same to your spirit house. By keeping the evil (and good) spirits happy, they will not enter your house. The spirit houses built alongside luxury hotels and the headquarters of large corporations were enormous dolls' abodes, and far larger and smarter than thousands of real homes lived in by the poor.

CHIANG MAI, in the north of Thailand - and I loved the train journey. It took an age to chug out of Bangkok and its suburbs and I was fascinated to see hundreds of families living right by the railway line, sitting in large groups on the line next to ours, drinking, playing games or cooking on large woks balanced over small open fires. I could have dropped a coin straight down into the woks from my carriage window. Children played basketball and other games in the dust and on great mounds of sand right beside us, as we gathered speed, heading north.

Palms, banana trees, mimosa and flame of the forest lined the track and, not far from the city, we whizzed past a very smart little colonnaded platform, all shut up, but bang in front of the royal palace across the road - the King's platform. The carriage was large and open with tall metal luggage shelves reaching up to the ceiling, beside each pair of seats. I sat opposite an ancient Thai man in gym shoes, with no teeth, very dark glasses and a kind of Arab shemagh slung elegantly round his neck. I locked my rucksack onto the luggage rack, opposite my top bunk. As it got dark, and the country houses appeared among the rice paddies, so I noticed each tiny spirit house lit up like a Christmas tree, beside its host house - it was so pretty.

I had ordered supper - chicken and cashew nuts with fried rice, shrimp and noodle soup, fruit and tea. My Thai friend opposite ordered a huge bottle of German beer and two glasses and proceeded to share it with me. He (or his wife) had been clever enough to pack a hot picnic and he insisted I had one of his beef kebabs (a huge piece of flat beef on a small wooden skewer) and an indistinguishable batter patty. The kebab was yummy, the patty - fish I think - was disgusting, but I ate it with big smiles and thank you's; he would not share mine. My lemony soup contained one vast prawn, shell and all, which, along with everything else was delicious.

Soon afterwards efficient men in Nazi-looking uniforms with peaked hats and revolvers came through the carriage and organised the beds. A cupboard, like a huge airline stowage locker, was swung down from above suspended on wide straps. A bed was made up inside it and curtains attached. The large window below (how wonderful, eating supper with a warm breeze blowing in from the wide open window as we whizzed along) was covered with steel mesh drawn up like a grille, and as we vacated our seats, they too were converted into another bed. Hey presto! The toothless one climbed into his, and I climbed up to mine, and it was all very comfy. I can reliably report that the Buddhist monk on the bunk opposite me read a tabloid newspaper, slept in his swathes of saffron robes and used green toothpaste. We all slept in our clothes.

MORNING, and it was heavenly; at six o'clock I had to sport my sunglasses, as I drank an early morning cup of tea. We chugged laboriously up forested hills and across valleys, with temples here and there and past colourful little stations swathed in fluttering national flags, urns of flowers, palm trees and bougainvillea. Our beds had been stowed away at five o'clock and breakfast trays flew up and down the aisle. I elected for tea and a piece of toast, as it was too early for a huge fry-up after a curry supper. It seemed dotty spreading butter with a spoon. In Thailand you are never given a knife and it is very rude to use one.

At seven o'clock we reached Chiang Mai, the much-visited, renowned northern hill resort, and I am afraid to say, my heart sank. It was horribly busy, noisy and smelly. As I write this, I am leaving tomorrow and I cannot say I have enjoyed it much. Dreadful, clogging traffic and a shopaholics' paradise. However, the day market and night bazaar are fun, the latter a razzamatazz for tourists, the former selling fruit such as lychees, mangosteen, rambutans (a red, prickly fruit about the size of a plum) loofahs and jack fruit - great huge spiny things, and lots of little stalls selling instant Thai food, cooked in large woks.

I teamed up with a Swiss girl the morning I arrived and took a pick-up truck taxi to the zoo and then walked on, up a high hill to see the most important Buddhist temple in the north. The temple itself was beautiful but, unlike Nepal, traders encroached the very precincts, selling everything from lotus flowers, jasmine garlands and candles as offerings (quite acceptable) to chocolate marshmallow Buddhas and other ghastly tourist tat. The zoo was very scruffy and sadly, as it was forty- five degrees (phew!) most of the animals had disappeared into the cool of their lairs and who could blame them. My room, at the guesthouse recommended by a girl at the Embassy in Bangkok, was a slum. All good backpacking stuff, but with mouldy walls, the lock hanging off the door by a whisker and a very weak fan; not much fun.

I took a pick-up taxi to a Buddhist centre on another day - a place of learning. Many of the trees had wise sayings nailed to them, many in English, such as 'A person with sweet words will feast you with an empty spoon' and 'Love is a flower garden to be watered by tears' all thoughtful stuff. I had also read of a herb garden and a forest not far away and was assured by the Irish landlady at our guesthouse, that it was fine to visit it alone. The 'forest' turned out to be a small glade of rather sickly looking spindly trees, the herb garden was a small fruit cage of plants in pots with no identification marks, and whenever I approached a monk, with a beaming smile and a request for directions, he would shrug his shoulders and walk quickly away. So much for a tourist attraction.

However, the system of pick-up truck taxis was excellent. Battered old red pick-up trucks with covered roofs and open-sided tailboards, cruised round town, looking for customers. A price was then negotiated through the front window and into the back you hopped. You often had a rather circuitous route to your destination while others were picked up and dropped off, but it was a really good system and as there weren't any designated pickup and set down points, you could hail one from anywhere to go to anywhere very cheaply. I joined a party from Eagle House where I was staying to see how local handicrafts were made.

I had been warned that it was merely a tour up and down a long street of factories, but quite interesting, and so it proved. We saw silver, precious stones, lacquer, wood, silk and paper umbrellas being produced at different locations. The silver and stones (there is a lot of lapis lazuli, emeralds, star sapphires, moonstones and jade in this part of the world) were pretty uninteresting - a few people, grinding and beating, without explanations, and then we were hurried into enormous shops selling the goods - the whole object, of course, was to get us to buy. The lacquer work, however, was fascinating to watch. The shape of the object is constructed from woven bamboo or wood and then twelve layers of lacquer are applied, smoothed in water between coats and dried naturally. We saw skilled workers gilding, etching, painting and even sticking minute pieces of chicken and duck eggshell onto the lacquer, to give different effects; some of it very pretty.

My fellow tourists - a French couple in their early twenties who spoke no English, and two British lads were great fun. (The men were both training as lawyers and one of them lived in Medonte Close in Fleet. I had lived there as a child in a large Victorian house named Medonte, later sold and transformed into the Close - how strange life is)

The Thai silk production line was also engrossing to watch. We all knew about silk worms and mulberry leaves, but to see the empty cocoons being boiled in a small cauldron set in front of an old woman, who gathered all the silk threads together over a spindle suspended above them, was really mesmerising. She calmly went on and on and on for hours, gathering all the tiny threads together into one thicker thread; each cocoon providing over five hundred metres of silk. We saw the worms, and the cocoons as they wove them, and finally the dyeing and the looms, followed by the inevitable huge showroom for purchases.

Then on to see teak and rosewood being carved. The finished pieces - extremely intricate, heavy tables, chairs, desks etc, weren't to our taste at all, but the craftsmanship was exquisite. Young girls sat in a large, airy hanger-like barn with an array of tools, chipping, scraping and chiselling delicate orchids and leaves, Buddhas and dragons or animal designs onto the tops, legs and sides of tables and other pieces of furniture. Mother of pearl was sawn into minute shapes and inlaid, such skilled work.

Best of all were the wonderful paper umbrellas. A liquid resin was extracted from the sa tree and poured into huge open tanks. Pieces of mesh, about four feet square, were then dipped into the liquid, and set upright in the sun to dry. Once dry, the paper could be peeled off the mesh squares in very thin sheets, and used to cover the umbrellas. All the tiny wooden struts and threads joining them were fashioned by hand with small knives, and the paper was varnished to give it strength and a certain amount of waterproofing.

Then came the painting. Wow! There were no bounds to the flights of imagination, and it was such fun to watch. Fans too, were made here. Some of the umbrellas were huge - perhaps twelve feet in diameter. The deft artists were keen to paint for us, free, on anything we had - backpacks, camera cases, bags and hats. They painted bamboo fronds and a couple of birds on a small canvas bag I had bought, and butterflies on my camera case, and before I knew it, on the camera itself. I was glad I wasn't carrying the green daysack I had borrowed - I don't suppose the owner would have appreciated orchids and lotus blossoms entwined round his back for evermore!

On the penultimate day in Chiang Mai, I attempted to arrange a tour, through my lodgings, to a National Park quite a distance away. I was told that as there were no other takers it was not possible, and the same thing had applied to a visit to an orchid and butterfly farm earlier in the week. As Eagle House had advertised 'tailor made tours', this disappointed me, and they would not even quote me a single price. A couple of other agencies in the town quoted me sky high prices, so that was that, as I didn't think it wise to go by taxi on my own. In the end, I spent the day swimming and writing cards and letters by the pool at a nearby luxury hotel. My very first swim of my travels and a lazy day in the sun; as I had been dreadfully sick all through the previous night, it was probably no bad thing (although I was very careful about sunbathing; it was forty-five degrees that day). The scent of the frangipani trees behind me, and the beautiful coconut palms swaying in the breeze beyond me, were wonderfully restful.

Thursday 11th July

I am now on the train journey back to Bangkok. The hotel had promised me an early call at half-past five; I was glad I had slept lightly and woken in time as no such call had materialised. I donned my heavy rucksack and left a silent Eagle House at six o'clock. I had to walk quite a way to find a tuk-tuk (motorised rickshaw), but now I am on my way - fourteen hours in the train back to Bangkok. The only signs of life in Chiang Mai at that early hour had been the occasional wraith-like Buddhist monks who slipped in and out of the shadows down side streets, their orange robes drifting behind them. They clutched large silver rimmed bowls in which they collected food, toiletries, and other necessities, handed out by charitable townsfolk from their homes.

We are whizzing past rice paddies now, in the shadow of the hills of Thailand. It is very hot, even at eight o'clock in the morning, and I am happy to be in the real countryside again, with the windows wide open. I am playing my music; Unchained Melody and Mozart are very calming as we pass lakes smothered in large pink lotus flowers, and banana groves.

I am horrified at how everyone in the train tips rubbish out of the window; everything is disposed of that way, bottles, cans, polystyrene bowls, plastic bags, just tossed out – yuk! And no one ever waves back to the children who wave to us from shacks, flats, on walls and in fields, but I do, always. There are monkeys all over the track next to ours as I write, by a temple . . . the scent of jasmine . . . small boys playing football. On this journey I have planned my next adventure, down to Malaysia. Wheee! . . .busy Bangkok, here I come again.

Yes, as busy as ever. Bangkok drivers spend an average of forty-four days a year in traffic jams, and the fastest selling items at petrol stations are cellular phones, televisions, food warmers and 'comfort loos' or car potties, all for these jammed-up motorists. I forgot to mention new friends I had met in Chiang Mai - Spook, Lynne and Sky Russell from Cape Town. He looks a bit like Bob Geldof - forty, long, long ponytail, extremely handsome, a botanist and film producer. Lynne, dark and beautiful, and Skye their daughter aged five and straight out of a Mabel Lucy Attwell book - freckled, with a froth of blonde corkscrew curls. We all warmed to each other, and I now have an invitation to Cape Town where they live - right on the beach in a rather remote, wild area; well, you never know.

On my return to Bangkok, I went to a happy hour at the Australian Embassy with David, as Kate wasn't feeling too well; a modern but very lovely building, with lush palms, shrubs, ponds and fountains both inside and out. I met an American girl, teaching in Bangkok. It is funny how little throwaway lines stick in your mind . . . she was commenting on the pleasant fact that she didn't have to pass through a metal detector (for guns and knives) each morning at school, as she had had to in New York State. What a world.

During the next few days there was a flurry of postal activity for me in the Dufall household. I had letters and faxes from my family and many friends. Letters mean so much to me here, regardless of all the fun I am having. I spoke to my brother Hugh and to my mother on the phone; I plan to take David and Kate out to dinner and discover I have won fifty pounds on Ernie - perfect!

<u>Sunday 14th July</u>

Bangkok lives up to its reputation again. When the third taxi I hail at Kate's, agrees to switch on his meter (most won't) he takes me to the wrong hotel, and we spend another frustrating meter-ticking twenty minutes finding the Oriental Hotel, from where I have planned to catch the river bus. At what is reputed to be the smartest hotel in Bangkok (the Dufalls think otherwise) I have got my act ready. As the elegant doorman opens my taxi door and I alight, with sunhat, rucksack, bumbag, carrier bag containing my water bottle, lunch and camera (not your average millionaire hotel resident) I put on my sunhat above a stunning smile, and in the poshest voice imaginable say how lovely it is to be back at the Oriental, and that I am just going to catch the river bus ('Which way is it? I can't quite remember') and that I will pop back for a drink later. Two porters joined us, and drew me maps and wrote notes in Thai of where I should alight; I definitely got the impression that they thought me a totally eccentric English woman . . . good.

True to form, since this is Bangkok, the crowded and extremely fast riverboat missed out my stop altogether, dropping me on the wrong side of the river. I had to walk about a mile with my heavy rucksack, albeit the smaller khaki one - the heat was stifling - in and out of the traffic, to find a rickshaw. Eventually I reached the Southern Bus Station, quite a way out of the city, and luckily the next bus to Kanchanaburi left ten minutes later. I thought I would spoil myself and travel on an air-conditioned bus for the three-hour journey - one pound sixty against seventy-three pence. It was a cooking day.

KANCHANABURI

I have such mixed feelings about my journey here . . . such unspeakable, unimaginable atrocities were perpetrated along the River Kwai . . . and only last Christmas an English girl was murdered here by a monk, though I have not reminded anyone in England of this. I also feel a need, having been so moved by all I have read, to say a prayer beside the six thousand British graves.

The journey was comfortable and speedy, through lush, rural countryside, with many old sugar and pineapple processing plants set back from the road. Kan, as it is called, is a bustling little town and on arrival I visited the excellent TAT (tourist office) to pick up maps of the area. I hopped on the back of a motorbike taxi and we sped off to the Jolly Frog Backpackers' where I had planned to stay. It was jolly!

It consisted of a collection of straw roofed, open-sided buildings, surrounded with bougainvillea, palms and lots of other gorgeous greenery. Bedrooms were in one storey or verandah'd two storey houses, surrounding a small lawn on the bank of the River Kwai. It was very busy when I arrived at lunchtime, a good sign. The Jolly Frog had had a good write up in the South East Asia Lonely Planet book, bought at vast expense in Chiang Mai, but totally invaluable. My little single room with frilly nylon curtains, mozzie screens and a fan, cost me about two pounds; there is a real mozzie problem here by the river. My room was up an outside ladder on the verandah floor, above the lawn and river. After settling in, I went to find out about trips to Hellfire Pass, some seventy kilometres further upriver, where the allied prisoners had had to cut a pass through solid rock in fearful heat and monsoon with very little food or water. I had gathered the Pass was difficult to reach and I was a bit concerned - I didn't want to go alone by hiring a bike or truck, or go with just one unknown guide - a dilemma.

I was directed to Uncle Sam who ran tours to the various local attractions. Most of the young (there was no one over twenty five in my guest house, it seemed) come here to visit the vast caves, temples, spectacular waterfalls and the disco riverboats plying the river, though many do visit the main war cemetery in the centre of the town. Sam seemed a really delightful man, but his Hellfire Pass tour was for a minimum of two people, at 550 bahts each (fourteen pounds) though he could take me on my own for 800 bahts (twenty one pounds). This was too expensive for me. I returned to the Jolly Frog via the large cemetery in the town.

About five thousand British prisoners of war are buried here. I had read various books of David Dufalls, on the Thai-Burma railway construction, and in this place lay the victims of this dreadful project. I knew the cemetery visit would upset me, and it did. Thousands of POWs aged from seventeen to well into their fifties were transported up by rail from Singapore and Malaya in cattle trucks, with little food and water for five hot, humid days and nights.

The Japanese planned to link up railway lines throughout Thailand and Burma, a vital supply route for them, and it was estimated that this project would take five years to complete. The Japanese insisted it would take eighteen months. The route lay north west of Bangkok through thick jungle, over the River Kwai Yai and over the western mountain range up into Burma.

Thirteen thousand Australian, thirty thousand British, eighteen thousand Dutch and seven hundred American troops, with two hundred thousand 'liberated' Thais, Burmese, Malayan and Indian workers completed the four hundred and fifteen kilometre line in seventeen months. Over a hundred thousand died. There were many soldiers buried there from British county regiments and several naval, Royal Marine, and RAF men. Three British Special Forces captains had died on the same day, December 16th 1941, and sailors from HMS Sultan, HMS Repulse and HMS Prince of Wales had died there in July 1943. An Argyll and Sutherland Highlander, Major MacKellar had won an MC and Bar. What men these were. On one gravestone I read 'James lies here in this foreign land, please place a flower for me. Mum'. I picked a small yellow, trumpet shaped flower and placed it for her on the Scotsman's grave, then returned, pensively, to my guesthouse.

That evening at supper, for no particular reason, I chose to sit at an empty table for four, rather than at one for two. After a while, a young Chinese-looking couple asked if they could join me. It turned out that they were from Singapore, and, having just arrived, were planning some tours of the area. I casually mentioned Sam's Hellfire Pass tour, which included drinking water for the day, lunch near a waterfall and a return journey by train over the Kwai bridge back to Kanchanaburi. They were interested and I was delighted. After supper we walked to find Sam and arranged that he would pick us up the next morning.

I woke very early, and after a cold shower, wrote letters by the river in the garden. I had been quite taken by surprise to find how calm, almost serene, Kanchanaburi was and how warm and peaceful. It is difficult to explain. It had a feeling I really couldn't quite put my finger on, and certainly hadn't expected. With an estimated thirty nine deaths for every kilometre of track, one, it is said, for every single sleeper on the line (hence the name Death Railway) it didn't seem right not to feel a desperate sadness. And yet, the overwhelming feeling I got was of forgiveness. Never, never to forget, but yes, to forgive.

At eight thirty, Poon, Lee and I (they were 'Mr Poon and Miss Lee' and please would I call them Poon and Lee - I never did discover their first names) climbed into the back of Sam's red pick-up truck. His brother drove; it was wonderfully cool as we sped along, and dear Sam was a delight. He pointed out so much to me and answered my endless questions. We passed fields of sugar cane, and tapioca, a pretty crop with a mass of many-fingered umbrella shaped leaves held out and up off a central stem. Lining the road were papaya, coconut palm and eucalyptus trees. The soil was very red, brighter even than Devonian soil, and in the distance, jungle covered, rocky hills, many of them sharply pointed, ran north, as far as I could see.

We sped past women in coolie hats outside their homesteads, laying out coconuts, bananas, carobs and pineapples for sale, in the shade of bamboo groves. It was real Thailand, with very little traffic and country people going lazily about their business in the stifling heat. Some time later we turned off the road onto a red dirt track and, seventy kilometres from Kanchanaburi, reached the head of the pass.

The POWs, working in eighteen-hour shifts round the clock for six weeks, were forced to excavate solid limestone cliffs to a depth of eighty feet over a distance of two hundred and forty feet. Built in only three weeks, Hellfire Pass alone claimed one thousand, eight hundred lives. Minimal food and water was provided, their shoes and clothes rotted away in the worst monsoon for decades and, apart from dying of malaria, dysentery, ulcers, and other diseases, many were beaten to death. Sleepers were hewn from teak trees and, once the pass was excavated with a minimum of tools, the POWs were forced to lay over nine hundred yards of track each day. Asians were also 'conscripted' to work on the line. The Japanese would advertise a film show in a rural area, and families would stream in to watch it. Afterwards, the women and children were herded out through the door, but the men locked in, to be marched away later to work on the line.

It was an eerie place, still remote and totally unspoilt. The Australians, as custodians of the pass, had dedicated one or two memorial plaques along the way to those who died, and to one man in particular. Sir Edward 'Weary' Dunlop, an Australian and the much-loved and revered allied Camp Commandant and surgeon who unveiled the first plaque in 1987. His ashes were scattered here in 1994 - on both occasions at the Anzac Day ceremony on March 25th. We walked the length of the pass, and then on along the deserted track for some distance. You could clearly see where the prisoners' tools had been used to hammer down through the rock face, and several teak sleepers were still embedded in the track. I found a very heavy screw with a large round top, about six inches long, but somehow this wasn't the place for souvenirs, and I replaced it amongst the stones. I was so very glad to have come.

Hellfire Pass, Thailand

The pick-up truck was waiting for us at a pre-arranged point beside the track, with ice and water, and we were driven, a somewhat subdued party, to a spot further back along the line beside a pretty waterfall. I cooled my feet and decided to try and climb up it a little way - it wasn't steep. Of course I slipped, grazed my elbow, and made a real mess of my trousers and white T-shirt, much to everyone's amusement. We then had a wonderfully spicy Thai lunch at a roadside café, laid out on trestle tables under a grove of coconut palms. Juicy pomelos for pudding - much nicer than the ones we get at home.

Then we raced against time in the little red pick-up truck and just caught the train, along the same line, a short distance away. The station was just a sign and a small building, and on we hopped for an hour's train journey through fields of tapioca and pineapples, with the dark green hills towering not far beyond. Each tiny halt, hardly a station, was a blaze of colour - bougainvillea, hibiscus and frangipani trees - and the scent, in the heat of the afternoon as we chugged along, was delicious. We passed over embankments and through cuttings and I tried to imagine

51

the price paid to complete the route. The Kwai river meandered below us, in the hot sun, and finally we clattered over the bridge itself, back into Kanchanaburi.

We alighted and took a few photographs. What a memorable journey! It was hot at forty degrees centigrade. Sam took us back via the small J.E.A.T.H. War Museum, the initials standing for Japan, England, America, Thailand and Holland - the countries involved in the war in this area. It was extremely interesting, with POWs memorabilia, diaries and drawings, and is run by Thai monks. I wrote the same thing in the visitors' book as I had at the cemetery - ('Cynny Sharp, Goose Cottage, England - Thank you for our freedom') then returned home to the Jolly Frog and a cold shower.

I had one more thing to do; I wanted to visit the second, smaller and less frequently visited war cemetery at Chung Kai across the river, but again, how to do it? One boatman wanted 400 bahts (over ten pounds) for the ten-minute trip, but Sam eventually found a young boy who would pick me up from the Jolly Frog raft the next morning, for 200 baht. He swooshed in to collect me, as the Thai army were racing an enormously long Dragon boat downriver. It was full of jungle-green clad soldiers wearing Foreign Legion style caps with peaks, and a square flap at the back. On every other dip of the small squat paddles, they would shout in unison, as tug-of-war teams do; it was quite something to see - perhaps thirty soldiers paddling a long, slim boat with a thin, pointed bow and a master dressed in scarlet, standing amidships and shouting loudest of all.

I set off with my boatman at about the speed an aeroplane achieves just before it leaves the ground. It was all I could do to keep my sunglasses on and I wondered if my stud earrings would survive! It was wonderfully exhilarating, the prow of the narrow gondola-like boat lifting high in the air as I clung on. We shot past floating restaurants and raft houses and up a tributary of the River Kwai. We then slowed down, and after a short time stopped at some stone steps leading up to the cemetery. Quiet, sunny . . . I walked through the trees to the graveyard.

It was magnificent, and a fitting tribute to those who lay there. Row upon row of square plaques stood between small, brilliant flowering bushes. Many bright butterflies floated among them and gardeners in large pointed bamboo coolie hats hoed and snipped; it was a breathtaking place. The boatman had agreed to wait for half an hour and I walked slowly between the rows. Many Dutch and a few Malay and Indian soldiers were buried here though most were British men.

Beside my whistle (for emergencies), earplugs and a Second World War songsheet, I had brought with me from England a couple of church service sheets, with familiar hymns and prayers, printed on them. I had cut one out, secured it in a sturdy plastic envelope and, in the absence of any wire, bought a Thai cut-throat razor, stuck on to a metal handle. I bent this in half, protected the blade with the wrapping, and stuck it through the plastic envelope. Just before leaving, I stood quietly before one of the graves, and left my prayer in the soil beside it.

CABBAGES AND CONDOMS

Bangkok - Thursday 18th July

Last night I went out with Kate and some other girls. I have had faxes from my mother and from my son Jasper who also rang last night, which was a lovely surprise. Just as the phone rang in the Dufalls' house, a bird flew into the sitting room and straight up the open-plan stairs to the landing above, followed at great speed by the two Siamese cats, who shot from furniture to fish bowl, to terracotta pot (broke it) to stairs in pursuit - all in the space of about three seconds!

Back to our night out. Kate (Australian), Barbara and Nathalie (New Zealanders), Catriona (UK/New Zealand) and I met in a smart hotel, and, after a drink, walked to the most unusual restaurant I think I have ever been to. Named 'Cabbages and Condoms', it was opened in 1984 in a quiet, tree-lined soi (small street) in the middle of Bangkok, between the 'Darling Turkish Bathhouse' and the 'Non-Scalpel Vasectomy Centre'. A man named Mechai Viravaidya had founded the PDA (Population & Community Development Association) a non-profit making organisation, in 1974, to try and curb Thailand's soaring birth and Aids rate.

The restaurant, with tables both inside (the 'Vasectomy Bar' and 'Condom Room') and outside, is renowned for its wonderful food and unusual decor. On the walls, framed displays of condom packages from around the world made compelling reading. Large, shallow, round bamboo trays acting as frames proclaimed the name of the country selling these items - most in their wonderfully colourful original packets . . . even the plush carpet had pictures of condoms woven into it, with different names - The Pilot (propeller on the end), The Diver (plus fins) etc. I was riveted by it all! The idea was that 'birth control should be as obtainable and cheap as vegetables', hence its name. All the profit from the restaurant goes to fund work in HIV Clinics, Family Planning Centres, to preventing child prostitution, and offering vasectomies. As a way of spreading the message of safe sex the PDA had given out more than five thousand condom-decorated key ring 'survival kits' to delegates attending a recent World Bank and International Monetary Fund Conference in Bangkok.

Condoms are called 'Mechais' in Thailand, after this amazing man. After my initial disbelief, I really could not argue with the arrangement. We had a superb Thai meal, many giggles and made far too much noise. Barbara was PA to the New Zealand Ambassador, Nathalie and Kate both proconsuls in the New Zealand and British Embassies, and Catriona was en route from St John's Wood to New Zealand to see her mother. On our way out we visited the Cabbages & Condoms Handicraft shop - apart from the inevitable key-rings, flowers and brooches for sale made out of pretty coloured condoms, there were beautiful wooden bowls and silk sarongs, made by single mothers and others whom the PDA supports; it really was a most enlightened idea. Outside, the final joke came as we passed a large sign proclaiming 'I am afraid we do not have after dinner mints. Please help yourself to a condom instead' and below, two boxes marked 'modest' and 'moderate'. Each of the girls took three or four and gave them all to me, much to the amusement of the gawping taxi drivers. We left the lovely leafy greenery of the restaurant garden, a cascade of tiny, twinkling starry white lights festooning the trees, and went our separate ways. What fun!

Friday 19th July

I rang the Longmans, the friends in Dorset who had made all my Thai fun possible; through them I have met so many wonderful people, beginning with the Dufalls. David came to say goodbye at six in the morning - I was still asleep, and Kate bade me a very fond farewell a bit later and left for work. Later that morning, I found a lovely card from them both, wishing me well and giving me more Sydney addresses to add to the list I already have. How kind people are. With the card was a blue and gold pen scattered with moons and stars . . . to sign this book with one day; what an appropriate present for an inveterate scribbler. And so, goodbye to Thailand. It's cooking hot again, and nothing changes; the taxi driver tries to overcharge me, then adjusts his rear view mirror with much ceremony, so that he can see me better . . . the usual practice. And so to 'Humpalong' Station (I never could pronounce Hualamphong) and to Malaysia.

Someone has written from England to ask me what has inspired, worried or frightened me, and whom, of all the people I have met so far, I shall remember? The people: well, dear Jagdish and his splendid family will always mean Nepal to me. The gentle kindness of her people and the childlike awe and enthusiasm Jagdish and I shared in the mountains. The Tibetan girls, Raisa and Ro Kaiya at the Potala Hotel were great fun, Biju at the school in Bhaktpur was kind and gentle, and Jan Salter, the painter, an interesting woman. In Thailand, the Dufalls have been real stars, welcoming me back from up-country forays, and giving me wonderful meals and a cool bedroom haven. Spook (rhymes with 'book'), Lynne and Skye in Chiang Mai were such fun, and Michelle adventurous and interesting. Back in Bangkok I have enjoyed Barbara's company, and I shall certainly miss being addressed as 'Memsahib' or 'Mud-um Seeneey' when I return to Hampshire.

On the subject of heat and liquid, I have learned a great deal. While trying to sleep in my stifling room in Chiang Mai my body perspired like mad and the instinctive thing to do was to wipe it away, thus defeating the body's self-cooling system. By not doing so, what little air there was from breeze or fan, cooled me wonderfully. I drink a great deal of water all day, occasionally lassi which I love (fruit, yoghurt and ice liquidized together), or fresh lemon and lime juices. On the train back from Chiang Mai, though drinking constantly throughout the fourteen-hour journey, I went to the loo only once; that is how hot it was. The body really is an extraordinary machine.

I don't think so far, anything has worried me. I know I cannot walk far with both my rucksacks fully packed, and this is frustrating, but I grit my teeth and manage somehow. The heat is extremely energy-sapping, far more than I realise, and as I write, I am recovering from my train journey down here to Penang, which, I'll describe in a minute; it was very easy, just physically tiring.

I was badly frightened once, and thought I would omit the incident from my journal - but as it still sticks in my mind . . . It was in the jungle, at Chitwan in Nepal. One afternoon, as Jigmy and I stood on the elephant mounting platform, he made it quite plain to me that he would prefer me to go alone on the elephant safari; he had 'things to do'. This I did. I don't consider myself a faint-hearted girl but the elephant driver's behaviour that day really did scare me. If he saw any game - deer, rhino, wild buffalo - he would beat the elephant with the short harpoon he carried and stick it into the beast until blood was drawn and the elephant was clearly annoyed. He would then encourage the elephant to charge blindly through the fifteen-foot tall grass at great speed, trumpeting, and frightening all the animals badly.

The driver thought it great sport and the elephant would sway from side to side and growl, deep in its belly - most alarming. The elephant driver laughed wildly, took no notice at all of my protestations (and anyway, spoke no English) and he even dismounted at one point, to pick something up. A Japanese tourist had been killed by a rhino the previous week, so I knew the risks only too well. I returned, shaken, and Jigmy was nowhere to be seen. Hours later I insisted he should accompany me another time and told him why; he just laughed.

To date, I have felt safe; never complacent, but as confident as I can be on my own. I have realised that the only time I am likely to meet those of my own age with the same interests, is more likely to be whilst staying with friends. The places I stay in are often fairly rough, though usually clean, and perfectly adequate. I tend to see other forty-somethings at five-star poolsides, and in expensive restaurants. In the main they are very much tourists; I am of necessity a traveller. The traveller sees the country at ground level, breathes it, experiences it, lives it. This usually allows two things the tourist cannot provide - more time and less money. If you are going to really travel, it is going to take longer, and on a day-to-day basis cost less. So says my 'South East Asia Lonely Planet on a Shoestring' and that's about it. Travellers take trains and buses, eat at local roadside bars and walk a lot; most, of my own age and stage, don't!

What has inspired me? Above all, so far, the Himalayas, those colossal, towering, snowy mountains. Meaning 'Ice Mansion' in Nepalese, they soared almost out of our world, majestic and mighty. The effect they had on me, and others I have talked to since, was electrifying. I was often moved to tears and felt great surges of joy and euphoria when amongst them - a magical feeling. The people of Nepal are such lovely, undemanding people, who find their pleasure in simple things, often making the most of so very little, and undeterred by hardship. Their hospitality is boundless; I well remember the sick granny, lying on her rush mat behind a curtain in a tiny village, whispering to her small grandchildren, urging them to bring us mats to sit on, as we rested for tea, high in the hills. Yes, inspiring.

Kanchanaburi on the River Kwai moved me greatly. The terrible loss of life so very far from home, in unimaginable circumstances, brought different tears; of horror and disbelief and of the deepest gratitude for the sacrifices made in that alien place. I have felt much and I have felt deeply.

JAMBU AND SCOTCH

Later

The night train from Bangkok left at half past three in the afternoon on the dot. It was quite full and my carriage held swarms of young Malays returning from a religious seminar in Thailand. One of them, a young fat man with a loud voice, struck up an immediate friendship with a wild-eyed unshaven German backpacker. They sat cross-legged on their seats opposite each other having a loud religious discussion - bordering on argument - for the entire twenty-one hour journey; they were still at it when I went to bed. One of the Malays offered fruit round the carriage and gave me a piece. Looking like a pale green pepper but rather more pear-shaped, I bit into it and found it wonderfully crisp and clean-tasting, like a sweet radish. It was a jambu.

The day wore on, and I consulted my Lonely Planet on where to stay and what to see in Penang. I had filled my water bottle for the journey and bought fruit: rambutans, spiky lychees, and bunches of yellow grape-like longans still on their long stalks, to eat on the way. I ordered a curry supper - rather different this time, and I missed my friend in the gym shoes. I ordered tea and toast for breakfast. As I finished supper, I realised a kind of cocktail party was going on, with much hilarity, in the minuscule space between my carriage and the loos, and gradually it spilt over right beside me; I was on the end seat and that's when I met Joe and Linda.

They were the best sort of Americans, garrulous, full of bonhomie, and gathering everyone they came across into their fold, with interest and jollity. Linda was tanned an impossible mahogany colour. Her hair, rather obviously dyed white blonde a million times, hung down lifelessly like a wig, but she was full of life and fun, accompanying her brother on a jaunt through Thailand. Joe, who worked for a tobacco company, was round and nice-looking, with bright white American teeth and a gorgeous smile. With introductions all round, they immediately ordered another bottle of Scotch and a pail of ice and off they went again, cosily sitting opposite me in a seat for one, plying me with whisky and quizzing me on life, death, and my adventures. I moved back to their seats with them until the 'Nazis' arrived to make up our beds, and regretfully I bade them goodbye around midnight. They got off at the Thai coast bound for the islands and I gave Linda my flight details to Bali (she was very tempted to join me) we swore lifelong friendship and swapped addresses. 'Goose Cottage' seemed very tame beside her '4001 some Boulevard, Fort Lauderdale, Florida'.

I slept a little but found it difficult with the carriage lights blazing and people getting in and out at different stations throughout the night, although my bed was comfortable. I put my money belt under my pillow, (containing travellers cheques, passport etc) and kept my small zipped bag with camera, radio, water and books etc by my feet in bed, while the rest of my precious things, my binoculars, clothes and papers, were locked in my big rucksack padlocked to the upper luggage shelves. The smaller khaki rucksack I use for my washing things, a towel, more books and clothes in case I get stranded; this all seems to work.

On the morning of Saturday 20th July I eagerly awaited the border crossing. The Thai countryside was pleasant, and much the same as that I had seen on my journey to Chiang Mai; rice, bananas, coconuts and tapioca (sounds like the start of a recipe). At eight o'clock we reached the Thai-Malaysian border at Padang Besar and were all ushered off the train - a great palaver, with all our luggage. We went through Immigration just inside the station building and then through Customs. The officials made me unpack my smaller rucksack, purely out of boredom I think and questioned me about my umbrella (I ask you!) tucked down the side, and then waved me on. Immediately and quite extraordinarily the countryside and train attendants changed and it was not my imagination.

BUTTERFLIES AND BUFFALOES

We gathered speed, passing serried ranks of rubber trees and many different kinds of palms, grown for their oil. The railway officials were much gentler, kinder people, always ready to talk and give advice unlike the rather dismissive Thais. On we went, stopping at many stations, large and small, where local tradesmen would leap aboard with globe-like bamboo baskets of fruit, meals of rice and curry wrapped in newspaper and buckets of coke and Fanta buried in ice - all madly expensive.

We reached Butterworth at noon and I immediately made for the ferry to the island of Penang. As in so many ports and airports, it was a long hike and that's when I realised my limitations on carrying all my gear at once. I managed, but with some discomfort, mainly to my shoulders. I had packed all the heaviest things in the middle and on top, as decreed by my daughter Gemma, but it was HEAVY! The approach, some three kilometres over the water to Georgetown reminded me so much of sailing into Portsmouth. Fort Cornwallis, built in the 1700s by the British, who first settled there, commands a dominant position over the water, and many of the buildings are old and now much faded Colonial homes.

And so, I arrived in Georgetown, the capital of Penang. The rickshaws here gave you the feeling of being pushed along in a wheelbarrow. The driver pedals behind you and you sit, together with your gear, in a seat rather like the scoop of a digger. A bit worrying - as you can't see him steering - inching past buses and across busy main roads. I found The White House Hotel (recommended by someone in England) and it was clean, which was all I needed right then. It was tiled from floor to head height throughout with shiny white tiles, just like a hospital or some similar institution. With coloured tiled floors and vast, high ceilinged corridors, it made me think of a lunatic asylum. I was tired, but wanted to see the town . . .

The first thing I noticed, on buying a map of the island, was how many British names there were. 'Lebuh' is the word for street, and I found Lebuh Campbell, Lebuh Argyll and Maxwell, Carnarvon (sic), MacAlister, Herriot, Farquhar, Leith. The phonetically spelt English signs were so funny - 'Teksi' for taxi, 'Farmasi' for chemist and 'Take Dat Photo Shop'. My hotel was in Chinatown, a wonderfully colourful, busy area, full of tailors' shops, noodle stalls and goldsmiths. I had some lunch, a fried chapati and dhal, one scooped up with the other, at a tiny café and noticed they sold amongst the cokes and Fantas and other drinks - iced Horlicks; I must try some one day. Curry Kapitan is another local speciality; the story goes that a Dutch sea captain asked his cabin boy what was for supper - 'Curry, Kapitan' he replied, and it's been on the menu in Georgetown ever since. It was strange to see so many Muslims, many of the women heavily veiled, and Chinese temples were often just round the corner from Buddhist or Hindi places of worship. Sadly, the well-known E & O (Eastern and Oriental) Hotel built by Raffles was boarded up undergoing renovation, so the Gin Sling will have to wait.

That night I emerged showered and hungry from the asylum, to find the annual city parade in full swing. Hundreds of people, many of them children, lined the roads to watch vastly long and brilliantly-coloured Chinese paper dragons, orchid covered floats and decorated water buffaloes parading happily along in the warm night air; what fun! I found a small restaurant, just a bar really, and had some rice and curry and a lemon soda. I then walked for a while before turning in - the Chinese quarter was full of music, vendors, old men in bars chewing the cud, and throngs of meandering families.

The next morning I wandered up to St George's Cemetery, just beyond my hotel. Here were buried many of the first settlers and it was quite fascinating. The graves dated from the sixteenth century until the late eighteen hundreds, and gave a poignant insight into the hardships of life in those days. Many of the children did not survive infancy; three children only months old were buried together with their mother and a last baby - she had died in childbirth. Young officers and sailors, ships' engineers and women who had perished at sea, on the long journey south, were finally buried here. Officials of the East India Company - often Head Administrators of the settlement at only twenty-seven, had died here of jungle fever - malaria, I suppose. One entire family had perished overnight, 'of disease' and another man, a British Major, had been 'Murdered by Chinese robbers in the night'. What a hard, alien life it must have been for European settlers.

Later that day I made for the beach. Nathalie (the New Zealander, at The Cabbages & Condoms supper) had told me about a good guesthouse right on the water at Batu Ferringhi, about fifteen kilometres to the north. Shalinis Guest House was lovely. Not particularly smart, but fairly new. I had a room with a large double bed, overlooking the verandah and only fifty yards away from a mile of white sand. The surf was very loud and wonderful to live by all day as it crashed and swished on the sand, and three noisy cockerels living next door joined in, crowing at intervals all day long as they strutted on the sand which made me laugh.

The fat mama who ran the guesthouse made me a mug of tea and a bowl of fruit salad each morning for breakfast - papaya, pineapple, melon and banana. Gorgeous, and I ate it watching the sea, on the little verandah. The pineapple was wonderfully fragrant, and much more intense in flavour than our imported ones, as were the bananas. About a quarter of a mile in either direction along the sand, were vast hotels with pools and sun beds and all the paraphernalia . . . I would sit in a favourite spot and watch the fun - the jet skis, and long, yellow inflatable 'banana' boats towed speedily behind motor boats with people sitting astride the huge banana. From each hotel you could parascend, taking off from the beach and doing a wide circuit out to sea - great fun to watch. One day a man walked by, then walked back and sat and chatted to me. His business was 'water sports and massage'. I said I didn't want to pay for either, but a free ride on a jet ski would be fun . . . he went away, returning about half an hour later with the offer of a free massage (in my room) - 'of course' he said 'you can't be naked on the beach' What a pity I didn't fancy him . . .!

After a couple of days sorting out letters, finances and writing cards, I caught a bus back into Georgetown one morning, and out again part of the way, to the Botanical Gardens. After alighting, I walked about a mile and found a marvellous stall - just two plastic tables, chairs and a tiny griddle, in the gravel car park by the gardens' entrance. I had a yummy chapati and dhal (eaten with the hands) for just sixty cents (fifteen pence). It is so easy to spend a lot in Malaysia (half an hour on a jet ski for 40 Malaysian Ringets - about ten pounds) and yet so easy to spend very little. A reasonable curry (though too much rice) costs about three pounds in a restaurant, but a smaller plate of wonderfully spicy noodles, ginger, chicken and prawns at one of the roadside stalls, only costs about fifty pence.

On working out my finances, having budgeted twenty two pounds a day, approximately, for my entire trip, I found that in Nepal, where I had had to pay for accommodation (when not on treks) I had spent an average of twenty one pounds per day which included a decent wedding present for my brother, and presents for my family within this. In Thailand (despite my free lodgings in Bangkok) I spent an average of thirty pounds per day. I am now being extremely careful, aiming to live on about ten pounds a day for a few weeks. A room here is on average the equivalent of six pounds fifty and food is wonderfully reasonable, as I have explained. Bangkok cost me a fortune in taxis as the Dufalls lived off the bus route and I often met David or Kate after work at the Embassy, or some other venue - again by taxi. Travellers coming up through Malaysia say how expensive it is after Bali; I say how inexpensive it is after Thailand.

Sign on my bus to the Botanical Gardens in four languages - Chinese, Malay, Thai and English – 'Please do not spit".

I loved the botanical gardens, with its long velvety sweeps of grass, huge oriental trees, beautiful palms and orchids. I sat on a seat in the shade and wrote this. As I sat so peacefully, a Muslim family walked up the hill - all as black as midnight, mother in full sail with veil and yashmak, and only her eyes showing, dressed completely in black, while her three enchanting small daughters bounced along in impossibly frilled dresses, walking with their father, who was clad in shorts. I called to him that his little daughters were the prettiest things I had seen in the gardens, and asked if I might take a photo of them. They then asked if they could have one of me, and I posed with the three identically dressed little girls, for their father. As they left, the children waved coyly to me all the way up the hill, until they were out of sight.

A day later on the beach, I was chatting to a Latvian girl, when up skidded a beach bum on his jet ski, with a great swoosh of seawater. They show off like mad, aiming at the beach at frightening speed, and literally driving their machines out of the water and up the sand until they stop, then stepping elegantly off for a coke, to pose, or seek a passenger. Miss Latvia and I said we were definitely not interested in a half hour's spin for twenty ringets, but I called that I would love a few minutes for free and, hey presto I was on board! It was smashing fun, and my new friend took a couple of photos of me as I sped past.

<u>Saturday 27th July</u>

I have had a sore throat for a couple of days and have felt very tired. It is exceedingly hot, and I have discovered the hard way that not only must one replace the water and salt lost, but also other body salts such as potassium, not readily found in food here. My sleep pattern is up the creek; I have slept on some days until ten o'clock and on others I walk along the mile of wonderful sand just beyond my room, as the sun rises.

Today I took a bus to the butterfly farm, about ten kilometres further up the coast; at least, as near to it as I could get. The bus driver dropped me at a roundabout and said 'You walk', and so I did, only a kilometre, but I was still feeling rather feeble. I hummed 'Mad dogs and Englishmen' to myself but once there, I was enchanted. The term 'butterfly farm' is unpleasant; even butterfly world or something similar would be better. I found myself in a huge wire cage, with masses of roomy sunshine for the butterflies and moths, amongst hibiscus, orchids and other magnificent flowers. Butterflies I had seen high above me in the jungle, or floating across the wide gorges of Nepal, were now close enough to touch, and so wondrous to behold. Brilliantly iridescent, large and majestic or delicately transparent, tiny jewels, deep blue, or yellow and black spotted - they were all gorgeous. My favourite was quite a large black butterfly, its wings opening to reveal a deep velvet blue, like a painted night sky, with tiny white points, like stars, shimmering in the blue. I watched it for a long time, floating and dipping for nectar among the orchids.

I spent quite a while there, and also saw scorpions, tarantulas, water scorpions, geckos, and beetles with bodies four inches in diameter. On emerging I didn't feel much like repeating my walk back to the bus, and on the spur of the moment bought one of those Isotonic fizzy drinks, a can of 100 Plus I think it was, containing glucose, potassium and Vitamin C, and other energy giving goodies. It was effective almost immediately, and I felt quite back to normal again. I remembered buying one on my way back from Kanchanaburi, and how very much better I had felt, almost instantaneously, in that dreadfully hot minibus.

Oh, how I miss everyone! Knowing I will not get any post for another two weeks is hard, but only because I have been dallying here awhile. Once I am on the move again to Ipoh on Monday, I hope the longing will lessen.

Our minds are so extraordinary. In the middle of Malaysia, surrounded by so many exotic sights and sounds, I dreamt last night that the Archers were all forced to leave Ambridge. By half past four, I had saved them all, single-handed!

As I was gargling last night (with salt as my mother has advised me to) I was joined in unison by the resident dove, who lives above the shower room. She cooed away merrily, and, if I shut my mouth and gargled, I could at a long stretch, have been another dove. There are lots of two and four legged beasties here. Three little pye-dogs join me whenever I walk along the beach, and odd shaped kittens frolic in the sand. They have very short, stumpy tails and thick hindquarters and back legs - most peculiar. The three resident cockerels scratch and scuff in the dust and sand, occasionally staging spectacular fights right opposite our verandah, egged on by all the locals. Small lizards run up and down the walls, both inside and outside the guesthouse. I've watched them having mosquito suppers under the strip lights, which I thoroughly approve of. Mynah birds with startlingly bright beady yellow eyes, watch us eating meals on the verandah, and enormous crows (they look more like jackdaws - I'm not exactly sure what they are, but they're huge) find any morsel of food left by picnickers. This morning as I was sitting on the verandah, one flew past me with a large paper plate in his strong beak and proceeded to peck it completely clean of rice, or whatever, by balancing it in his claws on a large, flat frond of a palm tree - comical to watch.

Tuesday 30th July - Ipoh, Malaysia

I left Batu Ferringhi in a bit of a hurry on Sunday, realising at breakfast time that as it was the Prophet Mohammed's Birthday that day, and a public holiday the next, the beach would be swarming with Moslem families and very noisy. I packed my two rucksacks speedily - it's fun to change plans on the spur of the moment - and just managed it to the bus stop. Being frugal, I resented paying Malaysian Ringgit (RM) 18 (£4.50) for a taxi back to Georgetown when I knew the bus fare was RM1.50 (under 50p). The bus was hideously overcrowded and I perched beside a fat man, slid off my large sack and all three of us shared the seat. I felt so sorry for the poor Moslem girls in that heat, with their heads permanently covered by a tudung; even in the sea, they paddle fully clothed. As I got off the bus in Georgetown, I met a fellow traveller, Craig from Glasgow, with the broadest of accents.

He and I found D'Budget Hostel (which I recommended to him; I am now becoming one of the knowledgeable travellers) and checked in. RM 8 (£2) for a dorm room seemed great, as I'm still on half measures for a couple of weeks to catch up after Bangkok. My room was tiny with two bunk beds (an upper one already occupied by a towel and other belongings) and I bagged the other top one, wondering who my companion was. The showers and loos were very clean. Leaving my big rucksack locked up and the other stacked behind it in a corner by the bed, I set off to re-explore Georgetown. Having got to know some of the locals out at the beach and learnt about the food, Georgetown now seemed somehow much more familiar and I was more into the Malaysian way of life of course, than I had been the day I arrived. I found a bustling open-air café selling 'chicken rice' and ordered a steaming bowl along with some iced coffee. I've also sampled fried noodles, banana leaf curry (a selection of curries served on a huge banana leaf, rather than a plate, straight on to the table, with pickles etc to accompany it) and murtabak (dough rolled extremely thinly, folded and fried on a griddle) served with dhal, and cuttlefish curry.

I saw Craig across the street and, hailing him, he joined me. The 'chicken rice' consists of a plate of plain white rice, a bowl of succulent strips of steamed chicken and a bowl of clear chicken soup, with the odd vegetable floating in it, which you spoon together on to the rice. Delicious, and only RM 3 (70p). I haven't been brave enough to try the 'Seafood Porridge' yet - I merely imagine it. I then continued my tour of Georgetown, and Craig went off to seek out friends.

As I was reading the information board outside one of the wonderful old Colonial buildings, I caught up with a couple who were around about my age and looked as if they might be army or diplomatic sort of people (frightfully British). As we were both on a 'Colonial Route' of various old buildings we met up again at Fort Cornwallis (where the British first landed in the 1700s) and got talking. They were very nice, and I asked them if they would do me a favour and ring my Mother on their return to England the following week; just to say they had seen me and that I was well. I tried to give them some local currency, but they wouldn't hear of it.

I returned to D'Budget to find my room-mate there . . . .a good-looking Spaniard of about thirty, named Carlos, with black curly hair. I wasn't at all sure at first about the idea of sharing with him, but as he made himself scarce when I arrived and knocked on our door politely later, in case I was undressed, I decided he was probably okay.

Later I met up with a rather boring woman of my age for supper. I'd struck up a conversation with her in the Botanical Gardens, we had swapped details and she'd suggested I look her up if I returned to Georgetown, which I did - and wished I hadn't. She was also on her own, (her husband had left her for two 'tarts', she said) and with oodles of money, she complained about everything. Whilst travelling you must try your utmost not to Criticise, Complain or Compare; it is really important to try and make the best of it all, and when, coming out of the café, we almost tripped over a large rat, she launched off into a tirade about the Chinese - I just giggled. She was planning to travel for five years . . . good luck to her.

I slept rather fitfully that night, with the door of the room unlocked, being more concerned with fleeing from Carlos if the need arose, than with anyone entering. He had been sitting cross-legged on his bunk meditating when I returned at ten o'clock, and turned out to be a perfect room-mate and didn't snore, fart or leap, while I kept my precious things safely at the end of my sleep-sheet by my toes. In the morning I borrowed his Rough Guide to look up accommodation in Melaka, Singapore and Bali, while he went for breakfast. On his return, he handed me a lovely map he had drawn of a place he was going to stay at in Bali, and with a cheery 'Once more into the brunch!' (how I laughed) he slung on his backpack and departed. About twenty minutes later, as I was standing starkers drying my hair in front of the fan, he reappeared, knocking first, with lots of maps of Kuala Lumpur, Singapore and Bali for me, and said that he hoped so much we'd meet again 'Seeny'.

I just had time for a quick breakfast, a walk to see St George's Anglican Church (sadly, locked) and another wonderfully ornate Chinese 'clan meeting house' before I had to vacate my room. I downed a can of the excellent 100 Plus, said a prayer for strength and donned my kit. It was terribly hot, but determination won and I reached the bus office about half a mile away without too much difficulty.

BALA

The coach journey to Ipoh was very interesting. Rather than crossing over on the ferry, we drove over the Penang Bridge, some eight kilometres long, the longest one in SE Asia, linking the island of Penang with the mainland. The three-hour trip to Ipoh cost less than three pounds - excellent value. We passed mile upon mile of coconut and palm plantations, beside the toll expressway, and many small coloured sunshades on the hard shoulder under which farming families, living on the edge of the plantations, would sell bananas, rambutans, and the huge spiny jackfruit. I had no idea there were so many different kinds of palm trees, and as the coach laboured up hugely steep mountain cuttings and then sped down the other side, I saw vast rubber palm estates and banana trees, and high forested hills. It was very hot, and the coach windows were shaded with bright blue satin curtains most of them drawn to keep out the sun - except mine. I apologised to the Moslem girl next to me (they must all have been boiled in their veils) explaining that I wanted to look at her country, and she fully understood.

IPOH - I reclaimed my big rucksack from the underbelly of the coach (insisting on having the other one inside with me) and caught a taxi to the hotel I'd plumped for. It was a rather dingy Chinese-run establishment, but seemed okay. I tried to haggle with the clerk over the price (RM 23 - £6) but he wouldn't budge. Then, rather overcome with being here, after all those years of hearing my grandmother Meta talk about Ipoh, I told the clerk my reason for coming; that my father had been born here in 1919 (he died in 1971) and that my grandfather had been a barrister here for over thirty years, living in Ipoh, and had died in Kuala Lumpur in 1937. The clerk, Mr Toh Kam Toon then told me he would take me in his car to St John's Church (with which Grandpa Joe had had close connections) on his way home, but that I must be ready in ten minutes. I found my room, dumped my bags and off we went.

A little while afterwards, having been dropped off (Toon had promised to collect me in a short while) I stood on the priest's doorstep, quite suddenly in floods of tears. It was a lovely old wooden, shuttered Malay house with a long verandah, behind the church; and that is how the priest found me. Dr Batumalai, a tall, black, kindly man of fifty, told me to take my time; he thought I had done something terrible. It was so hot, and I was tired and very emotional indeed, thinking of my father and my grandparents, once in this very spot, so very far from England. I ended up in his kitchen, having wonderfully strong tea, with him, his wife, and Ezekiel, a young Malay trainee priest, who had also just arrived. I demolished quite a few biscuits I'm afraid, not having had anything to eat since breakfast time. Then Toon peered in, and ended up joining us. Dr Batumalai told me to come back the following morning and I could then see inside the church (which was locked). Dear old Mr Toon, (aged seventy-eight) drove me back to my hotel, taking a route past lots of old Colonial buildings and law offices, especially for my benefit. I had cuttlefish curry supper very near my hotel, and bought cakes in a smart little bakery, which I later shared with the next porter on duty - Mr Yong.

Today has been just as extraordinary. I caught a bus half way to the church after a fairly revolting breakfast. I will try any food almost without exception, but I cannot stomach murtabak and dhal, or curried anything for breakfast. I wanted very black tea but I think I was given milky sweet Horlicks, and the palm oil spread on my toast was . . . but mustn't Complain!

St John's church was very Scottish, plain, simple and almost austere, with wonderful wicker-backed and seated pews, which must have been nice and cool. It was funny being in a large church and almost passing out with the heat. I said prayers, and Dr Batumalai brought me a cool drink and it was very peaceful. He has invited me to a church meeting of some sort in the church on Thursday. As I walked back towards the centre of the town, I wondered how on earth I could find out more about Grandpa Joe.

The very smart Ipoh Club, bordering the large green area in the town centre, was strictly for members, unless you were taken as a guest. I was walking past the law courts, when I saw a large Indian in a huge black turban, carrying what were obviously legal briefs, across the road towards me. (I have had enough practise identifying lawyers in Winchester). I stopped him, explained very quickly what I wanted, and he wrote down for me the name of the senior partner of a top legal firm in Ipoh and told me where to find him; he was seventy-six he told me (take note for what transpired later).

I eventually found the office and was ushered in by a pretty sari-clad girl. Mr W.E. Balasingam is a splendid man, smart, nice-looking, with a mischievous twinkle in his eyes; we hit it off immediately. He said there had only been two firms of lawyers in Ipoh in the 1910-1930s period including his, and that my grandfather had probably belonged to the other firm. He took a photocopy of the sketchy details I had and said that he would take me to lunch in the Ipoh Club tomorrow and we could then chat. He also asked me - in general banter - how old I thought he was. Of course I knew, so I said, looking him up and down, 'Oh, let's see, er, late fifties or early sixties?' He chuckled and was delighted; 'that old?' he asked.

I returned to the street and tried unsuccessfully to find my way to one of the oldest restaurants in Ipoh. (Restaurant here in Malaysia, especially if an old one, means a large, high-ceilinged room, open to the street, with fans, lots of metal or plastic tables and chairs and excellent cheap food). I got completely lost, and asked a woman for directions. I ended up (when they realised I was alone) being driven by them (her father drove and there was mother, sister, my friend, daughter and me - all in a smallish car) right to the door of the restaurant I had been looking for. People here are wonderfully kind and I didn't know how to thank them enough - I had been miles off course.

It was a very busy place with no free tables, so I asked a young couple if I could join them. I ordered noodles with chicken and prawns (it comes in a large soup bowl with stock and chopsticks) and fresh lime juice. You are expected to pay as soon as the food comes, and quick as a flash, the husband at the table with me, paid for everything I ate. Once again I was delighted and grateful. They asked me all about England and my journey and kept asking if I wanted anything else to eat, so I had another lime juice on him - what fantastic kindness to a complete stranger.

When we parted, I sat for a while on an old stone seat beside the green (the old cricket pitch), flanked by old Colonial buildings, and took in all that had happened. I just had to ring my mother and tell her.

I walked back to my hotel via The Railway Station Hotel. The station itself is housed in an incredible building known as the Taj Mahal of Ipoh. It is a huge, white, domed building, dating from the mid 1800s, an impressive Moorish architectural landmark, in front of which is a lovely garden. Inside this wonderful building is the elegant hotel, and not, I guarantee, like any other station hotel in the world. I ordered a large glass of iced coffee on the verandah, which runs all round the palatial building, and sat in a big, puffy chair, above the jasmine and palms in the garden below, to finish writing a letter and some cards. I'll bet Granny often came here. She was fondly remembered as a very talkative, utterly charming woman, a great character and a terrific snob; it is said she was the very first European woman to visit the Cameron Highlands, which is where I may go next. And so, the close of a lively couple of days.

Wednesday 31st July - and another whirlwind day. I am quite convinced I am being helped from on high; my life has turned into a social whirl, which is extraordinary considering I knew no one when I arrived . . .

The day began at seven o'clock, when I changed hotels. I really don't expect much for my money, but if you pay for a room and: you cannot see after dark as the six inch strip light is in the bathroom, the shower doesn't work and the dribble of water from the tap just off the floor is your only means of washing, the wire grille replacing the top few inches of my walls means I can hear the Chinese Madame at her desk in the corridor until three am and the Ladies of the Night doing business in the next room while my fan has one speed only - off the Beaufort scale at about Force twelve . . . you are entitled to find other lodgings. You should have seen me, trying to sleep with a blindfold on, a scarf, to block out the blazing lights from Madame's empire on three sides of my room, and to keep my hair from taking off in the blast from the ceiling fan; it was both comical and uncomfortable. The only good thing was that I knew no mozzie would get me as they couldn't stay airborne long enough in the downdraught, to nip!

Much consternation from Toon, but I explained kindly and promised I would still keep our date that evening. He is picking me up at eight o'clock. As I write this, I have no idea what for, but I think to see the night-lights of Ipoh (very spectacular apparently) and his home. He was seventy-eight if you recall, and very frail, so no worries on my part.

To move hotels I traipsed up and down the street with my belongings hastily packed in rucksack liners, plastic bags etc much to the amusement of the Chinese community. My next room has a well-behaved fan, western loo, fantastic if ancient shower and a decent light - all for only a few pennies more. Next, I rang Mr Balasingam to check whether I could wear a sleeveless dress for lunch (the Club is very smart) and he replied on no account and, as his morning appointment was cancelled, would I come as soon as I could.

I tore back to the new hotel from the phone box, took a screwed up skirt and silk blouse over to a boutique across the road and asked if I could iron them. Another amazingly kind Ipohian, the salesgirl ironed them both, thought I was totally eccentric and asked me to tell her about my lunch, which I promised I would. I tore back, dug into the depths of my rucksack again, for necklace, scent, sandals, bracelet and in a flash, Geriatric Backpacker was transformed into . . . well anyway I didn't think I looked too bad!

I caught a taxi as a treat - the heat was terrific - and arrived at Bala's office (gave up on his name and everyone calls him that) at about eleven. He greeted me warmly and had placed a large brown envelope in front of my chair, opposite his on his vast lawyers desk. I thought perhaps it was some information I was seeking. I was touched to find it contained pages of sayings and quotations ('If you have built castles in the air, Your labour is not lost, That is where it should be, Now put the foundation under it' - and 'To love and to be loved is to feel the Sun on both sides' are two that I particularly liked) and extraordinary articles on exercise, health and other topics. How could he possibly have known I really enjoy words and poems?

We chatted for ages, and he called his staff in to bring water for me, and large envelopes (when I told him I had photocopied my diary to send home to my family) and asked if there was any other help he could give me. He rang a partner in another law firm and we arranged to call on him on our way out to lunch. Bala was a wonderful man, extremely courteous and gentlemanly but extraordinarily frank with me on such a short acquaintance. He is obviously revered by his firm, the oldest in Malaysia, dating from 1876. Eventually, after much baring of souls and hearts (ah, how often have I been privy to the secrets of my friends across the world) we went for lunch.

On the way we popped into the offices of the law firm of Maxwell, Kenion, Cowdy & Jones where I was introduced to a Mr James Devadason. He showed me a rather smart coffee table book, entitled The Malayan Judiciary, and directed me to a photograph within the pages, taken in July 1928, on the occasion of the opening of the Supreme Court Building in Ipoh by the then British Resident. In the first row at the top, twelfth man along was Joseph Dunford Wood. Thrilled to bits I leapt up, much to their amusement. There was my grandfather and it was only the second or third photograph I had ever seen of him! Photocopies were hastily made for me.

Bala and I then crossed the large wide cricket pitch, the white wooden rails running round it shaded by palms and frangipani trees. Past the colonial buildings and Chinese shops bordering them, the venerable Indian advocate and the mad Englishwoman walking to lunch in a club I knew my grandparents had belonged to. What an incredible journey this is turning out to be. Up steep steps at one end of the green, it was a beautiful club overlooking the old town centre. With huge, lazily revolving ceiling fans, panelling, wicker steamer chairs and a band playing discreetly for the diners, I had to pinch myself. I savoured the prawn, salmon, crab and caviar salad (Bala had told me 'the sky's the limit!') and then I had quite delicious grilled snapper, crème caramel and coffee. Oh, wow - rather a welcome change from the usual street noodle stalls, much as I enjoy them. Bala and I were away; we did not draw breath for an hour, and he told me some wicked jokes! Naughty Bala then told me that his morning appointment, postponed until the next day, had been cancelled by his secretary on his orders. 'I can see that Judge any time, but you are only here for one more day' and he asked me if I would have lunch with him again the next day, once I'd finished my arranged appointment to meet the Maxwell, Kenion and Co's senior partner. After a fond and grateful farewell on a busy main road, he headed back to his office.

The opening of the Supreme Court Building in Ipoh, July 1928.
My grandfather, Joseph Dunford Wood is third from the right in the back row.

A DATE WITH TOON

I walked to the Perak Museum (Ipoh is the capital of Perak State) housed in a wonderful old nineteenth century wooden Colonial palace; all interesting stuff about tin mining, forestry, rubber etc. I then walked (feeling a bit stupid in dinky sandals and silk blouse) up the side of a vast highway, to seek out two or three very old colonial bungalows, which James Devadason had told me were the only ones still in existence in Ipoh. Lorries, taxis and mopeds roared past me, many of the drivers tooting and waving madly as I picked my way up the central reservation and then alongside the wide roads (it's my jungle hat that attracts attention and I just ignore it now). It was searingly hot, and after much searching near a roundabout, I found the bungalows.

Two old, wooden, black and white painted, partially clinker-built bungalows on stilts, or rather on stone triangles, a cross between trig points and staddlestones. I disturbed a Moslem couple in what had obviously been the servants' quarters (now their home) joined by steps and a covered open walkway to the back door of the bungalow. When I explained my mission they didn't mind a bit, and showed me round the house, now Government-owned and used by visiting officials. It was absolutely fascinating.

The rooms were arranged in a circle with tall, elegant wooden double doors opening off the main sitting-room and similar double doors opening into the next room and so on, until the last pair of doors opened on to the sitting room once again. The whole wooden building had very high airy ceilings, ancient GEC fans and old-fashioned Bakelite light switches. Shutters around each room opened both at floor level and at window height, with narrow shutters on the walls connecting each room. There was no glass to be seen, and around the higher part of the walls wooden trelliswork allowed the air to circulate. It was rather like an Arthur Rackham house from a fairy story, or a Somerset Maughan tale . . . by the time I left, quite a little party had gathered on the steps to bid me farewell - the husband, his veiled wife, their small son and the local policeman, who'd come to see why I was wandering about. 'Remember us, when you are back in England!' they shouted after me.

Eventually back at my hotel (another long story - a fascinating political/social discussion with three others in a share-taxi en route, on Malaysia, men, Prince Charles and the Empire) I rummaged around for my second and final screwed up silk shirt and tore over to the boutique to have it ironed before it closed. The girl was highly amused that I had another date and kept me talking for half an hour, on marriage, (hers was in a week's time) my travels, Chinese food and hotels. The Malaysians love talking! I then wrote this journal for a while and listened to the World News on my small radio.

At eight o'clock, Toon collected me in his tiny car and off we sped past the cinema he had managed for twenty-five years. He drove me round the city for a while and then out to the most extraordinary Woolley's Food Centre. Sited in a large hangar-like building (open sided, of course) many hundreds of plastic tables and chairs were arranged, with over thirty food stalls ranged around them, selling Chinese, Malay and Indian food. The idea is to wander around and choose, and then sit down at a numbered table (ours had '97' painted in the middle of it) and drinks are brought. You then order the first dish, which is delivered to your table, and when that is demolished you get up and order another and so on. Dear Toon, the Chinese reception clerk from the Cathay Hotel, wouldn't let me pay for anything. I had star fruit juice and he had lotus root juice - both a little bitter, but very refreshing, then Sa Hor Fun (noodles with chicken, spring onions and seafood sauce) and satay sticks - pork, with a scrumptious nutty sauce, then Woo Kok and Char Siew Pan - Chinese steamed, pork-filled balls, one breadcrumbed, the other a light white bread. Delicious!

Large families had taken over groups of tables and there was a wonderfully festive air about the place. Our meal finished, it was quite late, and Toon drove me back to my hotel. What a day! On Friday I shall leave Ipoh and travel up to the Cameron Highlands for a few days. I long to collect mail I know is awaiting me in Kuala Lumpur but I cannot arrive there too soon as; (a) it's too expensive for me to stay there for more than a day or two and (b) as it's such a busy city, I really don't want to be there for long and (c) I will make for Singapore and my next flight on August 19th after that. It is half past eleven - I must shower and sleep now, but I had to write of all that has befallen me today – Wow, WHAT a day!

NT

Thursday 1st August

Today I began with trying a banana murtabak for breakfast in a bar across the road called 'Dins Cafe'. This is folded dough cooked on a griddle, and a possible Malaysian compromise for breakfast, so I thought. The salt and oil used on the griddle didn't really help, but it was 'interesting' (as we say about food when we won't be re-ordering) and then the owner asked if I would like some gravy. Chicken gravy he meant and insisted I tried it - in the end curry might have been a better bet.

My meeting with the lawyer James Devadason was fun. His grandfather had been British and his grandmother Malay, and he was a star, looking up church records for me (he is on the St John's Council) to see if there was any mention of my grandfather, or possibly my father's christening, although he may well have been christened back in Scotland, on Tiree. We drew a blank. He was then very keen for me to meet the senior partner, Datuk NT Rajah, and I was escorted by James up to the penthouse at the very top of their offices, with a really wonderful view of Ipoh (the 'green' I keep referring to, was below us, twelve acres set aside by the British to mark Queen Victoria's Jubilee).

Mr Rajah joined us for tea; he was a grand old boy, and I soon had them laughing over some tale or other. I learnt so much about the production of rubber and tea from them, the (now halted) deforestation of the Cameron Highlands, resulting in a warmer climate up there than had been experienced in the past, and about the racial mixes in Malaysia (50% Malays, 48% Chinese, 2% Indians and others). All most interesting. I had asked James whether there was anything I could do in return for his kindness, once I had returned to England. Two things, he said. To try and find out more about the Maxwell who had founded the firm (not difficult, as he had illustrious parents (Governor of the Gold Coast, knighted, Lincoln's Inn etc) and also more about his own grandfather. I promised to try.

Dear old Bala I knew would sell his soul for video copies of 'Beau Geste' with Gary Cooper, Robert Preston and Ray Milland and of the 'Charge of the Light Brigade' with Errol Flynn and Olivia de Havilland - a tall order, but I really will try. I took my leave of the two men, having been invited out to dinner tonight with Mr Rajah and his wife at the Perak Golf Club. Wow again! James rang to cancel my church appointment that night, telling me it was a boring committee meeting and he wasn't sure why the vicar had invited me.

I then hot-footed it round the corner to Bala's office, via the Hong Kong Bank, where I suffered the indignity of having my credit card rejected when requesting cash against it; grrr. An expensive call to Kuala Lumpur followed - still rejected - I know what the problem is and I used my second card instead with no problem. My bank can untangle that one for me. (Despite adequate funds for the seven months, the card company still set a monthly ceiling, which, as it is August 1st, I must have reached for July, blast them).

Bala was a bit quiet, I thought, and, if I was really honest, I think perhaps he was a little put out by my having spent so long at Maxwell's and having a supper date with them. Men! Anyway, once again we strolled leisurely across that beautiful green, to the Ipoh Club. It is such a special treat for me to dine like that. Everyone there knew him and he introduced me to friends at other tables. Later, after more scrummy seafood, followed by papaya, watermelon and coffee, I sat in his cool office, under the big ceiling fan, with all the windows wide open and with his help and stationery, I packed up copies of this journal for my family.

Back at my hotel, after fond cheek kisses, Bala and I parted (he has made me promise to ring him on Monday). I then once again dashed over with blouse number one (which, by some twist of fate I had actually washed the night before) for ironing. It seemed the new girl in the boutique knew all about me, can't think why!

Oh! Over coffee earlier that day, it was just hinted at by Mr Rajah that I might like to borrow the company flat in the Cameron Highlands. Gosh! That would make a change from dingy hotels (although they do have a certain frontiersman kind of charm, especially the Chinese ones). I'll wait and see if anything more is mentioned about it tonight.

Tonight came and went, and it was a very nice evening. 'NT' (as he had asked me to call him) Rajah and his nice wife Gnana picked me up in their comfy old Mercedes, and we drove to their home. Gnana, a slim, very good-looking woman was dressed casually in trousers and a heavenly Italian silk shirt. Their home was cool, marble-floored and absolutely huge and as we sat and drank whisky and water, and gin and tonic, their daughter appeared. I liked Arun enormously. She was thirty-three, with two small children and was living with her parents, sadly separated from her husband. She was very beautiful, with cascading curly black hair and wonderful dark eyes, which lit up when she discovered that I lived near Salisbury, as she had been to school at Sherborne. She had loved the area and we chatted at length about pubs and teashops and the English countryside.

We then drove to the Perak Golf Club, a large building with beautiful floodlit palms at the entrance, wide balconies and a spacious, pretty dining room. Gnana ordered all sorts of good things for us; sweet and sour fish, Chinese venison, tofu, chicken dishes and rice. Everything was quite delicious and I was still busily eating when the others had had enough, much to their amusement. On our way home we took a detour to a Chinese food centre very like the one Toon had taken me to, where we chose a selection of extraordinary Chinese cakes. Some were the colours of blancmange, in pink, white and green layers, others steamed and stuffed with brown sugar and coconut and wrapped in palm leaf strips. We drove home and wolfed them with large glasses of iced water. The lovely thing was that I felt replete, but not at all full or heavy. Their food is light and very tasty and almost devoid of any fat, grease or stodge. Later Gnana and NT drove me back to my hotel, with instructions on where to pick up the key to the company flat, from their Cameron Highlands office. I was over the moon, for the umpteenth time that week.

As I climbed the stairs from the street to the hotel reception desk, I saw the friendly young waiter from a restaurant I had frequented a couple of times, sitting in a chair, and guessed correctly he was waiting for me. Earlier in the week he had expressed a wish to work in London and asked if I could help him. Not really, I had said, but I would give him a list of hotels and said he ought to send a reference and find out about work permits from our Embassy in Kuala Lumpur. After greeting him I wrote him a list of hotels and advised him on wording a letter. Then, without looking directly at me he said very casually 'Oh, and can I have your address?' I laughed and said did he really think I travelled round the world giving my address to complete strangers? 'Good try' I said and he respected my wishes; I just wrote 'Cynny Sharp, Hampshire, England' on his bit of paper. We said goodnight and I had a quiet chuckle at the varied events of that day.

THE CAMERON HIGHLANDS

Next morning Friday 2nd August, and I dashed across the road and up to the beastly Cathay Hotel to say goodbye to Toon. He advised me on buses to the Cameron Highlands and we parted fondly. What a nice old boy. Then, as arranged, I sent my first fortnightly check-in fax to Kate Dufall (with whom I had stayed in Bangkok; she had asked me to keep in touch as I was travelling alone). I gave her my onward address and movements and wished her a happy birthday.

On returning to my hotel I found the old boy on reception working out bills on an ancient ebony abacus. I loaded my world onto my back once more and crossed the road to catch bus No 1 to Kampar, three quarters of an hour away. Thank goodness I had decided against having breakfast - you will realise why in a minute.

The bus bowled along past charming old wooden Malay houses on stilts, set amid lush gardens, the wood mellowed and lightened by the sun. I chatted to a young Malay girl named Tan (I now realise you call all Malaysians by their surnames) who had helped me aboard with my rucksacks. In Kampar I caught a second bus to Tapah, both small towns bustling with women in saris with wonderful jewellery and strings of orchids in their hair. Others, wearing austere full length black robes and yashmaks with only their eyes peeping out, mingled with Chinese women clutching small porcelain-skinned children with jet black hair, wearing western clothes - baggy trousers and T-shirts. Malaysian children sported fresh green and white school uniforms, with pinafore dresses or shorts. The mixture of races was fascinating.

My next bus had lost its door, and all the windows rattled. The smell of the oleander bushes lining the road was delicious; it was very hot indeed. We crossed rivers and sped between palm oil plantations to Tapah. This is the taking-off point for the Cameron Highlands and I waited an hour for the next bus; again, an opportunity for a spot of people-watching. A fat, spoilt, Indian boy of about six years old threw a tantrum and almost unwound his plump and wobbly mother's sari, much to the bus queue's amusement. I noticed a tiny girl dressed in a wonderfully frilly blue and white dress. Her little head was completely shaven, she wore flip-flops and would have made the perfect bridesmaid. I asked her father, to whom she was clinging, if I might photograph her. 'Yes, but why'? he asked; 'Because she looks so beautiful' I answered, and so I did.

I am not quite sure how I can describe my next bus journey, climbing fifteen hundred feet up to Tana Rata in the hills. Imagine this - it took a little under two hours and the big bus drove steadily at about 50mph. I had read in my Lonely Planet that 'All the bus drivers on this route seem to be frustrated racing-car drivers, and the journey can be fairly hair-raising'. This book never exaggerates. I had asked about taxis (sixteen pounds). The entire journey of four hours, on three buses, was to cost me under two pounds. So, when the time came to board the bus, I carefully chose a seat over the wheels on the driver's side, as all the traffic in Malaysia drives on the left. This way I would be furthest away from the precipices.

THE JOURNEY

Glory be! As I said, it took a little under two hours, and in that time we negotiated six hundred and fifty-two (perversely I counted them for fun) hairpin bends. One after the other after the other, and as we all clung on to the seats, window bars and our luggage, the bus swung wildly to the right, to the left, to the right, to the left. I was quite bruised on arrival all along my right side, having been constantly jarred against the bus. It was hair raising, real David Attenborough stuff, as we careered under vines suspended from banana trees and strung across the road, orchids growing between the massive rocks overhanging our route, tall, weird palms and the deepest, tallest jungle I had seen since Nepal.

Bamboo huts perched on impossibly tall, spindly stilts were built out high above the valleys, and my little frilly friend and her father got out in the middle of nowhere, so they must have lived in one of them. We swung past waterfalls and groups of men under small shelters constructed of banana leaves and palm, selling jackfruit and all sorts of roots and long, fat, green carob-like pods I could not identify. The settlements up here were very remote and I had read that tribesmen with poisoned blowpipes had inhabited these slopes until fairly recently. The bus hooted continuously as almost all the corners were completely blind, and many times I shut my eyes as we passed within inches of oncoming vehicles. I have never been on a journey like it! Thank God I hadn't had any food since the night before. And I made a mental note to choose the same seat again, even more importantly going back down, as the steepest cliffs would be down to the left.

I was mentally and physically exhausted on arrival. I was also pretty tired after all the excitement of Ipoh and so the large, airy flat, with balconies on two sides overlooking the jungle hills and the small town of Tanah Rata was real heaven. It was sparsely furnished, but with three bedrooms (with their own bathrooms) a nice kitchen, a television (I watched some of the Olympics), sliding glass doors to the balconies and attractive bamboo furniture, quite perfect for me. For the first time since leaving home, I have space, privacy, hot water, and can cook meals and walk about with nothing on – what luxury. At this point I remembered my mother telling me that my grandmother was reputedly the first white woman to visit the Cameron Highlands in the 1930's. How intriguing.

Monday 5th August

The temperature up here is wonderful, about twenty-one degrees so just right. Tanah Rata is, as the books describe 'a fine plateau, with gentle slopes, shut in by lofty mountains'. Tea, every imaginable vegetable and strawberries are grown here, and in some hotels you can order English cream teas! On Friday and Saturday I relaxed and went to bed early and began planning a long walk.

On Saturday at supper in a local café, I met a friendly Danish girl who had worked in Wareham and knew Dorset well. We met up again yesterday and, with boots and my bergen, we set out at ten o'clock into the jungle on a quite well marked (to begin with) trail, expecting to walk for about three and a half hours. Brigitte was fun and as we swapped stories of our travels we both agreed we would not have liked to have walked that haphazard path alone. We had planned quite an arduous route and, after seeing another couple of signs they abruptly ended. The jungle walks were marked 1-12 and we had decided to start on 8 and join 6 then 5 and 2, across the hills, ending up in a village about an hour north of ours and the final settlement up here. We occasionally rested and drank water, my can of 100 Plus and her Coke, fully expecting to be back for lunch.

Quite suddenly the trail petered out completely, down by a swampy stream where a grove of huge-leafed banana trees crowded in the water. The rocks all round us rose hundreds of feet, with exposed tree roots snaking at our feet and almost impenetrable jungle canopy above us. Twelve-foot high trees that I recognised as small houseplants at home grew beneath thick palm (as opposed to palm trees) with little sky visible. I had a torch and Gore-Tex mac in my rucksack, but little water left and no food or jumper, or my whistle, and I soon realised what a complete fool I was. Brigitte wasn't as fit as me and we were both tiring rapidly as we climbed a rock face in the right direction. Almost immediately it plunged down again, so we employed hands and bum mode to descend. And so it continued for several hours, until quite suddenly I noticed a small black irrigation pipe snaking along the bottom of a narrow stream. We followed it for fifty yards or so and found a well-trodden path. After another hour we arrived at a clearing where we spied a row of glasshouses.

I had begun to think we might have a job finding our way home before dark. At four o'clock, we emerged through a collection of orchid-filled greenhouses into the village, exhausted, filthy and quite shaken. It had served us right. I made a mental note always to take food, a whistle, spare clothes, a compass and some sort of ground covering in future. We had been led to believe that the trails were well-trodden, even litter-strewn in places and fairly tame going. Huh!

We ate curry and drank lassi in a small café and later caught a share-taxi down the hill to Brigitte's guesthouse, where we unashamedly indulged in a cream tea: scones, jam, clotted cream, butter, the lot. I then walked the mile home down the hill rather stiffly, after we had planned to meet up again in Malaka or perhaps in Bali. I went to bed very early and woke up horribly stiff. Today I have done useful things, such as booking my bus to Kuala Lumpur for Friday, finding a present for NT Rajah, (a dusty bottle of Pimms in an ancient Chinese grocers) and writing to my friends and family. Tomorrow I am off on a tour of the area, which seems the only way I can see all the tea plantations etc without having my own transport. Only three more days until I get my mail.

A STEAMBOAT

<u>Tuesday 6th August</u>

Last night I ate out - some fried rice, and honey melon juice to drink. These drinks are delicious, my favourite being watermelon juice, a heavenly flavour without the fiddle of all the pips. I would so love to try the local speciality here, called a Steamboat. It's a Cameron Highlands' version of a fondue, with meat, fish, eggs, and all sorts of vegetables, which you place in little metal baskets with long handles (rather like large tea-strainers) and then immerse in hot chicken or vegetable broth. Sadly restaurants will only serve it to a minimum of two people and I had watched others tucking in. Brigitte and I had planned to sample one after our walk, but our day didn't quite turn out that way; perhaps I can find someone to share one with . . .

The Imam was at it again at dawn; I am not irreligious, but to have been woken very early on several mornings by the holy man, wailing mournfully in prayer over the valley was not on. This happens about five o'clock and he is so loud, the Mosque being high on a hill overlooking Tanah Rata.

Later - I began today on the wrong foot. My watch had gone haywire and thinking I was in plenty of time for my sightseeing trip I rose at six thirty, only to find from the good old BBC World Service that it was nine o'clock. My tour had been due to leave at a quarter to. I showered, downed tea, melon and mango and ran down to make my peace with the tour office, planning instead to go on the next tour. I have never quite figured out the alarm on my watch.

Well, I was the only one on the tour bus, which was good, as I was able to make best buddies of the driver/guide, and ask him all sorts of obscure questions. We began by climbing beyond the next village in the minibus, round and round and round the bends once more until, quite suddenly, the jungle fell away, and there to our right undulating gently away into the distance grew row upon row, mile upon mile of clipped tea bushes. They looked velvety and healthy, a glorious glossy green in the bright sun, and a wonderful sight. We climbed on and up, with stunning views across the estate, until we reached the Boh Plantation. There, joined by three young English girls, we were shown the various processes used in the production of tea leaves and tea bags from the tender top shoots of the tea plants. They are sheared off by hand rather than picked. We watched a machine looking like a hovering, inflated hoover bag, being guided over the tops of the tea bushes by two men, one on either side of the row. This is a small mechanical device for snipping off the topmost shoots. The smell was glorious!

The estate had been in the Russell family ever since tea was first planted here in 1926; the Russells live in Kuala Lumpur. The processing machines, sifting gear, conveyor belts and grinders were all the original ones and the high-ceilinged wooden sheds which housed them, were fragrant with the aroma of tea (which belongs to the camellia family). It was just like putting your head into an enormous tea caddy. None of the Boh tea is exported, as demand is high at home and the very best grade of tea is bought up at source by Singaporean hotels, so cannot be purchased. The whole process was fascinating.

I then left the girls and walked slowly down the hill, visiting a rose farm, established by another Englishman in 1934, an apiary (the bees were absolutely tiny), a strawberry and vegetable farm, and an excellent market. The strawberries were grown in two ways. Either, at a height of about four foot off the ground in very long plastic pipes, with a narrow strip cut out along the top (like a horseshoe-shaped gutter) with small drainage holes at one foot intervals underneath; or in round, plastic, holey bags, one bag for each plant, placed directly on the ground, each bag about a foot high. Neither way necessitated any weeding at all, and they were covered overhead with plastic corrugated open-sided roofing. My guide identified all the various fruits and vegetables for me and I bought some tree tomatoes, pendulous, purple things, looking rather like pointed plums (a fruit, apparently - I will try one tomorrow) and miniature plum tomatoes, and strawberries.

For lunch today, prior to my trip, I had had a delicious omelette, cooked for me at a stall in town and which I ate cold, with tomatoes, avocado and some rambutans. The beauty of living in this flat is that I can buy local food and eat it here; it is difficult preparing and eating food in a small room in a guesthouse, and anyway, street stalls are so cheap to eat at. I do miss raw vegetables though as everything here seems to be fried, curried, steamed or stir-fried. I also tried a petai looking just like a huge broad bean with a bitter and very strong sweet/sour taste, which suddenly hits you. The beans were contained in the long, fat, green carob-like pods I had seen earlier. It is such fun trying all these peculiar things!

Today, having just rung Kuala Lumpur to make a booking for a dorm room (bunks) at the Travellers' Moon Hostel at two pounds a night, I was summoned to the lawyers' office beneath the flat and asked to ring Bala immediately. Imagine my surprise when he told me he had made arrangements for me to stay with his daughter and her family in Kuala Lumpur, for as long as I liked.

I am absolutely convinced I am leading a charmed life in Malaysia. I am to ring Bala's daughter Victoria, on Thursday to confirm the plan. I am once again stunned by this kind offer. It will be wonderful to have a room of my own in which to read my letters and listen to the radio. I am always wary of revealing that I have such a smashing and expensive little radio in a bunk bed arrangement, with strangers. Talking of strange beds, I am fully qualified in knowing how to test for bed bugs now, and also learnt in Ipoh that the only way to sleep in extreme heat, is to shower in your sarong and then go to bed in it dripping wet!

<u>Wednesday 7th August</u>

Happy Birthday to my darling daughter; she is twenty-four today. I shall ring her later and do hope she likes the flowers I ordered, and isn't about to go dashing off to Crete, as I can't quite remember her holiday dates. I also have all my fingers and toes crossed for my son Jasper's 42nd Street, which he is producing and which opens on The Fringe in Edinburgh on Friday. I am so proud of him. He says there's an article about it in The Scotsman that he will keep for me.

Well, Old Yeller was at it again early this morning, at precisely five thirty-three, and I am sure he was wailing even more loudly than usual. However, I am sure someone benefits from him and I hope it makes them feel better. I had a lovely feeling as I woke, of being borne gently down the length of Malaysia on a cushion of kindness and concern, being handed carefully from one family to another, all totally unexpected and unasked for by me. Great fun and very happy-making. A quiet day.

Thursday 8th August

Yesterday, and all through the night, great banks of rain and thunder came rolling over the mountains, and I wondered if there would be a chance to walk again. Determined to do so, when it brightened up a bit, I packed all the things I should have taken before, as well as goodies for my lunch. The trails are so badly marked that, together with a Spanish couple, I spent some time ferreting around trying to find where mine began. Once I'd found it, it was wonderful.

The cloud was very low and although the path was quite good, I could at first see only about ten yards ahead of me. Mist swirled through the huge trees, ferns and creepers, and the path fell away very steeply to the right, down into dense jungle. It was real Harrison Ford country. A local boy of about sixteen came through the mist towards me on the narrow path, with what I thought was a fishing rod, but turned out to be a blowpipe, some seven feet long. He also had two Malaysian knives, one long and sharp, the other blunt-ended and heavy, tucked into his belt. I hailed him and he told me in broken English, that he was 'shooting birds' but had not found any, and he passed me by. The rain began and I put on Gemma's Gore-Tex jacket, hood up, and made sure everything was stowed away inside the plastic liner in my bergen. It is so useful and comfortable, and I use it a great deal. I tucked my camera down my front. I was using a slide film given to me by Jagdish, to try and capture the eerie, misty jungle, the huge dripping banana leaves, trailing vines and dense vegetation bordering my route. Once I found an absolutely enormous dead leaf, about three feet long and a foot wide.

I continued along the narrow track for about an hour and a half, and slowly the mist lifted. I had been told by Danes I'd met over a meal some days ago, that this particular path just stopped dead at some point at a construction site and I was much saddened when I reached it. Rape, desecration, these words were appropriate. Quite suddenly the lush jungle vegetation came to an abrupt end and vast wide areas of ochre-coloured earth lay bare of any green thing. I could not make up my mind whether to photograph it or not; it was so dreadful to witness. Man has much to answer for, in the name of some hotelier or speculator . . . and so I had to retrace my steps. I soon came across the Spaniards I'd met previously, who told me they had just seen a large green four-inch long scorpion; how exciting - sadly I didn't see one.

At another point, as rain began to fall again, I stood close to a huge tree on the path to change my camera film beneath my hood. It was very dark and drippy and still, and as I glanced behind me with film, plastic film pot, camera case etc. all carefully balanced, I caught sight of an almost hidden brown face, sharp black eyes, curly hair and a huge long stick, which was definitely not part of the vegetation. A blowpipe. The eyes looked straight at me, and for a second I could not believe what I had seen as I had heard no sound whatsoever. I stayed motionless for a minute, my mind racing, and then pulled myself together, telling myself this was a much used path and although I knew there was an Aborigine village somewhere above me, surely little brown chaps didn't go around firing poisoned blow darts at foreigners . . . I crept away noiselessly and never saw him again. I had had absolutely nowhere to hide and nowhere to go on that narrow path and yet curiously, apart from one split second, I was not afraid.

I made my way back slowly, as the roots, fallen trees across my path and stream beds I crossed were very slippery with the rain. The sun came out and at one point I came to a high clearing where I could see the jungle hills folding into each other far below me like a child's painting, the low cloud swirling over and between the folds; quite wonderful. As the sun warmed the foliage, I smelt what I can only describe as the fruity vanilla perfume of some unseen flower, warm and fragrant. Almost at the end, or rather back at the beginning, of the path I found an exposed tree root overlooking the track in the sun and I sat to have my lunch and watch the birds.

Walking with Brigitte I had seen an enormous green and yellow woodpecker half way up an old tree trunk, prodding for insects with his beak. He had a large and beautiful bright yellow shock of feathers down the back of his head just like a mohican haircut. I must look him up some day. This time I saw a pair of tiny green birds with long, curved beaks, which hovered fleetingly at a flower, drawing out the nectar from inside; they were honey-suckers. I had seen one earlier, identified by the guide in the rose garden at the tea plantation. I was entranced watching them on the edge of the jungle among the banana trees in the warm sun. The final triumph of my walk was to see a perfectly beautiful butterfly, obviously attracted by the bright yellow cuffs of my jacket. I had seen the same species in Penang at the butterfly farm and was thrilled to bits to see it in the wild. Very large, with a wingspan of perhaps eight inches, it was triangular in shape, black with a brilliant emerald band across the middle of both wings - quite spectacular and I was so excited to see it.

Back in the flat at about five thirty, there was a knock at the door and there was Aruna. She was the daughter of the senior member of the law firm who had lent me the flat if you remember, very attractive, thirty-three, separated and a lawyer. I had met her with her parents in Ipoh. She had come up on business to the office here in Tanah Rata and was staying in the flat until Saturday. It was really lovely to see her, and after showers we shared some of my whisky. Then we hit the town and had a Steamboat, to which she treated me. I had been longing to try one and it was truly delicious.

A large metal pan in the shape of a spring-form cake tin with small central funnel is placed over a flame and filled with chicken broth. We then cooked all sorts of goodies in the simmering liquid - prawns, cuttlefish, squid, chicken, tiny fish balls, Japanese tofu, quails eggs, watercress and other leafy greens and mushrooms. The last thing you put in having devoured the rest, is a plate of very thin noodles, followed immediately by two fresh eggs, which you break and stir into the broth. As the noodles cook, the eggs thicken the broth, so you eat it all together. Small bowls and porcelain spoons and chopsticks are provided; I loved it. Aruna and I chatted about our loves and lives and I learnt so much again, about the ways of the country and of her parents' (originally from Sri Lanka) attitude to her divorce and of Chinese marriages and men. On our way back up to the flat I bought chocolate for us both and that will be that for me for food, until I get to Kuala Lumpur tomorrow afternoon. The thought of that drive down the hill has already dispelled any thoughts of breakfast or lunch!

THE KANAGARATNAMS

Tuesday 13th August, Kuala Lumpur

The last few days have been so happy, thanks to the wonderful family I have been invited to stay with here in Kuala Lumpur. The coach journey was comfortable and much less dramatic than the outward journey in the tearaway local bus, apart from the fact that the huge spare tyre on the seat beside me blocked the emergency exit. I read my book 'Captain Corelli's Mandolin', and did not eat or drink a morsel until we were on the main highway, and almost at Kuala Lumpur.

Once there, loaded up with my life again, I hailed a taxi and made straight for the post office. I had heard much from fellow travellers about the traffic noise, pollution etc in Kuala Lumpur and had thought I would just pass through to collect mail. How much I would have missed! It is one of the most breathtaking cities I have been fortunate enough to visit. Palatial white Moorish architecture, extravagant confections of minarets, spiral stairways, barley twist columns, balconies and courtyards, stand alone in splendour, beside ultra-modern, sleek and beautiful skyscrapers, sparkling towers, gleaming white multi-storey car parks spilling over with bougainvillea, ferns and lush trailing climbers. Everywhere there are palms, fountains, small parks, flowers on wild plots. I loved it.

The post office was one such beautiful, towering, white skyscraper, with an enormous globe positioned on the forecourt, wide, elegant marble steps, a pretty pool and a spotless, airy interior. I was full of anticipation and found no mail under the S's, but a card saying 'SHARP bulk collection'. Yippee! And awaiting me were nine letters. I was over the moon. I sat on a seat inside the post office for an hour, beaming away, reading all the news, surrounded by my belongings and gave most of the stamps to the resident loitering local philatelist.

Later I made my way to the famous and very beautiful railway station to wait for Bala's daughter Victoria. She and her family live on the outskirts of the city in a large bungalow full of fans, wide windows and spacious rooms. I shared a bedroom and bathroom with Renata who was twenty-one. Her sister Verna, was twenty-four and both girls were exceedingly pretty, tall and leggy with beautiful dark, shining eyes. Victoria is just a few months older than me and Kana an executive with a Swiss company is fourteen years her senior.

Originally from Sri Lanka, they were all such fun and teased me constantly, calling me 'Memsahib' and pulling my leg about 'foreign labour' as I helped with the washing up, dustbins, etc. They all worked full-time, and we ate out every night at all sorts of different places, from excellent seafood restaurants to Indian curry houses and Chinese noodle stalls, where they were well known. Living with the Kanagaratnams was an incredibly gastronomic experience. They bought me fruit to try for breakfast; custard apples and Vietnamese dragon fruit, and I in turn helped where I could with the chores. One evening after yet another delectable meal out, Kana drove us round the city centre which was magical and thronged with people. 'You notice they are all Malay - the Chinese are too busy making money' he chuckled. It was a veritable fairyland of sparkling lights, spotlit fountains, street cafés, flags and music.

The next day I visited the Kuala Lumpur bird park, which is beautifully laid out. My greatest thrill was to see a group of different hornbills and, most exciting, to hear their deep, throaty honk, confirming my suspicion that I had heard them both at Chitwan and in the Cameron Highlands, though I hadn't actually seen them.

At the weekend, Victoria drove me to the Kuala Lumpur National Monument, an open space on which is built a War Memorial rather like the Cenotaph, commemorating those who had died in both World Wars, and in the 1948-1957 emergency. Another memorial sculpture depicted seven fighting men, with guns, a flag and fallen comrades, fashioned by the same sculptor responsible for the Iwo Jima monument in Washington; it was most impressive. Water, fountains, graceful swaying fan palms, the prettiest bronze water lilies and lots of marble surrounded the area, which is magnificent.

We then drove on to see a gigantic restaurant, floating on a lake. Constructed of wood and beautifully carved with open spaces here and there on the floor, in which the water was lit from below, it had jolly red plastic chairs and red-clothed tables as far as the eye could see. It must have seated four or five hundred people, with a stage in the middle where dancers performed in the evenings. Pretty decorations and jumbo flower-filled boats gave one the impression of being on the deck of a ship at sea.

Outside and opposite the restaurant, we heard a high-pitched whining sound, and walked over to investigate. A tarmac track had been laid out on an open patch of ground, winding round small grass hillocks and verges. Many people, young and old, sat on benches and in a small grandstand, watching men and boys with remote controls guiding their model racing cars round the track at terrific speed. It was great fun to watch - occasionally one lost a tyre or turned somersaults in the air as they hit a hillock or one another - great excitement, and of course no one got hurt. We thought it a really imaginative use of a small plot of land, and lovely to see so many parents and children enjoying the spectacle rather than lazing at home in front of videos and televisions all weekend.

Another day, I had an excellent haircut for a pound, as did Victoria, in a tiny, bustling Chinese hairdresser's flat, in a very poor area of the city, overflowing with both customers and family, chatting noisily.

I bought a train ticket to Singapore for nine pounds, electing to make the six-hour journey by rail for a change and as it is much easier crossing the border and going through customs by train rather than by coach.

One memorable day Verna drove me to St Mary's Cathedral in the heart of the city, where my grandfather's funeral service had been held on 24th September 1937. The Cathedral was the size of a small parish church, and so wonderfully English despite the whirring fans. Magnificent flower arrangements adorned the altar and font, and around the walls poignant memorials to Colonial families made fascinating reading. In the 1920's a man aged thirty-nine, 'Governor of British North Borneo' was 'killed by a fall from his horse' and another 'Chaplains' Warden from 1926-28, who 'gave his life in saving his children from drowning' was remembered.

I found my grandfather's burial entry in a huge leather-bound church book dating from 1876: 'J. Dunford Wood' and the date; place of residence Ipoh; profession, Barrister-at-law; in amongst other burials of planters, Colonial Government officials (who very often died young) and many children aged ten, twelve or merely infants hours old or stillborn. Grandpa Joe had been buried nearby, but in the 1960s the graves had been moved to a plot some miles away at Cheras, when an Islamic building (Pusat Islam) was erected on the original site. I felt and Verna agreed, that a further search at Cheras would yield very little if anything.

The morning after I arrived at Victoria's I mentioned to the family that I had the address in Kuala Lumpur of an old Chinese man whom I knew had been alive in 1988, and who was the last remaining member of my grandfather's staff. I asked if the address meant anything to the family, as there was no record of him in the telephone directory. To my utter astonishment, considering Kuala Lumpur is a huge city, I discovered the man lived three roads away from where I was staying!

Verna drove me to find it with little difficulty, and there was the very house. I rang the bell and a young man came to the gate. Yes, Mr Yeoh lived here and yes, he was in - I could not believe my luck. The old boy had written to a distant cousin of mine, whom I'd never met, after seeing an article in the Malay Post in 1988 on how she was searching for information about her great uncle, my grandfather. Despite his help she didn't manage to come up with much, and so I was continuing the search.

Mr Yeoh was a marvellous old boy. Clad only in shorts, with a hugely distended tummy beneath them and rather unhealthy looking legs, he was most hospitable and intrigued that I had come to find him. Aged seventy-eight, he had worked as a typist for my lawyer grandfather at the age of eighteen. He had had to dress completely in white ('Spick and span' he said) and due to the slump in those days, had worked without any pay for the first three months. He told me my grandfather was a tall and very intelligent man who took great delight in bullying the Malay Judges in the lower courts with his superior knowledge of the law. However, the European judges in the High Court were a different matter. He had atrocious handwriting, and often couldn't decipher what he had written himself just a few days earlier. He was apparently 'Very henpecked' by my grandmother who was a 'Very jealous woman' according to Mr Yeoh - of what he could not really explain. Grandpa Joe had had his own firm, called J. Dunford Wood, at Hale road in Ipoh, where the lawyers' offices remain today. I'm afraid to say he was apparently a heavy drinker and was sometimes half-drunk in court. He eventually suffered a heart attack in a Kuala Lumpur hotel and was immediately rushed to the nearest public hospital by the hotel staff, where he died.

An added bit of historical information from Mr Yeoh was that in those days KLM ran flying boats from Penang to London, which took eight days, whilst the journey by sea took a month.

Well, I am about to depart from Malaysia, a country I really didn't know a lot about and which I have loved. I have once again, and mostly due to the wonderful families I have met, learned so much. I have travelled on the hair-raising little pink mini buses round Kuala Lumpur in which twenty-five sitting and ten standing is the law though twenty-five of each is the norm. I have removed my shoes yet again before entering a house, as is usual in the whole of South East Asia (bliss both for hot feet and for the housewife) and I have been amused by the many motorcyclists and scooterists racing down the Malay highways with jackets or shirts worn back to front over their clothes to keep them clean in the traffic! I have been to church with Victoria and Ernest - the Kuala Lumpur Tamil Methodist Church service was both interesting and fun. Conducted in Malay and English, we sang hymns I knew well, with swaying and clapping added and the sermon given by the priest (who could have doubled for Michael Jackson complete with dark glasses) was all about marriage - an indoctrinal lecture aimed at the young Indians in the congregation, but highly amusing, nonetheless ('The wedding ring is the smallest handcuff in the world' . . . and he coined the word 'Mismated'. Does it exist?).

I talked for hours to Victoria, and also to her daughter Verna who, at twenty-four, found the compulsory tradition of young people living with their parents until the day they get married, and then with their parents-in-law, in the case of a girl, rather stifling. (She has put in her papers to emigrate to Australia, having spent three very happy years there at University.) I explained, at their request, and as simply as possible, the reasons for the rifts within our Royal Family and why Prince Philip isn't King.

Lastly, I visited Malaka, the oldest city in Malaysia, colonised by the Portuguese, the Dutch and, in between, twice by the British. On the way we passed a horrific looking camp for Boat People (now empty) and then for a day I became a fully-fledged Tourist following-the-tour-leader in sheeplike fashion along with thirty-odd others, variously sporting beer guts, Gucci tennis shades, dyed hair, camcorders, sun specs on gold chains, and overflowing shorts. God give me squat loos and toothless locals any day! It was an interesting visit, and the best way to see the colourful old city of Malaka from Kuala Lumpur in such a short time.

On the way there, slim, elegant rubber trees, girdled with small cups to catch their latex, grew as far as the eye could see beyond the expressway, giving way to mile upon mile of lush palm trees, grown for their nut oil. Reaching Malaka, we were rushed at breakneck speed, from one 'photo opportunity' to another. St Peter's church, the oldest Catholic church in Malaysia built in 1710, then down to the sea to watch fishermen wading chest-high into the water to catch anchovies in enormous, collapsible 'Y' shaped nets, then onwards to the 'padang', a large grass arena where the Malaysian flag was first raised in 1957.

I broke away by the sea to watch spellbound as a large pied kingfisher dived for his lunch and herons waded haughtily through the mangrove bushes. My reverie was broken by a Brazilian standing next to me, whose mobile phone buzzed noisily and who dropped his binoculars in his haste to answer Rio or wherever. Every second person in Malaysia has a dratted mobile phone, and they cut the air on trains, buses, and beaches - maddening.

Before I left Kuala Lumpur, both my mother and my son Jasper sent me newsy faxes and Verna drove me all the way into the GPO on the off-chance that there might be a long-promised letter there from my brother Hugh, which there was - how welcome. He writes so well, from his heart, and I love him for it.

With banks of electronic gadgets in the Kanagaratnam household - gate-opening bleepers, light dimmers, CD players etc. and a table with seven remote control devices on it, I asked if I might watch a video on my last day. For two hours that evening, I sat mesmerised with Victoria and the girls on plush seats in their darkened 'theatre', as they showed me films and concerts on their incredible laser-discs (LD's) with, it seemed, fighter planes, warriors and drummers screaming and booming in from all round the room. I had no idea such things existed!

My final responsible act, prior to leaving for Singapore and much to Verna's amusement, was to remove and throw away a tiny two inch leaf of cannabis, pressed with other Himalayan leaves and flowers, for their fragile beauty, inside the pages of my book, in case some ferocious Singaporean sniffer-dog tore out the last two chapters which I hadn't yet read.

We all bade each other a touchingly emotional farewell, with cards and presents exchanged (I had bought them English jams, marmalade and lots of different kinds of biscuits from the Kuala Lumpur branch of M & S). I was even given a lovely little present and a picnic for the train from a work-mate of Victoria's, whom I had met in the back seat of Victoria's car, and who had later asked me to supper. Verna, bless her, had made me a new journal, as this one is almost finished. Hers is great fun and includes a photo of her entire family.

Finally, a thought, spied in an opulent cosmetics shop in Kuala Lumpur 'Beauty is not a matter of looking young, but of looking good'. Hooray to that!

On the morning of my departure, everyone rose early to see me off and Victoria loaded me up with carrot cake, cooked noodles, fruit and cans of 100 Plus. We were both tearful as I'd almost become part of the family and they had begged me to stay on a bit longer, but I wanted to see a little of Singapore before taking to the air again onwards to Bali. Ernest, about to take his final law exam that day, drove me to the wonderful railway station and dear Bala, who was staying with them, accompanied us. He saw me off on the sleek and beautiful train, and I knew in my heart I would probably never see him again as he is seventy-nine, and has no intention of coming to England. Kuala Lumpur looked gently magical in the misty morning, as we slid south. What a stunningly beautiful city.

The train gave me a foretaste of Singapore. Impossibly clean, smooth-riding and with a constant supply of films on the over-sized television screen, one either end of the carriage, catering for half the passengers facing one way, and half the other. A small child of about four proceeded to munch his way through a whole packet of Cocoa Pops cereal as we sped through the jungle, but all the children were very good - God bless the video!

THE CUPBOARD

On arrival in Singapore everyone embarked and joined a long queue at the platform Passport Control (the Malaysians had processed us on the train) which was tedious with my heavy rucksack aloft. However I was soon on my way by taxi to the GPO for my post. I am not sure how best I can explain the heady exhilaration of collecting mail. To reach the main post office in some foreign, far-away city, by taxi, rail, bus or on foot with my heavy load, usually panting and extremely hot, and then to ask for the box or drawer marked 'S' and to sort through and recognise the writing - Gemma's, Jasper's, my mother's - my heart leaps, and it always amazes me that such flimsy forms, envelopes and cards can find their way across half the world, to bring me encouragement, news, and so much love.

On this occasion, a marvellous welcome to Singapore awaited me with masses of news from my family and half a dozen friends. I always finish this joyful task if not in emotional tears, then very misty-eyed, and later spend hours reading and re-reading every letter on my bed, in a park, on a bench or in a café. To know that friends are thinking of me, and missing me is very heart-warming. Next, somewhere to stay . . .

Friday 16th August

I am writing this on a pretty wooden bench beside a fountain at Raffles Hotel. It is the most delicious haven of palms, verandahs, and distant music, described by Joseph Conrad as a 'straggling building of bricks, as light and airy as a birdcage'. It is breathtakingly pretty, and, as I've been sitting here in my long blue and white Malaysian batik dress and straw jungle hat, three people have asked to be photographed with me! Obligingly I have posed beside the fountain, with the balconies beyond. Perhaps I look a trifle 'Passage to India'-ish; I shall soon begin charging them. I should have loved to have bought inexpensive souvenirs for the family, but inexpensive here means a tea towel at fifteen pounds and postcards in packs of four for over three pounds.

In talking to other travellers in other lands, I had heard of a hostel here called New Sandy's Place, very cheap and well situated just off Orchard Road, the shopping mecca. Having mastered the excellent bus and MRT (tube) connections, I rang the place (I had rung before leaving Kuala Lumpur, but they wouldn't keep me a room - first come first served, they'd said) and the owner told me to stand stock still by the phone, and she would come and collect me.

Five minute later the owner arrived and after tripping across a rather soggy field with stepping-stones in places, between two cloud-scraping five star hotels, I was shown a 'small room'. The light is on the wall outside, the bed is a foam mattress on the floor, the sort you fold in three and put on garden furniture, a tiny table beside the bed holds my jewels and pots and this little den is just four foot six inches wide (I can kneel on the bed/floor and place both palms flat against opposite walls) and six foot six inches long. Lying down and stretching my toes, I can touch the door. I took it and am now living in a cupboard!

The Cupboard, Singapore

At eighteen Singapore dollars (about eight pounds) I'm delighted, as reasonable accommodation in Singapore starts at about thirty pounds per night. It is merely somewhere to lay my head and I'll be out all day. Oh, and there is a clean loo and shower with instant hot water, right opposite The Cupboard, and free tea, coffee and fruit are offered for breakfast. The Cupboard has large air vents opening on to a multi-storey car park, ah well. It is the weekend and will hopefully be quieter. You can't have everything . . .

Saturday 17th August

The night went quite well, with a good fan above me and my clothes suspended on string and coat-hangers from the ceiling. Yesterday, besides mooning over Raffles Hotel, I visited St Andrew's Cathedral. It's glossy, gleaming white exterior results from the use of Madras Chunam, a mixture of shell lime, egg white and sugar.

I needed a quiet few minutes to pray for my friend John, whose son, I hear from home, was killed in a car accident at the beginning of July. He was in his twenties and on his way home from London. John's wife died five years ago. There is nothing to say, but pray and my heart goes out to him.

I sat at the back of the Cathedral in a cool cane-seated pew, and reflected on so much. Carpe Diem, and gratitude for everyone I have met and for all I've seen and done.

Later on I rang a Singaporean ex-Brigadier, a friend of London friends of mine whom they had contacted on my behalf. He said he and his wife would be delighted to give me dinner that evening. For the rest of the day I meandered, enjoying the city. Singapore is impossibly clean, tidy efficient and new. The absence of litter is nice, but I can see why Malaysians and others tend to scoff at the place. The people sit po-faced on the MRT and buses, eyes closed, plugged into their Walkmans, no one looks really happy, and you are considered a real devil if you take more than a week's holiday a year, from work. I was often helped by earnest young men, whilst studying my map. I met one who worked as cabin staff for Cathay Pacific, and loved coming to England 'For the Body Shop and the Changing of the Guard' - an interesting mixture!

The city is amazing. Winking red lights revolve at the roadside wherever a taxi is required, electronic boards at bus stops flash up information on the length of your wait and for the destinations of the next buses, the MRT tracks are sealed behind a glass wall, so that you can never actually touch the trains and they stop exactly in line with the doors in the glass wall, so that the two doors open simultaneously and automatically when the train stops. You must have the exact bus fare which you feed into a machine once aboard and take a ticket, or feed a card into another machine and the fare is automatically deducted and the card spat out, like a phone card; thus the driver never handles any money.

My evening with the Brigadier and his wife was terrific fun and most interesting. They drove me out to the eastern shore in their swish car, where I gobbled up steamed crabs, mammoth prawns, chicken, scallops, noodles, asparagus and Tiger beer. He has a top-hole job as President and Managing Director of one of Singapore's government-run utility companies, and they were both so kind. Stepping out of my cupboard in earrings, sandals, scent and smarty-pants gear, caused me much amusement. Perhaps I should entitle my journal 'From Cupboard to Cadillac'!

They drove me all round the city afterwards, and the beauty was enchanting. The tall, gleaming, metallic hotels, domed Colonial halls and Chinese wooden-shuttered shops, painted in ice cream colours, silhouetted and spotlit in the warm night. Strings of tiny white lights were festooned like pearl necklaces from the branches of trees, lining the wide roads and everywhere there were statues, fountains, spires and grand palm-fringed entrances lit up in the sultry night. We stopped at a block of high-rise flats, as the couple wanted me to see how ordinary people lived (they'd have had a fit if they had known about The Cupboard!) and en route bought a pudding called Ice Kachang at one of the hawkers' stalls, a cheap, self-service equivalent of our roadside cafés. A seven-inch high pyramid of grated ice mixed with bright pink syrup, milk and sugar, peas, lurid green worm-shaped jelly, beans and chewy white palm seeds . . . quite something!

The housing estate was splendid, with every facility you could imagine (doctor, post office, hairdresser, supermarket etc) within the complex, and pretty landscaped flowerbeds winding round the buildings. We took a lift to the twenty-fourth floor, to see the stupendous view, high, high above the traffic below, before driving home. They dropped me at the MRT station near to my lodgings, and I tripped across the field once more, in the dark, having been assured by the landlady that it was safe at night, and in the event there was a mega-watt contractors' light illuminating my path.

<u>Sunday 18th August</u>

I suppose it does sound a bit odd, to come to this incredible city with the sole aim, if I didn't do anything else, of finding a coffee shop in some anonymous back road, where the local men congregate on Sunday mornings to gossip and drink coffee. They bring with them their caged birds, which they suspend from an overhead trellis and who sing merrily away to each other for hours. Well then, odd I am.

I rose at six o'clock on Sunday morning with map at the ready, and set off. The Sunday morning bird-singing session has become rather a feature locally and although I was the first European to arrive that morning, many other travellers soon bowled up in taxis, on local buses and on foot, to join the merriment. It was such fun! Slim, crested birds locally known as Jumbos, coloured chestnut, black and white, hopped about in tall, pointed bamboo cages, swaying alongside each other from the trellis. Tiny 'white eyes', minuscule, sleek little green and yellow birds, sang their hearts out in beautiful, round, carved bamboo cages further along. Larger birds, China thrushes, were more sedate, swinging in airy, grand cages as they serenaded their friends.

More and more men arrived, some with three or four cages, slipping off or unzipping what my father would have called 'bath hats' - cage covers to keep their birds clean and safe until they were swinging in the air next to their chums. I chatted to lots of the local men and one bought me coffee and I teased them when they answered my question on what did they talk about each Sunday? 'Birds' he said and I enquired of which variety, feathered or two-legged, and they slapped their thighs and roared with laughter in amusement - didn't seem to have heard that one! I stayed for ages. It was such a simple, cheerful gathering, and, although the thought of captive birds is pretty appalling, the birds themselves seemed to really love it, and the trilling, chirruping and wild singing was so joyful!

I met a nice American couple who joined my table. They lived in Jakarta and knew Bali very well. They offered to fax me lots of good budget information, for me to collect from the owner of a luxury hotel on Bali, whom they knew well. Wonderful! Then, with the afternoon ahead of me, I left that remarkable, happy scene, now crowded with local men and row upon row of swinging, singing birds, and headed back to the city.

I had been given so much information about Singapore - you absolutely must go to: the Jurong Bird Park, Zoo, Orchid Garden, Sentosa Island, etc. I was still quite tired and the heat was oppressive so, having seen two bird parks (in Chiang Mai and Kuala Lumpur) a zoo (Chiang Mai and on my safaris) and orchids in Nepal, I made instead for the Botanical Gardens. It was sheer heaven. I love trees and even though, yes, they are planted here by man, they are given space to flourish and are looked after as well as any landowner would his estate. The colour, variety and scent on the breeze, as I strolled around, were so refreshing after the concrete and glass of the city.

A lake bordered with huge monkey pot trees and other majestic species, was alive with small turtles, paddling furiously in the sunshine. They carried such wonderfully marked shells, but I didn't think my camera would capture them, just below the surface of the water. I walked beside enormous kapok trees and small ponds covered with china blue lilies and up a path lined with slim palms called sealing wax palms, on account of their bright red stems (I had thought, when I had seen them in Kuala Lumpur, that they had been painted). I brushed past powder puff trees and marvelled at the wispy pink and white clouds of flowers, reminding me of my grandmother's swansdown powder puffs. Every bench seemed to be occupied, but at last I found one in deep shade, under a low, spreading Rose of Venezuela bush. There I sat and wrote this. I need to catch up often when I see so much, and I cannot write in my cupboard, with no daylight and a forty-watt (and that's being generous) light bulb. I wrote to friends who are to be married and to all who had written me the twenty-one letters I had collected over the past week. Later, a spectacular thunderstorm sent strollers, revellers and large families scurrying for shelter, but those few hours had been really lovely.

Monday 19th August

I am rather glad I had not planned to stay here longer. Victoria and the family were rather rude about the place and the Singaporeans. At the risk of being libelled, I found them dutiful, bow-legged and smug. I am generalising I know, but it seems their lives are lived by the five big 'C's' - Car, Cash, Credit Cards, Condominium and Career. They were very helpful if I was studying my map in the street, or on the MRT, but always got a little dig in, not only about Singapore being the only place to live, but also about how awful - dirty, poor, dull - every other country was. Many of them, old and bowed or young and twig-like (reminding me of elegant little stick insects) walked as if they had air bags between their legs - I never did discover why!

I left my cupboard at eleven in the morning having sat on the floor and caught up with this diary - I'm not sure I could live in this wee, dark space voluntarily for much longer. I shouldered my packs (about twenty-two kilos altogether, I later discovered) and caught the MRT into the city and checked at the Post office for mail. I had to walk quite a way again in the searing heat but eventually caught the airbus to Chiangi airport from outside a large hotel. Thanks to a tip in my Lonely Planet, I had an excellent meal of chicken curry, watermelon juice, cabbage and a coconut bun for about a pound, in the hawkers food centre down in Chiangi airport's basement, a great place where all the staff eat. My flight to Bali was one of the best, with Garuda Indonesian Airlines, lots of room, no one beside me and a yummy crab, duck and parfait supper.

BALI

I arrived in Bali at eight o'clock in the evening and asked an English girl with two friends if I might share a taxi. I did so, the taxi dropped me off and I hiked round looking for a room. Quite a few places were full but I eventually found one. A very pretty little bungalow, set amidst winding paths, bridges, pools of goldfish, palms and clouds of brilliant flowers. This was my home for a couple of days while I decided what to do and where to go. I collected a book sent by my mother from the post office, and tried many times unsuccessfully to ring England to tell my family where I was. In the end I gave up with my phone card and resorted to one of the Wartel Telecommunications shops for tourists, which cost a fortune. I spoke to my mother and gave her the telephone number of the place I had booked to stay in from the following day, at Ubud up in the hills.

I am very tired. For the last three weeks I have had a really fantastic time, but with many late nights, bus, train and plane journeys and, worst of all walking fully loaded in the thirty degree heat, I knew I needed to rest for a while. My bungalow was an oasis of calm. Just a few yards away, beyond the little bridges and thick stone walls, life was very different. Imagine Benidorm, Blackpool, Bournemouth, Baywatch and Kathmandu all rolled into one, and there you have Kuta in Bali! A seething, ear-splitting mass of hawkers, surfers, trippers, cafés - the very worst place I have come across so far.

However, Kuta beach is real heaven. I bought two roasted sweetcorn from a barrow for my supper one night, and sat on the sand just as the sun went down. The sands are wonderfully wide and miles long, with surfing conditions even the young Australians return to time and time again. But the volume of traffic, the dust, western cafés and cheap shops just added to my longing to find peace, rest, green things and sky. As I wandered back after eating my sweetcorn, I bumped into a couple I'd chatted to the day before, as we had waited by the luggage reclaim after our flight. It was quite a coincidence to have seen them again, considering how many thousands of people live in, and visit Kuta.

John and Debbie were Canadians, about my age, and had lived in Canada, South Africa and Thailand. He was an engineer, and they were about to go and live in Sumatra. They insisted I had a drink with them and after tonic water (quinine keeps the mozzies away) and a Bali Hai beer, this became supper and they treated me to a delicious salad and chocolate cake. They were nice, we found a place with excellent 60s music and while I happily baby-sat their video camera and other expensive goodies, they danced cheek to cheek. They had been apart for almost eight months and adored being together again. I am now bidden to Sumatra as soon as I can make it.

Next day I packed up once more and just before I caught a shuttle minibus up to Ubud, I chatted to a Dutch couple from Amsterdam, whose lost luggage was either in London, Brunei or Java which made my fatigue seem a very minor problem. The minibus took an hour and a half to clear Kuta, picking up passengers from guesthouses all round the town. The bus was stifling and airless, but we soon climbed away from the coast and bowled along through the unbelievable emerald green of tier upon tier of terraced rice paddies.

Ubud was cooler, much prettier than Kuta and the cultural centre of Bali. Painting, dancing, carving - all are here. I was dropped at the cottages I had painstakingly researched from my book and rung the previous day to book a room. No room now, they said - sorry, and I had a complete and utter sense of humour failure. I was exhausted and I am afraid I yelled and screamed and told them all they were wuzzers and what was the point of ringing and being told I had a room if they then changed their minds? I extracted yet another bit of paper with a guesthouse name, given to me by two Danish girls in Thailand, and the proprietor rang them for me. Eventually the owner came and collected me, promising me a room. I had had it by now.

The retreat I had sought was a small cottage, divided into two, set amongst the watery paddy fields with narrow, raised paths to reach it, and surrounded with palms, hibiscus and oleander bushes. At last! I negotiated a price (three pounds fifty) and the owner said he would include breakfast. When I had recovered my composure and unpacked a bit, I took up his offer of a mountain bike to borrow and pedalled the two kilometres into town. I collected the fax on Bali information, sent from Java to the Ubud hotel by the couple I'd met in Singapore (bless them for remembering, I'll send them a card) bought water and had a meal. A good friend in England knows and loves Ubud and I have looked out her recommendations on where to eat. As I biked slowly back, I saw a great 'V' of white birds high in the sky, flying towards me. I thought at first they were seagulls, as they might well have been at home, but to my amazement I realised, as they soared overhead, that they were herons and surely an omen that I have come to the right place?

Thursday 22nd August

Ever since I arrived here yesterday there has been a steady stream of the owner's brothers and nephews coming to see me. At first I was naturally wary, but when a little procession wound its way down the narrow path between the watery paddy fields, bearing cup and saucer, spoon, sugar and an enormous thermos of tea, free and unasked for, I reckoned they were on my side. There are only two little bungalows here and they are not listed in the Lonely Planet. I had been a bit upset on my arrival and I am not the usual sort of traveller (due to maturity and solo mode of travel) so perhaps I was rather a novelty.

As I tried to sleep last night I wrestled with the problem of once again being out of contact with my family. My mother only had the telephone number of the first place, which was full. I decided I would fax a friend in the morning with details of my whereabouts and plans. She could then pass it on to my mother. To fax Mum from abroad requires making two phone calls, the first to tell her to switch her phone to fax! Perhaps I am slightly unnerved by the tragic news of John Walker's son's death; and feel I need to be contactable, in this lovely, but faraway place.

In the early hours of the following morning I was woken by an urgent knocking on the thick wooden door. Surely not breakfast? There was one of the brothers in the half-light pleading with me to come out 'Englan'! Englan'! telerone! telerone!' he cried. I found undies, and still in my filmy Indian nightie (too hot, but mozzie proof) I followed him, locking my room with the padlock fit for Windsor Castle, as I half-suspected it might be some plot. I considered: I was completely out of contact from home and had dismissed the idea of telling full-up guest house No 1 to give any callers the telephone number of guest house No 2, just too complicated with the language barrier.

In the owner's tiny thatched office high in the Balinese hills, as the dawn mist drifted over newly planted rice, and the palm leaves dripped after the night rain, over the airwaves was my darling daughter Gemma, loud and clear from Putney! It was wonderful and the answer to my many fervent prayers of the previous night. We talked for ages - I protested but she was adamant - wanting to know how I was and to tell me she was off on holiday to Turkey the next morning. Oh joy, to know that all is well and that my family now know where I am. The owner's brother beamed away listening to me. It was ten past five in the morning as I picked my way back to my little home in the paddy fields, much, much happier. Someone, somewhere is surely looking after me, as I've thought before.

BAGPUSS AND THE FROGS

<u>Wednesday 28th August</u>

Bali: I am almost lost for language to describe my first week of wide-eyed delight on this luscious island. Everywhere is simple beauty. The six monthly festival of Galungan for which huge bamboo arches, called pendors, line the roads, was celebrated only a few weeks ago, and they are still in place. Made of intricately woven bamboo and coconut leaf, often tipped with corn tassels, they arch widely over and swing gently above the narrow roads and paths, giving a fairytale quality to each village. Music can be heard everywhere. Bamboo wind chimes, melodiously low, swing outside the many small shops, and over the rice fields ingenious little windmills clack musically up and down the scale to ward off the birds. In temples and restaurants, bamboo and metal xylophones are played with great dexterity all day long, and customers lounge happily on huge round floor cushions at low tables enjoying the bell-like tinkling.

Every morning a member of each Balinese family or business, places offerings to the Gods at the entrance to their 'homestay' or house, either on the path or the floor - miniscule woven palm baskets of rice grains and other scraps of food, bright flower petals and perhaps an incense stick. These are replaced daily, on steps, street corners and counters; Bali is a Hindu island, unlike the rest of Moslem Indonesia.

Each village around Ubud where I am staying, is a self-contained craft centre. One village will be a hive of activity as wood-carvers saw and chisel and intricately fret and paint, their porches a mass of chippings and sawdust. In the next village silversmiths, painters, or batik fabric workshops will line the narrow streets. Beyond the small houses, in the countryside, terraced rice paddies give a magical beauty to the landscape as they descend impossibly steeply, one glittering narrow watery strip below another, the little emerald green tufts of young rice equally spaced while the still water reflects the palms or clouds above. Deep gorges cradle fast-flowing rivers and streams, and the fertile volcanic soil produces superb fruits and vegetables, while speckled hens roam the ploughed soil.

The wider areas of rice fields on the gentler slopes are tranquil in the sun. Farmers work tirelessly, often bent double, in their large conical coolie hats, while flocks of white egrets paddle in the distance. Duck herders with long poles lead their brown, quacking charges through the villages in the early morning, to feed on the harvested paddies, pecking them clean of stray rice grains, ready for planting again.

Bali is blessed, apart from her wonderfully fertile land, with fine-featured, good-looking people. The men, many extremely old, work in the fields and jungles, carrying heavy loads of logs, vegetables or bricks on poles balanced across their shoulders. At other times they sit around in the sun gossiping, in Manchester United T-shirts, sporting hibiscus flowers behind their ears.

The women are extremely beautiful and often wear the Balinese dress; a lace bodice, sarong and wide sash, in brilliant, jewel colours. They walk elegantly, with tall baskets or wide trays balanced on their heads, and in the evenings wash their clothes in the streams, and themselves and their children in the village trough, bare breasted, and ducking down when strangers pass. The women also work in the fields, in wide bamboo hats, their small babies slung across their backs, curled in cotton papooses, and the older women live with their children and grandchildren, wearing merely a sarong from the waist, as was the custom in days gone by. Children fly splendid homemade kites, or fish in the rice paddies and the older ones race about on motor scooters and work in the many cafés and hotels. They are quite delightful people, kind and unruffled by anything.

Over the course of the week I got to know my young landlord and his family very well, and they in turn took me to their hearts. Alit, the boss, is twenty-six and driving me one day on a three hour round trip to Kuta (for mail, before I disappear to the coast on the other side of the island) he told me a lot about their Hindu beliefs, which seem to hinge on the fundamental acceptance that your life is planned by the Gods. Thus they do not worry overly about things, but just content themselves with knowing that what is, was meant to be.

Alit is very handsome and runs an excellent business with a small tour company alongside his cottage accommodation. His brother Rai and their friend Ketut were comical. After I had had a marvellous day's jaunt out with Ketut one day, on the back of his moped, singing 'Michael row the boat ashore' at the tops of our voices (his English was very bad, but I taught him the chorus) we now cry 'Alleluia!' every time we see each other. Ketut is twenty-two with a wonderfully broad smile, and he brings me an enormous thermos of tea at six o' clock in the morning, calling 'Alleluia, mees Seeny!' through the door, before sweeping my verandah. Rai is shyer, bringing me fruit salad and jaffle for breakfast about half past eight. Jaffle is a toasted sandwich with sealed edges, filled with egg and tomato, or banana, or jam, and quite scrumptious.

Both he and Ketut are mad about my small binoculars. Borrowing them as I eat my breakfast sitting in my bamboo chair with radio, letters and diary, they sit on the step in front of me, taking it in turns to spy on 'Women!' in the rice fields stretching before us, and once to watch Japanese girls swimming in a pool some distance down the road. Dayu, Alit's wife is twenty-four, the same age as my daughter, and very petite and pretty. We both giggled together madly, when she insisted on lending me her traditional Balinese dress to visit a temple and I had to force my breasts into her very small, tight, boned corset. My cleavage ended up almost in line with my shoulders! Their six-month old baby is gorgeous. Named Bagus, I renamed him 'Bagpuss' after the children's storybook at home, and it has stuck. He is carried around for much of the day tucked under Ketut's arm or strapped across his grandmother's back and is an immensely happy little boy. Alit lends me a mountain bike whenever I want one, as we are a good ten minutes ride from Ubud village, and

Ketut and I dashed off on his moped at no minutes' notice one day to catch the post. They are all so kind.

Alit was in full agreement with me, when I said I didn't think the Gods had wanted me to go to the original guesthouse, but to come to him. I love my cottage. As I have already described, it looks out across the rice fields, and in the pond just below my step, frogs honk, burp, croak and plop all night, making such a kerfuffle that, much as it amuses me, I have had to resort to my earplugs. I think they have a boss-frog and, starting from the occasional deep honk, a commanding and very throaty croak begins. Rapidly hundreds of others join in and they get louder and louder as they crescendo into a real din - I wish now I had brought my tape recorder.

From my wide wicker armchair I watched tiny, olive-backed sunbirds suspended over the huge sunset-coloured hibiscus flowers only feet away from me, the little birds' long curved beaks burrowing deep in the flowers to gather the nectar. Once, as I sat quietly on my verandah, a brilliant blue and white kingfisher, with a bright red beak, dived down to my pond and plucked out one of the small fish Ketut had released unadvisedly, into the water only half an hour before. It was a Javanese kingfisher and, as he flew off he left one of his turquoise feathers behind for me on the water.

To one side of my cottage is an ancient and very beautiful Balinese temple, recently opened as an art gallery, and often during the day the sound of gongs, xylophones or singing, floats over the walls. With villagers peacefully planting rice before me in the warm sun and the huge volcano in the far and hazy distance, it is a magical scene. There is so much tradition in this culture. Young Bagus was honoured at a Hindu ceremony when one month and seven days old, then again at three months and at six months. There will be a further temple ceremony in his honour when he is a year old.

Once a year, in March, Bali has a Silent Day when no one at all leaves his or her home and all is utterly tranquil, whilst every six months each temple (and there may be three or four in a town) holds a festival. I witnessed such an occasion on my moped jaunt with Ketut. As we watched under the biggest banyan tree I have ever seen - as tall as my village church spire at home and hundreds of years old - women and children bearing offerings of fruit, leaves and sweetmeats in bamboo baskets and palm boxes piled high on their heads, streamed out of the temple, down into the gorge below us, across the river and up the hill opposite. Brilliantly dressed in shimmering sarongs with wide sashes, they laughed and chattered as they walked with their small children, the men following in equally colourful sarongs with white bandannas round their black hair. It was a breathtaking spectacle, and in the week that followed I saw many such processions. The memory of those happy, beautiful, devout people streaming across the gorge will always remain with me.

Festival day, Bali

On a different note, I have found a good place to eat just round the corner. It is far from smart, but clean and cheap and the local workman and shop assistants also eat there. Ubud is a mecca for painters, sculptors and craftsmen from many lands, who often settle here, and those who seek and admire their work, holiday here. Consequently there are a great number of charming little restaurants in Ubud, with superb food and spectacular views over the rice paddies and jungle and often prices to match.

My place is a hive of activity, with a dozen young boys and girls aged from about ten to their twenties, serving and cooking. Different booths bordering the restaurant prepare and cook Javanese, Balinese (much the same), Chinese or Indian dishes. Being European and on my own, I was immediately surrounded by the young, wanting me to teach them English, to help them practise writing it (in between cooking and serving) and poring over my photos of home. I learnt their names - Jonah is a little fat boy who loves my torch and watch; Deffi, at eleven is very pretty and asks me about my garden in England. She was incredulous to learn that no, we don't have palm trees or coconuts growing there, and 'rice fields in England?' again no, and it's very difficult explaining what exactly we do have. Phoo-too (I never did learn how to spell it) a gorgeous-looking chap of twenty wants to marry my daughter Gemma, having seen her photo. Sobren, also in his twenties, spent ages writing words and asking me to correct them. We had one potentially sticky moment when lots of boys crowded round me, laughing, and Sobren wrote 'dic like fuct?' and I thought, here we go, but it transpired he was asking me whether 'thick' was like 'fat' which left me wondering at the way my mind works. Not for the first time I wished I had brought something more with me - postcards or photos of my house (I have only a few) of my village at home and of England.

One of the cooks in his thirties, and madly good-looking, asked me for a date. He is well travelled and articulate, but I am wary. I can eat here for about two pounds fifty a day, but do occasionally tire of rice and noodles. One day I tried the famous Es Buah dish, a pudding of ice crystals mixed with chocolate milk, all sorts of fruit and fresh tomatoes (which are used as both a fruit and a vegetable here) and surprisingly it was quite delicious. Fresh fruits - pineapple, pawpaw, lime, or avocado, are chosen and whizzed into juices as you wait, and taste heavenly - the addition of a little chocolate syrup with the pineapple, and sugar with the avocado are yummy. Gado gado is a salad including prawn crackers and peanut sauce, and I've eaten searingly spicy Javanese chicken, with chillies and lemon grass, and Kodok (frog) pancakes.

I am feeling much more rested. My rucksacks' combined weight is now about twenty-two kilos, so with my tan and muscles developing nicely I might apply to 'Gladiators' on my return! I have found that Tiger Balm soothes mozzie bites and at long last I have finished my malaria tablets. The final disaster had happened in the ultra smart Citibank in Singapore early one morning where, not having had enough breakfast to absorb the very strong pill, I was violently sick in their staff loo, but fine thereafter.

There is SO much to buy in Bali. Gorgeous sarongs, jewellery and carvings and I have to rein myself in - do I really need bamboo wind chimes for Goose Cottage?

ALLELUIA!

One day I toured the island with Rai in Alit's white jeep, knowing I would otherwise never see the beautiful mountain temples and other lovely places recommended to me by my Jakarta friends. Rising at four-thirty in the morning, Rai and I meandered through Bali at forty miles an hour watching the mist clear high on Mount Agung and Mount Gurang Batur, the main peaks on the crater rim of the huge volcano.

By five o 'clock the villages were alive with the business of the day; women with baskets of vegetables on their heads and men off to market, driving pick-ups loaded high with coconuts, people and fishing nets. Older men pedalled bicycles from a bygone era with scythes over their shoulders and smartly uniformed children walked to school. Rai enquired anxiously as to whether I had my 'glasses' with me and while I gazed out from high above the crater, as the cloud and mist cleared to reveal a beautiful shining lake, with orchards below it, and towering lava peaks above, Rai scoured the villages with my binoculars for 'women' - how I laughed! He loved looking at other distant things, but always teased me about his 'women' and I would nudge him and point if I spied one on the horizon.

We drove slowly on through hot and dusty little villages where in the afternoons men gathered to stage cockfights, carrying their prized possessions in baskets on motorbikes, or under their arms, tail feathers fluttering. We visited a tenth century monastery cut into cliffs of lava, an eerie place of ancient worship, deep in a jungle gorge, with rice paddies and palms soaring in tiers above us.

Returning to Ubud for a couple of hours, Dayu dressed me in her very becoming brown batik sarong, brilliant yellow long-sleeved lacy bodice and a beautiful sash. Much to the amusement of the men, Rai and his 'Balinese woman' drove off again to farewell cries of 'Alleluia!' We drove for two hours through jungle valleys and across fertile hills, to a large and beautiful lake where, amid flowers and lawns, a small temple stood poised, half on the shore and half on an island. The scene was magically picturesque with the hills circling the lake in the swirling mist. Signs outside all the Balinese temples ask you not to touch the buildings, not to spit, throw rubbish, not to enter if you have a period and to dress correctly. Rai and I were each required to hire a white sash at one temple before entering, and Dayu was determined that I should be spared further outlay, by attiring me appropriately. The colours in which I was dressed were those reserved especially for visiting the temples. Other sarong, sash and bodice colour combinations are worn for festivals, cremations or parties.

On we drove, through a village famous for its colony of egrets - many hundreds of the elegant little white storks roost high in the palm and banyan trees at night, and I realised the great 'V' I had seen on my first evening, had been the egrets heading for this spot. Telegraph poles in Bali are often painted grass green, and blend in perfectly with the dense foliage. We had such a happy day, and our final visit was to Tanah Lot, a perfect fairytale temple, perched on a rocky outcrop by the sea and cut off at high tide. Tourists gather in their coachloads on the cliffs overlooking it, to watch the temple silhouetted against the sunset, through their Japanese camcorders, and tripod-mounted cameras. I joined them, jockeying for space to take a photo from the cliff-top restaurant, with cliff-top prices to match. My imagination allowed me to blot out the people, the commercialism and the hawkers, selling every imaginable horror, and to savour the sheer isolation and holiness of this incredible place. The wide black sands, the sea crashing on the sharp rocks below the temple, and the monks in saffron robes praying under the five-tiered temple roof, as the sun set over the Java Sea beyond.

On the way home Rai bought us steamed sweetcorn (steamed in their skins - why don't we cook them like this at home?) which were young and marvellously tasty, and a bag of fresh orange passion fruit, especially for 'my Balinese woman!' I had had so many compliments, from foreigners and Balinese alike, thumbs up for dressing as I had done to visit the temple from local women, even 'sexy!' from some Germans and I was asked to pose below the temple with a Japanese family. Contrary to my fleeting thought that they might not like the idea of a foreigner dressing in their traditional way, the Balinese thought it a tremendous compliment, and I was very touched - well done, Dayu. On our way home, as Rai and I sang our National Anthems, Ten Green Bottles and Unchained Melody, I chided him for driving slower and slower. 'I like to be with you' he said simply, and we got home eventually.

Oh, Bali, Bali - what a magical place! Those who read this may notice I haven't even been to the beaches yet - only in a fleeting few minutes in Kuta eating my sweetcorn, had I seen the famed sands. Friends have all alluded to my sitting in the sun, doing nothing, swimming, and what on earth was I going to do in Bali, for three weeks? Apart from the temples, of which there are several in Ubud, there are also superb art galleries, famous throughout South East Asia, many housed in ancient Balinese palaces and temples, and all the other places of interest I have described here.

Three months would not be long enough to take it all in and, not since Nepal have I been so completely overwhelmed with the beauty I have found. I only wish I had the time (and the funds) to visit Java and Sumatra, although women are strongly discouraged from travelling alone through the latter. I have again learnt so much - to my shame, that Singapore is a completely separate country from Malaysia which I had not realised, that tapioca is a root, grated and used for cooking (not the gelatinous frogspawn we know as tapioca - that is sago) and how inventive the Gods were when they created bamboo. It is the most incredible material, used for the building of houses, fences, furniture and decorations; for bird, cockerel and animal cages, for eating utensils, dishes, musical instruments, to cook with and in and even the sophisticated irrigation system here in Bali is made of bamboo: dams, levies and aqueducts making full use of the rivers and rains.

Later. The day before leaving Ubud, I watched a stunning outdoor display of Balinese dancing. The display I had seen last week in a thatched barn some way out of Ubud was the Kecak Fire and Trance dance, an incredible display of male dancing; fifty brown chanting men dressed in black and white checked sarongs tied with red sashes, danced with slim girls wearing glittering gold headdresses, their long black hair studded with orchids and their sarongs and bodices every colour of the rainbow. It was enchanting, very professional and exciting. The last dance involved the lighting of a fire on the dirt floor just feet in front of us, then, as the flaming coconut husks - lit with a liquid fuel of some sort – died into fiercely glowing embers, a man, supposedly in a trance, danced through them time and time again, dressed as a hobby horse made of raffia. As he kicked the coals around alarmingly to the drumming of the music, we all had to mind our bags, feet and legs.

This second performance I watched was equally fascinating. Small girls aged about ten and sumptuously dressed, with intricate frangipani, hibiscus and lotus blossom headdresses, small fans and tight, gold threaded sarongs, danced exquisitely to the traditional bamboo drums and xylophone music. They were followed by fierce and dramatically attired giants, men dressed as monkeys and a HUGE longhaired yak-like creature, with a gold mask face and snapping jaws. They danced in different rhythms to slow, harmonious music, or to angry drumming, strident chords. It was electrifying and the setting, in the twelfth century Ubud Palace, was quite perfect.

Well now, a man I sat next to at the dancing last night picked me up and I had a drink with him afterwards. He seemed quite nice in the darkness of the palace, but when he stood up he was about four foot six inches tall, with such disgusting tight little satin shorts on that you could practically see his buttocks (never mind his frontal trappings!) below a singlet (I think that's the right word) and during our conversation and the drink, I realised we had absolutely nothing in common. He thought Clinton wonderful, Saddam Hussein very wronged by the West and turned out to be FAJWID (Failed Australian Jew with Depression - his description not mine). He eventually delivered me home on the back of his rented moped, through well-lit lanes thronged with people.

On my last morning in Ubud, I cycled up to the photographers to hand in a final film and was hailed by four or five of my young restaurant friends as I whizzed past. I am so happy here! Despite the very narrow roads and terrible camber, I confidently bike everywhere now, made easier by the fact that the Balinese drive on the same side of the road as we do, which seems odd, in such a foreign country. Oh, I am quite enchanted with Bali! How could one not be, by a land where my shower water goes straight into the rice fields, where babies sleep snuggled beside branches of herbal leaves to ward off mosquitoes, and where no one ever bothers to actually go round roundabouts - they just take the shortest route. In many ways from what little I know of it, I think it must be very like Tahiti - quite beautiful, lush and still full of local traditions, festivals and music, despite the many foreign visitors. I adore it. Every new day when I awake, I feel as if I am a blank piece of paper, or a clean blackboard, wondering what will be written on me, that day, and whose footsteps will walk with mine . . . Remind me of this please, on some dark, English winter's day.

And now to the sea and a new adventure. Carpe Diem once again.

TULAMBEN

I set off at mid-morning on the hour and a half bus journey to Tulamben on the east coast of Bali. I had decided against going to the Gili Islands at the last minute, as many travellers had told me there were masses of mosquitoes and dengue fever there, and that the beach houses were now very expensive. So Alit and I put our heads together and came up with Tulamben, a very quiet spot beneath a small volcano, with black sand and incredibly clear water.

The journey took five hours and involved four buses and minibuses, picking up, and dropping off people like me (well, mainly half my age) at several locations throughout eastern Bali. Surfboards and diving equipment were loaded and unloaded, together with rucksacks and bags and at about four o'clock we arrived at Tulamben. We had travelled up and down huge volcanic hills and through rice paddies and jungle, and the terrain was rockier and very parched as we finally descended to the eastern coast. My abiding memory of the journey was of a small bamboo hut set in dense jungle, the door thrown wide open to reveal a women busy at her sewing machine - a fleeting vignette, as we whizzed by. Once again in every village and town there were shoals of mopeds buzzing about, but everyone drove carefully and considerately in busy areas, despite the fact that they just cruised up to the roundabouts and took the shortest (if highly illegal) route. I was alarmed at first, but soon got used to it and oddly it seemed to work!

On arrival I scouted about for somewhere to stay, wanting if possible a view of the sea, or of trees and flowers at least. It was scorchingly hot and the man in the 'tourist office' (beach bar) was unusually uncooperative, and much more interested in the fact that I was alone and where was I from and 'How long you stay?' than the fact that I was loaded to the gunwales, very hot, and in need of a room. He showed me some horrible place behind a café, looking out on to a concrete wall with piles of rubbish to one side. Eventually I plumped for a rather upmarket collection of luscious thatched bungalows, set privately amid a profusion of bright pink and white bougainvillea, coconut palms and other beautiful plants. With its own small restaurant right by the sea, and a beautiful little room, it was fantastic.

Later. My room is ten pounds a night and far more than I have ever paid, but I have a sun-lounger, a fan and a verandah screened with flowers just yards from the sea. There are no shops here, nothing but this small private complex, one other like it and a few beach bars. So, I shall eat carefully and just enjoy the room and the sea. I have been practising my German with a very nice family and surprisingly remember quite a lot. There are French and English people staying here too and almost all come to dive and snorkel - the wreck of the USS Liberty sunk in the war, is only yards off the shore in very shallow water, attracting large fish, I am told. One of my first tasks was to contact Alit back in Ubud to tell him where I am staying, as I had agreed to do, just in case - the old 'being in contact' feeling again. However there are no telephone lines at all in this part of Bali (how wonderful) but the fellow behind the desk called up his sister on his radio, and she called Alit with her number and my whereabouts.

There is no sand here but this doesn't matter as there are masses of black rocks, large and small, to lie on and against, and the water is as clear as glass. On donning my bathing things, I find I look a bit too thin. Nice in some ways, and not surprising with the heat and my biking and rucksack. However, once I am with my Australian friends, I dare say they will change my shape with barbecues and good living. I am so enjoying the peace here, catching up with this journal once again and writing long letters to a couple of friends. I shall try snorkelling soon, which I haven't done since the age of nine whilst living in Egypt. (My father had been in the British army there, and we fled in somewhat of a hurry, just prior to the Suez Crisis.)

Saturday 31st August

Today I will complete volume one of this marvellous journal of memories, made and given to me by my children. I could not have imagined that I would be given another, but rather that I would have to make do with bits of paper until I hit Australia, or accept the very rough and hairy paper produced here. However, dear Verna had made me one as a surprise present whilst I was in Kuala Lumpur, complete with a photo of all her family, a cheeky message, and much encouragement for the rest of my adventure - how fortunate I am.

Last night as I ate supper in the little open restaurant by the beach, a great balloon of a harvest moon rose from the sea and everyone stopped to watch. The huge copper orb swung slowly up into the sky, lightening, brightening and gleaming, until it shone through the palm trees swaying way above us, a spectacular sight. Later it seemed that all the stars in heaven appeared over my beach, thousands and thousands of them, and the Milky Way floated like a silvery veil over my cottage. What a glorious sight it was; I watched silently among the palm trees beneath the volcano and all night I heard the sound of the sea . . .

This morning Aline, my Belgian friend who is fifteen, and her brother Pascal, accompanied me into the sea and helped me don my snorkel and fit it properly. Then we were off, and a whole new world opened up. Even in the shallows, brilliant, violet-blue fish, as tiny as a finger nail, dashed between the rocks and coral, shoals of larger black and white tiger fish marched up and down and the most elegant angel fish, bright buttercup yellow, with wide black girths, tiny green fluttering fins and tail and long streamers - like radio aerials above, fed in the depths. I was mesmerised. What beauty, and only yards from my bedroom. It only costs a pound to hire flippers and a mask for the day and what fun it is.

Later.

Oh wow, this is an amazing experience! The water is as clear as an aquarium and I have swum past coral the colour of geraniums waving in the current, huge coral platters, fan coral and blue and yellow coral too. There are parrotfish, like little clowns and striped like a puffin's bill, and lime green fish, which appear luminous, with fluorescent pink gills. The shoals of tiny darting electric blue fish are like minuscule pieces of deep blue stained glass with the sun shining through them, swimming to and fro in large gangs and so enchanting.

In a couple of weeks I will be half way through my adventure. I will be very sad to leave South East Asia as I feel in a way that the really adventurous part of my journey will be over. We shall see.

ORIENTAL SWEETLIPS

Sunday 1st September

I am so pleased, as today I taught myself to dive for shells. I couldn't work it out at first. With my mask on but minus the air pipe, I would take a great breath of air and then try and glide down, but just could not reach the bottom, six or seven feet below. I could see a tiny pearl ormer shell shining under a rock and was determined to get it. Slowly, after many attempts, I found that just holding my breath and leaping up out of the water and then propelling myself down, worked. Less air and more momentum - what those watching on the shore thought I was doing, Lord knows!

I now have three or four lovely shells. There aren't many here amongst the coral. The parrot fish, wonderful green, red, blue and pink stripy fellows, milled round me, curious to know what this plunging object was up to - my old blue and white striped swimsuit must have made me look like a rather large fish. Oh! Today I saw a whole shoal of flying fish just off the shore, glittering and glinting in the sun - magical. Tomorrow I shall get up early and watch the blue-sailed fishing boats come into the bay about six o'clock - I wonder if they would take me out one morning?

Monday 2nd September

Today I rose at half past five in the morning and walked up the rocky headland at the western end of the bay. On the brow of the hill I watched the sun come up over a hidden, stony cove way below me and thought how lovely it would be to swim there, but foolish: it was cut off, completely private and if I got into difficulties, or was robbed, I would only have myself to blame - but what a shame. I had put one of the slide films given to me by Jagdish, into my camera, and took pictures of the rising sun. As I did so, I noticed two small boys cutting branches with a large knife and a sickle. They weren't more than four and six years old. They called to me and then sat shyly by me, as I photographed them against the huge volcano that towered over the bay. After asking me for money (this is the ugly face of tourism) - I was not carrying any - they skipped off down the hill, brandishing sickle and knife alarmingly.

Three months ago today, I flew away to Kathmandu, and, looking back, I am astounded at how much has happened since then, and how rich my life has been. I have been given so much, in the form of friendship, sights, sounds and knowledge and in my heart I thank everyone who has brought me safely and very happily this far. Special thanks go to my children for their unselfish encouragement and to my Mother who holds the bank account fort at home. Verna Kanagaratnam of Kuala Lumpur, thank you for this beautiful new journal and on I go . .

Soon after the little boys disappeared, I saw the huge fishing fleet skimming back over the horizon in the stiff breeze. There were over a hundred outrigger canoes and it was an amazing sight. The spidery boats with their blue sails rigged wishbone fashion, raced before the wind in groups and in slightly different directions depending on where their fishing villages lay. None seemed to be heading for my end of the bay. As I watched, I descended the hill and sat on the beach, resolved to walk to the other end tomorrow, where the first canoes home were already beaching. If I had used my sailors' sense, I would not have been so surprised when four outriggers suddenly swooshed into the bay together round the headland on which I had been watching. With wind and tide as it was they would obviously come in that way. I stood on the beach as they navigated shorewards and then helped to pull them up onto the shingle. The hulls were extremely narrow with primitive rudders and enormously wide, spindly outriggers so that they looked like colourful daddy-long-legs, as they came to rest on the shore. Painted white, red, green and pink, they were a handsome sight.

Later. It is quite remarkable how my quandaries are resolved in the course of my travels and suddenly the answer is there, right in front of me. I had spoken briefly to both an English and a Canadian girl (who'd teamed up to explore Bali) on the beach yesterday. Today I chatted to them again, we ended up having lunch together, and Fran the English girl told me all about Cairns, where she has been living and working for three months. She flies home (and thence on to Durham University) on Wednesday and has promised to ring Gemma for me. She also asked if there was anything she could take for me, and so I gave her all my photos. She was so nice, insisting I had her address and I know they will get there safely - I am delighted.

This evening I made friends with an interesting couple from California, both divorced, both charming. Chris Bradford called to me 'Done cookin'?'as I came in from sunbathing and just these couple of words led to a fascinating conversation over supper about diving. He and his very nice girlfriend Ray-Ann, travel the globe to diving locations, filming and photographing freelance and writing about what they see and find. I learned that Tulamben is a really special place, as you can dive and snorkel right off the beach, whereas in other places you have to take long trips out in dive boats. The coral and marine life here is superb, and they told me of extraordinary fish they had encountered.

Chris told me his amazing story of diving at ninety feet when he took off a glove to touch something and was promptly pecked sharply by a cormorant! They have promised to dive down near me to the shipwreck, while I snorkel above. For some quite irrational reason I cannot for the life of me fathom, I am very apprehensive about diving down close to it. I have tried to work it out; is it because it was originally torpedoed by the Japanese, and men died down there, or because I fear being sucked down into it, or because of the large fish which cruise round and inside it? Both latter fears seem silly. People dive and snorkel above it all day long, so I must try.

Tuesday 3rd September
I occasionally wish I had some transport here on Bali as I should still like to explore Lovina on the north coast, but I really cannot better this beautiful, remote spot, and another long journey seems a waste of a day. Many of the visitors passing through here, in couples, or foursomes, have bikes and so are freer whilst I must rely on local public transport.

As I returned from my fruit salad and banana pancake breakfast in the open-air restaurant, where I had once again watched the outriggers sailing breezily home, I found the morning's little offering to the Gods had been placed on my cottage doorstep; a tiny square of banana leaf holding grains of rice, flower petals and a stick of incense, to bring luck from the Gods.

From as early as four o'clock in the morning in the countries I have visited, you can hear men enjoying the disgusting habit of 'hoiking!' as they gutturally clear their throats and spit, the Chinese in particular do this - the women too. Now I know why my father used to do it occasionally, having spent much of his life in the Far East and much to my mother's irritation (and no doubt to our delight, as children)!

It is nine-thirty in the morning and the sun is already very powerful. Balinese girl porters are walking along the rocky shore, balancing gas canisters on their heads and festooned with diving paraphernalia, followed by a group of blonde, tanned enthusiasts. It is best to snorkel in a T-shirt, as the sun can do great damage to your skin, as you skim along the surface of the water. The French and Germans lie about oblivious, in the heat of the day, even discreetly topless which is absolutely taboo in this Hindu country, but the Australians and Americans are wiser about the ozone layer problems and the fact that we are more or less right on the Equator here (eighty degrees south of it) so I am very careful. In deference to the Balinese everyone here wears a sarong over their bathers, even to walk the short distance back to our cottages, which is as it should be. It is lovely wearing so few clothes for a change, and I think I shall be a devil and get a bikini in Australia. I am quite pleased with my figure, though I don't suppose it will stay this shape for long. The Germans staying here are unbelievable - they are all Big Guys, and the men have two main courses at every meal. No wonder they are so plump.

Observation - I have realised that there are two subjects that embrace the whole of South East Asia (and possibly the whole world) - the British royal family and football. If you can claim knowledge of either and preferably both, you will discover instant friendships in any land. I am a bit out of date, with my Luther Blissett and Watford wisdom, and should have had an up-to-date crash course from my son Jasper before I left.

I watched Chris and Ray-Ann don all their complicated gear and head for the deep again this morning. They tell me the Barrier Reef in Australia is forty miles offshore, and that Americans fly in to dive there expecting to do so right off the beach, as you can here, but that is not the case.

Wednesday 4th September

The last night, wanting a change from the food at my restaurant, I walked just a few steps up the beach and found a tiny beach bar with red checked tablecloths and coconut-leaf lampshades. I had a delicious grilled barracuda steak and salad, followed by pineapple fritters with chocolate sauce. Wicked and yummy! I had mentioned the place (which I had spied on my early morning foray) to a young couple who arrived yesterday.

Guy is English and teaching the language in Hiroshima, Japan, and his Japanese girlfriend Miyuki was sweet. They came and joined me and we drank arak cocktails (the local rice brandy) and all agreed on how spectacular Bali is. When I returned to my Paradise Cottages, Chris and Ray-Ann hailed me and I sat with them at a table in the restaurant while they played me the video they had taken that day whilst diving. It was quite unbelievable seeing huge starfish, brilliant corals, shaggy-finned lionfish and other beauties of the deep, on that tiny four-inch screen, from a hundred feet down in the ocean behind us. From their Coral Reef Identification book, I found the angel fish I had seen was in fact a 'Moorish Idol' and I recognised another as being an 'Oriental Sweetlips'.

This morning as I write, I am again eating breakfast in the dappled sunshine winking through the palm trees; tea with a slice of fresh lime, fruit salad of banana, papaya and fresh pineapple, also with fresh lime, and a delectable, crisp-edged banana pancake with honey - all this is free with the price of the room. Ray-Ann has just told me that their air fares from USA were over two thousand dollars each, and that the diving here is well worth that outlay and far better than that in the Caribbean.

I am so glad I popped in here on my way past. Chris was not feeling too well last night, so I donated him my very last two centimetres of Gatwick whisky. Tomorrow I leave this lovely place, and I am determined my children will come here one day, even if they are my age! The snorkelling on this reef has been one of the most incredible experiences I have ever enjoyed, and today was no exception. I saw lime green fish, eighteen inches long, with purple fins and yellow tails, a huge shoal of shimmering silver tuna following three divers, tiny bright yellow fish with blue tails, and a group of black and white fish, almost completely spherical, who swam just under the surface of the sea with me. There are forests of waving coral, sponges, sea anemones and urchins, clams and starfish and always the unbelievably beautiful fish. What a joy it is to see them so free, feeding, chasing, diving and spinning, just beneath the waves, just yards from me!

I snorkelled above the wreck today, but didn't enjoy it much. It seemed very strange to be swimming, in 1996, above a ship torpedoed in 1942 by the Japanese, with a friendly Japanese girl beside me in the water. You could clearly see the hull, on its side, and the broken mast and spars in the sand below. She had been taken in tow by a British destroyer but rough seas prevented them reaching a safe port, so they beached her here. Then when the volcano above Tulamben erupted in 1963 the lava pushed her further into the sea, thirty metres from the beach, and three metres under the surface at the highest point. I found it very eerie but still cannot work out why. I swam and chatted today to Guy and Miyuki and to Chris and Ray-Ann - a happy day, but there has been an influx of raucous Germans and young British yuppies lying about smoking and having endless massages from the local women - time I moved on.

Thursday 5th September

Whilst I was on the beach at five-thirty this morning, watching the sun rise up from the sea, I was joined by a kingfisher who sat on a rock ten yards from me, watching intently as the waves broke inches away from him. Twice he darted down and back again, swallowing something tasty. I didn't know that kingfishers fished in salt water. On the far horizon, through my binoculars I counted two hundred and seventy-four fishing boats whizzing home on the breeze. They looked like the bad guys in some cowboy and Indian film, masses of them suddenly appearing on the skyline from nowhere. The previous night I had watched night diving in progress; half a dozen divers, men and women, waded into the sea with powerful torches, and as they sank below the waves their light beams played through the water - a very strange and beautiful sight. At times, shining them upward and along, the patches of bright glittering light looked just like moonlight on the sea except that there was no moon. Very eerie.

The return journey to Ubud (a bit better - three hours and only two buses) was hot but fine, and driving through Bali is always such fun, as there is so much to see. Brown cows with wooden bells round their necks, clacking gently, were washed at village wells in the early morning sun, women washed clothes and small children and men washed their motor bikes - with Silvikrin shampoo! Small, black, very hairy pigs, slept under banana trees (I like pigs and these were gorgeous little beasts) and the village fighting cocks were carried lovingly by their owners in round bamboo cages to a meeting place in the village. There, up to a dozen cages were placed side by side, and the cockerels then gossiped all day, occasionally crowing loudly, until required for a fight. Wild orange amaryllis grew straight out of the ground by the roadside, and rain swept over the paddy fields.

FAREWELL TO HEAVEN

Back in Ubud I was welcomed so warmly by Alit and Dayu, and they promptly brought me a large thermos of tea through the teeming rain. Now I must copy this for my family, confirm my flight for Tuesday night arriving in Cairns, Australia the following day, and post everyone's letters. I only hope I have captured some of the essence of Bali in this journal - I never cease to be captivated, every single day. Oh, and Ray-Ann especially sought me out early this morning to say a fond goodbye, to give me her card ('Underwater Videographer') and assure me that I would be very welcome in Sacramento, California.

Friday 6th September

Early last night, the boys, Rai and Ketut told me I could go and watch a dance performance free at the wonderful art gallery next door, so I set off with Ketut along the narrow raised path between the rice paddies. The small stage in the gallery garden was brightly lit with arc lamps, the backdrop an intricately carved red stone temple gate, flanked with frangipani trees and beyond, the palms rustling in the night air. The only spectators were a few local Balinese and their children and I sat on the path with them and Ketut to watch.

It was enthralling. I later learned that the gallery organisers were auditioning several dance troupes from Ubud in order to pick the best for regular performances at the gallery. Their costumes were breathtaking. Sumptuous, gold silks and glittering head-dresses, flower-bedecked crowns and brilliant shimmering bodices above tight, wonderfully coloured sarongs, exceeding any of the lovely costumes I had previously seen. The Barong dance, centring on the huge, hairy, mythical lion, was superb. The creature, with a beard of human hair, danced mischievously by two men - one at either end - has long hair, feathers and bells all over his body - the children loved him. The dancing by the lovely girls has to be seen to be believed - at times like this I wish I had a dreaded video camera. They exercise extraordinary muscular control and great physical endurance and yet give the impression of effortless delicacy and femininity, using their hands, wide eyes, toes and fingers to amazing effect. I loved it all, especially sitting with the local people and savouring their enjoyment.

I woke during the night, at half past one, itching furiously. Escaping the rain, an entire battalion of ants was marching across my bed, many wandering off into my hair, ears, and all over my body en route. There were hundreds under my pillow when I lifted it up. Uggggh! I promptly shot out of bed and leapt into a cold shower, soaked my hair and spent the rest of the night in the other bed with its three centimetres of hard horsehair mattress.

I had worked out my finances earlier that day, trying to estimate how much I would need for the last few days in Indonesia - it's always a difficult calculation to make as you leave one country and arrive in another, and not forgetting the airport tax. I went to the bank and requested a little more money with my card, 'Twenty thousand rupiah, please'. My face fell a mile when the man said sorry, two hundred thousand rupiah was the minimum they would deal in. I pleaded with him that I was only here for another few days, but he was adamant. I suddenly realised that I was a few zeroes adrift and that I was asking him for the princely sum of six pounds – so two hundred thousand it was. The small plastic currency exchanger friends at home had given me has been one of my essentials.

Saturday 7th September

Yesterday I biked around Ubud, visiting various sites of interest previously passed by. I saw huge lotus pools by a restaurant announcing 'Due to the proximity of a major temple, we will not be offering beef' and a tiny laundry shop pronouncing 'We'll pick, delivere and punctual to you'! I feel very fit after my fortnight of biking, snorkelling and gossiping, and ever more confident on the roads. My hands and one buttock, grazed on the rocks, are mending well and once again I must face the prospect of leaving a lovely place and all the friends I have made here.

I am sure I am now fully qualified in packing and unpacking rucksacks. Not a centimetre of space is wasted in packing up, and as Gemma rightly predicted, by this time I know exactly what goes in where. When I stay for only a day or so in one place before a longer journey, as I shall tomorrow, I use just the smaller rucksack, leaving the large one full of things I won't need and securely locked. This cuts down considerably on the weight. What peace of mind those little Karrimor padlocks give me. Bought in an excellent shop near Euston station, they deter idle fingers and when in transit mode as explained, I can put my walkman, binoculars and radio etc in the top of the large sac and lock it. Nothing will deter outright theft of a complete rucksack, but there is definitely an honour code amongst us travellers - there has to be. Laundry is left drying outside our rooms, shoes on doorsteps, rucksacks with fellow travellers while you find a loo on stations, beaches and in towns, and people are very caring.

Sunday 8th September

About five-thirty last night I was chatting to the Balinese man I knew in the photographers' shop beside the wonderfully watery rice fields, when a figure walked by and I recognised Brigitte, the Danish girl with whom I had almost come to grief in the Cameron Highlands jungle. She knew I was in Bali and we were thrilled to meet again. After briefly visiting my cottage we had supper together. Since Malaysia she has travelled through Java and Sumatra, which was fascinating to hear about. She confirmed what I had already heard from others; that Sumatra is definitely to be avoided if you are a lone women traveller as you are constantly harassed sexually on buses, trains, everywhere, and it is very unpleasant. Java is culturally very interesting and Bali's mother country in a way. However, everyone agrees that Bali is very special, and like nowhere else they have ever visited and I so agree.

Yesterday I sold two books in a smart little second-hand book shop. Had there been someone to whom I could have given them, fine, but there wasn't, and I really couldn't afford the extra weight. For Captain Corelli's Mandolin, which I loved, and my South East Asia Lonely Planet, I got the fine sum of four pounds and with this I bought a tiny pair of frilly baby pants for the young Balinese girl in my café, who is very pregnant and who I know is desperately poor. I also gave Rai and Ketut fairly hefty tips this morning. It leaves me a bit short, but they have both been such fine friends, running me about on mopeds and sorting out ants. They have afforded me much amusement. Both were on my verandah again this morning with my binoculars, spying on faraway women - I will miss them.

Later. I kissed both men when I left (the whole of Bali were glued to the Mike Tyson fight on television), and they waved me out of sight on the bus. I sat next to a rather dull Lufthansa pilot working on the Far East hauls. He was however, very interesting on the subject of the so-called Tiger Countries - Thailand, Malaysia, Taiwan and Singapore, whose economies are leaping ahead, often faster than their people can keep up with as they suddenly live and breathe money, rather than farming or pursuing more traditional concerns. Everyone now wants to make lots of money, as I had found in Thailand.

I arrived in hot, busy Kuta at one o'clock in the afternoon and returned to the Gora Beach Inn, where I had previously stayed. Having to wait an hour for a room, I left my rucksacks there and found a hawker wheeling around soup on his bicycle. This way of eating is fast and cheap - he puts all sorts of goodies - rice balls, noodles, onions, meatballs, and vegetables into a china bowl, fills it up with hot soup and it only costs thirty pence. The idea is that you sit on the step of the nearest shop and eat it, then return the bowl to him – excellent. After a visit to a supermarket, where I bought two spring rolls, a bottle of water, some peanuts and bananas, I returned to find a room. I want to spend as little as possible until I have rung Gemma tomorrow, not knowing what that will cost.

<u>Monday 9th September</u>

On undressing last night, I investigated my pretty Thai pantaloons, as something had been pricking me for much of the day. They are rather complicated to undo, with a tie waist, and I had only had the opportunity of a completely dark, squat loo yesterday. I was horrified to find a two and a half inch needle attached to the cotton between the legs where I had been mending a bike-riding tear before I left Ubud - the rickety bus ride down to Kuta had been bone-shaking . . . gosh, the mind boggles! When I had showered and washed some clothes I ate the things I had bought for my supper, pleased that I had eaten for only one pound and fifty pence that day. I then promptly fell asleep at five-thirty in the afternoon until six o'clock this morning.

Later. I was determined to somehow buy a present or two for my mother and Gemma from a particularly gorgeous shop. I went to collect mail – lovely. Letters from family and friends and a card from Brian Lindley, a Wykeham Gallery artist who brings me doughnuts when he delivers his paintings - how nice of him to write. It cost me twelve pounds to ring Gemma. When at first I rang her shared London house, rather early in the morning, the answerphone was on; I couldn't believe no one was in on a Monday morning. I was unreasonably upset when I left a short message - it was so hot here, I had had to queue for the phone and I wanted to talk to her very much. I get rather emotional at these times. I rang again after fifteen minutes and left a more composed message and as I was doing so, Gemma picked up the receiver. All was well, and I will ring my mother and Jasper from Cairns.

Now to survive here for a final two days on a couple of pounds, a good challenge for me. I found a tiny backstreet café frequented by the locals, where a nasi goring and pineapple juice cost me ninety pence. Later in the day I sat on the beach for a while until the sun went down, and bought a steamed sweetcorn and an avocado for thirty pence each for supper. I still have water and some peanuts. My room is accounted for and I expect Garuda Airlines will give us a meal en route to Australia. My mother had sent me a credit card statement and on doing my sums I find I have so far spent £2,159, which includes phone calls on my Interglobe card. Dividing this by my daily budget of twenty-two pounds, I arrive at ninety-eight days - and tomorrow, 10th September will be my one hundredth day on the road, so all is well.

Kuta beach is fascinating. It must be two or three miles long, a fairytale sandy bay with long, high rolling surf and wonderful sunsets. I sat there for a few hours today, guessing the nationalities of all who passed me.

The young Australian beach babes and their surfer boyfriends all seem to have long, blonde curly hair and minimal clothing. Cleavages and brown bums protrude front and back respectively, despite which I think the babes come firmly second to the boards. The Japanese and Singaporeans dress primly in black and white, favouring white crocheted bowler-shaped hats and very long shorts for the men, almost meeting the white socks and trainers. The girls sport white T-shirts, black wavy mini skirts and huge platform sandals stuck on the end of their thin legs, or wear one-piece swimmys. Oh, and they are the camera-danglers too of course.

The Europeans tend to be white and skinny, beards or designer stubble for men and sensible bikinis for the girls, except for the French - back to bums and boobs again. The Germans couldn't care less about Hinduism and sunbathe topless. The Balinese promenade, watching these bare, tattooed, smoking women and bring their small children, dressed in ragged clothes - just shorts and bare feet. You can see single male tourists being targeted by the local shark boys with drugs, women or Rolexes. They squat together on the sand in little groups, two or three sharks per visitor and deals appear to be concluded.

Tuesday 10th September

I woke up very hungry and decided I was mad to try and live on peanuts and fruit all day. This is when I need a friend with me, to tell me not to be so stupid. I had to vacate my room at noon, but did not have to leave for the airport until seven in the evening. The prospect of seven hours on water and tuppence was crazy in the heat, so I cashed a few precious US dollar bills (I have a few left for crises) and ate curry and fruit juice in a café round the corner and felt better. I spent the day by the pool in a nearby hotel; three pounds, a complimentary soft drink and a large towel seemed money well spent. A large inflatable black kite, shaped like a rocket with a red pointed end and two huge black balloons at its base (well, I overheard some children being firmly told it was a 'rocket'!) hung in the sky at a forty-five degree angle all day - most disturbing, when you're only half dressed. Later, back at my hotel, (having left my rucksacks in the office) I took up the offer of a shower from two Japanese girls in the room next to the one I had had and eventually left for the airport at seven o' clock in the evening. I befriended an Englishman on the minibus

- Neil, in his twenties, travelling after University. He told me wonderfully hairy stories of travels in South Africa and Timor.

I could almost have stayed in Bali forever. With her twenty thousand temples, her relaxed, happy people and breathtaking landscape, who could blame me? It does seem incredible that on such a small island, so many people can energetically make so many beautiful things, often from virtually nothing save coconut shell, bamboo and palm. The Balinese believe 'heaven will be exactly like Bali'. Yes, I can believe that too and I shall never forget my time there.

BACK ON THE VEGEMITE TRAIL

We took off in an airbus and flew to Darwin in two and a half hours. A stop of forty-five minutes, enough time to read about the history of Darwin - photos of buttoned up, hatted Victorian women beside nearly-nude Aborigines, and we were off again, minus Neil and with a dozen seats each to chose from. Breakfast was served at about three o'clock in the morning Bali time and I dozed a little.

Wednesday/Thursday 11-12th September

As we approached Cairns we flew into the morning and an unbelievably fiery sunrise glowing across the far horizon, a deep bronze gold. Below us, high, forested hills rolled over the land and right to the sea, with dark rivers and the sunrise glinting on inlets and estuaries - it was magical. As we came in to land a beautiful sight caught my eye. A small flock of ibis, white stork-like birds with black heads and very long, curved, black bills, flew north, against the backdrop of forest and past our aircraft. We landed.

Prior to arriving in Darwin the cabin had been sprayed liberally with some odourless insecticide to protect Australia from nasty Asian crawlies, and after landing we emerged to be greeted with videos and signs proclaiming, beseeching, warning us to declare all and every item made of wood, leaves, feathers, skins and any food and vegetables. I had to produce my straw hat and basket and unpack both my rucksacks to extricate various small items. A woman beside me had the leather top on a Javanese native drum ripped off by the Customs man rather than face the inconvenience and expense of sending it to Sydney for examination. You cannot blame the authorities.

I emerged; into a new world of space and order, airport officials and of men and women in crisp, tropical shorts. A world of wide, wide roads, large wooden weatherboard houses with steps and verandahs, as I'd once seen in Virginia USA and I saw a sign announcing 'World Mountain Bike Championships, Cairns 12-22th September 1996' - in those wooded hills, I expect. I find dairy products again, milk and butter and cream, so beloved of our developed societies, and not missed at all by me so far. It is good though, to be able to drink from a tap again, and to have a hot shower whenever needed.

I am staying in the International Hostel, right on the seafront for six pounds a night. As I opened the door of my dorm room at seven o'clock in the morning, the sight that met me was so reminiscent of my daughter's school dormitory and later of her shared London flat. The worldly goods belonging to three girls from Sweden, Japan and Scotland respectively - clothes, books, letters and make-up carpeted every flat surface and they were all still fast asleep. The hostel is a wonderful place. I have a top bunk, looking out onto a small balcony and then out to sea. At high tide pelicans paddle past and small seaplanes take off, while spoonbills fish in the shallows. At low tide the mangrove swamp stretches four hundred metres from the shore and a large number of sea birds and waders run about on the mud.

Our hostel is a converted prison with five or six floors and corridors of rooms on one side looking over balconies down to a central area, floors below. There is a large kitchen with constantly boiling water and vast fridges where all the backpackers keep bags of food. There is constant pop music and wonderful staff who will book you bungee jumping, outback trekking, ballooning, trips on every kind of vessel imaginable to the Barrier Reef to snorkel and dive, or to the Tablelands (over which we'd flown) to skydive or white water raft. Visits were also on offer to the opal mines and to rap jump, (abseiling forwards) and to Cape Tribulation, where the rain forest meets the reef. For a few hours I was totally overwhelmed with the buzz of it all, disorientated by time and culture and in a kind of limbo. I made straight for the Post Office as soon as it opened. There, wonderful family letters awaited me including a large envelope from Jasper, with cuttings, photos, posters and programmes from his Edinburgh musical. I rang my family in England and after I had eaten something, felt almost normal again. I had fish for supper from a small stall and was joined by Lotta from Sweden who was becoming a vet courtesy of Liverpool University. She introduced me to 'Sub-Zero' alcoholic soda (mmm!) and told me of the trips she'd done from here. Armed with about seventy-six different brochures, I began to make plans.

Thursday, 12th September

It is odd to be back in an almost Western country again, and yet so much is different to home. Everyone in the shops is friendly and interested in you or in what they can do for you; huge air-conditioned buses towing luggage trailers glide past and most of the men in town wear striking bush hats. Shops, plazas and restaurants are stylish and fun and catamarans, speedboats, sailing dinghies and old pearl luggers sail in and out of the bay all day. Cairns is a most attractive, buzzing town with a holiday feel about it and I like it. I spent a few hours sitting on a bench at a table by the water writing this, as elegant ibises hopped up onto the esplanade from the mud flats to be fed crumbs by an old man, and green, red and yellow parakeets shrieked and fluttered noisily in the tree above me. I then bought a few things for lunch and a very sexy new swimmy. My present one has seen good service, bought in America in 1988! The new one looks like blue denim, is laced at the bosom and makes me look quite shapely. I'm off on the good ship 'Falla' tomorrow, a sixty-four foot pearl lugger, for a day on the Reef.

Saturday, 14th September

This hostel-living is rather like University. A communal kitchen, lots of twenty-somethings either frying vast pans full of bacon and eggs or vegetarians on the noodle and Vegemite trail. There are notices galore about washing up your own mess, don't use this fridge or you're Dead, and where to find the largest, cheapest mugs of beer. There is a notice-board crammed full of advertisements for lifts to Sydney, 4 x 4s to the outback, unused air tickets to Melbourne, diving gear for sale, a lift wanted to 'Alice' (Springs) and yacht crews wanted to sail to New Guinea. My room is sunny and adequate, though there is no chair or anywhere to hang clothes - just two bunks festooned with gear and the floor likewise.

I've met all kinds of creatures - Tracey, Australian, stud in navel, working on a fishing boat here, Mick, also Australian, just out of four months in jail in Bangkok for half-killing a man he caught practising as a paedophile. Mick's now really muddled up, having witnessed much homosexuality in prison and says he wants to be a missionary - we talked for ages. Lotta plays her didgeridoo in the evenings as we sit at tables in a corridor outside the kitchen; hilarious fun, it sounds like a cow farting most of the time.

Cairns is hot and still, early in the day but by mid-morning a cool breeze arrives. I wake about five o'clock, almost chilly in the room, under just a sheet. After my time in Ubud with no fan, and Malaysia, which was extremely hot and humid, this is very pleasant. It is spring here. My mother asked me how I was coping and whether I was used to the heat by now. Yes definitely, I love it. I cannot imagine England in January, as I sit here beside palms and pelicans. My back has also been fine. My rucksacks are heavy, but I strap them very tightly round my waist, to save my back leaning forward when walking, and rest when I can at bus stops etc, against a ledge on which to take some of the weight. Last night I was asked by a young fellow in the hostel, 'Are you the lady who has come down through Asia?' Fame at last!

FALLA

Sunday. At eight-thirty yesterday morning, I boarded the lovely old wooden pearl lugger 'Falla' for a diving and snorkelling trip out to the Barrier Reef. It was a day I will always remember. With a young crew of six (Troy, Cindy, Rick, Carmine and others.) and twenty assorted passengers we headed out of Cairns under sail. After coffee and tea, a life-saving briefing and a talk on safety, we were told about all the fish we'd see and those who wanted to scuba dive were kitted out. It was very hot indeed but glorious to be at sea, and I took the helm for a while and felt immensely happy. The crew were relaxed, professional and very funny.

As we approached the reef, I helped lower the sails and we anchored off the tiniest sand island I have ever seen. Set amidst an ocean of brilliant, sparkling clear turquoise water with large fish circling the boat, it was a heavenly spot. We all jumped in and dived or snorkelled between the island and 'Falla'. To dive cost an extra twenty pounds - the cost of the day out (at twenty-five pounds) was quite enough for me without that - and you can see just as much while snorkelling, you just can't touch so much. It was quite spectacular.

We identified many species of coral, shaped as their names described - staghorn, finger, brain and boulder corals, stunning bright blue sea stars (starfish) and clams five feet long, with thick, velvety, green-spangled 'lips'. A great Queensland groper fish came to investigate us and Katrin, an Irish girl and I teamed up (we had to snorkel in pairs as 'It cuts down your risk of shark attack by fifty per cent' we were told) and had great fun, gesticulating madly and pointing things out to each other. Lotta (who had sailed on 'Falla' the previous day) and I shared the cost of a disposable underwater camera. The photos are quite good.

Then back on board for an excellent lunch of salads, hunks of bread, cold meats and barbecued chicken with time to chat. Afterwards, the rubber boat ferried some of us over to the tiny cay (island). It was simply, indescribably, unbelievably beautiful. About a hundred yards long and half as wide it seemed a sliver of heaven ringed by the fragile coral. I left the rest of the party and sat at the far end with my toes in the crystal clear sea. Not for the first time I pinched myself and sent gratitude up into the blue and shed a few tears. I just could not believe where I was and what was before my eyes and that I really was in this beautiful place.

Later on, as about twelve of us sat on the sand, Troy explained how coral is formed and how it grows. On just one day of the year, three days after the full moon in November, the entire Great Barrier Reef spawns, thus nature gives the coral the best possible chance of re-growth, amongst so many hungry fish. It was a fascinating talk. Afterwards, as our hats, towels and other paraphernalia were ferried safely back on board for us, we all snorkelled together back to the boat, some distance away. Troy pointed out many interesting marine creatures on the way. He spied a white-tipped reef shark, a little chap only five feet long and harmless, hiding in a small cave nine feet below the surface, and he guided us down to see him. He was very handsome, slim, with a bright white tip to his tail.

Back on board, the crew related and acted out the history of 'Falla', accompanied by wine and cake all round. It was hysterically funny and worthy of The Edinburgh Fringe, for example a man wearing metal bucket on head with thick rope attached as air-pipe, acted as a Victorian pearl diver…we all sat around rocking with laughter, it was so funny. As I was gazing at the sea, a dolphin chose that moment to surface off the starboard bow; I instinctively shrieked 'Shark!' and everyone rushed up, to watch a dolphin ducking and diving through our bow wave. The crew teased me even more than they had all day - mainly on account of my Nepali sunhat, 'Love it, love it!' the fact that I came from 'Himpshire' and about my age; at the start of the 'Falla history' - 'In 1861, before some of us were born' - looking at me. The last fun of the day was a competition in which we all had to catch pieces of water-melon in open mouths from across the deck, the prize one can of beer 'And now! Representing Holland/Ireland/England/Denmark we have Christian!' and we all cheered and clapped as we took our turn. Of course they threw ten pieces of melon all at once at me, and the play-off was two and three pieces at once. Hilarious, but I didn't want the beer anyway. It was such a happy and interesting day.

This evening the hostel kitchen was full of vast Scandinavian amazons and tiny Japanese girls, all cooking furiously. I have spent a quiet day, writing and watching life on the sea here. So much goes on, as I have already described. My favourite sights are seaplanes taking off and pelicans landing. Tomorrow, another adventure.

TO PK'S WITH RUSSELL

I had answered an advertisement on the Woolworth's excellent notice board (which I had been told about by someone in Bali) for a 'Travelling companion, female with an interest in bushwalking, camping, nature, etc.' to accompany the advertiser up to Cape Tribulation. Last night, he turned up at the hostel, looking for me. It was rather awkward, I said perhaps, but only if another female accompanied us, and that I wouldn't camp (with him) but find a hostel. He said 'What about this girl' (pointing to an advertisement on our notice-board 'Liz, Room 36, wants a lift to Cape Trib'), so I found her, but she had already found a lift with someone called Russell.

Russell, Cape Tribulation, Queensland, Australia.

After much discussion I opted to go along with Russell too. I haven't met him yet, but he sounded okay on the phone. I'll leave my big rucksack in the hostel's lock-up room and take minimal things. I never had any real intention of travelling with the first man (Paul, a plumber from Cairns and self-confessed bush lover) and left a note for him to say no thanks. Feminine intuition (and mine is very keen) told me something was not quite right, and anyway, why was he advertising for a female companion?

<u>Sunday 15th September</u>

I bade fond farewells to Hisaka and Lotta this morning and have bought an Australia Lonely Planet from someone for twenty dollars. I thought I wouldn't really need one as I'd be staying with so many friends, but I hate going to places new and being ignorant of the history and famous landmarks, and facts about local transport. Now I feel well equipped. So, time for adventure once more. It is ten o'clock, I've woken Liz in room 36 and Russell is coming shortly - I wonder what he's like...

<u>Monday 16th September</u>

Er, well...he reminds me of a cross between Lord Bath and Willie Rushton; my family will no doubt be quite alarmed when they see the photos! However, within a few minutes of setting off, Liz and I learned he had been teetotal for six years and was very careful to see we always wore our seat belts. His 'Ute' ('utility vehicle' or pick-up truck to us) was wonderful. It was canary yellow, with enormous, thick tyres (two on each back wheel) and a petrol tank on which he could drive for three thousand kilometres. The large open tray at the back held a muddle of ropes, tyres, bags, oily rags and a large metal trunk rather like a school trunk. This we discovered was full of cooking gear, stove, pots, pans and tins of food. Russell, Liz and I all sat in the front.

We drove north out of Cairns on a good road and across a river and a sign 'Road subject to flooding - indicators show depth', beside wooden poles marked off up to four metres. Flooding up to three metres is quite usual. Fields of sugar cane and eucalyptus trees flanked the road, the hills rising steeply beyond them to the rain forest. A small 'Cane Railway' crossed the road at a place called Yorkeys Knob, a single gauge line, on which stood open-topped cane trucks. Russell was very relaxed, a good driver and a most amusing conversationalist. He farmed a ten thousand acre 'sheep-n-wheat' farm in Western Australia, with his father and two brothers. He had, over time, given lifts to lots of foreigners and even now kept in touch with English and German tourists he'd befriended years ago. Liz and I warmed to him. She was a very pretty English girl of twenty-six, travelling through Australia and New Zealand for a year having given up a media job in London.

On we drove in leisurely fashion, stopping at lookout points high above the glorious beaches. The road wound up the coast, with the steep hilly rain forest rising to mountains on our left and wide deserted beaches to our right, rocky at low tide with enormous rollers and overlooked by delicate eucalyptus trees. Humbug Reach came and went and we passed through a small town of little wooden houses on stilts, painted pale ice-cream colours, with verandahs and neatly mown grass around them. There was a cricket pitch in the town centre and a sign proclaiming 'Cricket

Piss-Up, All Welcome' and Russell said if he did drink, he'd be in there 'Like a dingo
- cheap piss, good comp'ny, nice town'. We came eventually to the Daintree River
after a diversion through the fashionable seaside town of Port Douglas with its
lovely beach, shops and smart apartments but a bland place on the surface anyway,
lacking much character. We crossed the river on a speedy chain ferry and Russell
paid the fee. He charged Liz and me five dollars (two pounds seventy each) for the
one hundred and fifty kilometre trip whilst a coach would have cost us over twenty
dollars.

Now we really were in bush country, with road signs warning of crocodiles and
of cassowaries, large emu-like birds, which sometimes run blindly across the road
into your path. Russell told us of some small station out west that completely ran
out of insect repellent in The Wet (wet season) and how it was discovered that two
or three parts Dettol to ten of baby oil did just as well. We passed solar-powered
telephone boxes and the road became very steep, rough and unsealed as they say
here (i.e. no tarmac). The dense, jungly rain forest now lined both sides of the road,
and we crossed many rivers, over ancient wooden plank bridges. We passed long
tracks leading to lodges catering for travellers and eventually arrived at Cape
Tribulation and PK's Jungle Village, which was much nicer than the name implies
and where Liz had planned to stay for a while.

It was a beautifully secluded small complex of log cabins, with a swimming-pool,
a bar and an open-sided common room. The central self-catering area afforded two
large gas hobs, and sinks at either end, whilst around the sides stood large fridges
and food storage lockers. All this in the rain forest, with excellent washing and
drying facilities, washrooms and a camping area.

I was keen to camp, in order to save money, and had discovered that Russell had
a small tent, two foam mattresses and other camping gear. He had also talked about
sleeping in the back of the 'ute'. We put up a small lime green igloo tent, which was
very easy (though there was no fly sheet so we hoped it wouldn't rain) and I asked
hesitantly if this was 'my' tent or 'ours'. 'Oh, ours' he replied. Dilemma. Liz (who
had checked into a cabin) and I were ninety-nine per cent sure he was just a pleasant,
harmless farmer, looking for company, and we were proved right. I had the option
of joining Liz on a spare bunk in her room, other tents were very close by and all
went well. It was a humming little camping spot, and as the other tents gradually left
over the days, so our pitch under the palms and stars was wonderfully peaceful.

I would sit cross-legged on the grass at eleven o'clock each night (one o'clock
GMT in England) and listen to the World Service news of Saddam Hussein making
trouble again. Waking on the first morning in the tent, I found it was nine o'clock
and I never sleep that late so I can't have been too worried about Russell. I often
chuckled at the incongruity of our situation. Liz's diary, she confided to me, sounded
even odder - 'Am at present travelling with an aged Australian hippie from the
outback and an upper middle class forty-nine year old English divorcee'.

In case you need reminding as regards Lord Bath and Willie Rushton . . . Russell
was about five foot four inches tall, exceedingly hairy, with a thick, vaguely trimmed
beard. A mop of rather long, straggly, matted hair topped this and edged the beard,

and he usually wore an ancient, equally matted, woolly maroon cap on top. He sported a dark shirt and trousers and construction boots, and in the evening a black and white gingham shirt was produced, though nothing else changed. The evil looking wrap-around sunglasses completed the picture of a seemingly thoroughly unsavoury character. What fun this is!

CAPE TRIBULATION

Cape Tribulation, named by Captain Cook when the Endeavour hit a reef there in 1770, is a stunningly beautiful place. Vaguely the shape of a dog's paw, it overlooks the Coral Sea and beyond that, the South Pacific Ocean. On either side of the headland, curved white beaches, wild and remote, are protected from the open seas by the coral reef. Dolphins and humpback whales come near to the shore at certain times of the year, sea eagles circle the headland diving for fish, and coconuts, unusual beans, seeds, fruits and leaves are left to bleach on the tide-line. There is a raised boardwalk through the mangrove swamps from PK's to reach the beaches, only a few minutes walk away. What makes them so extraordinarily beautiful are the thick green trees, creepers, ferns and bird calls of the tropical rainforest, which extend to the very fringes of the beaches. A good long walk beside Myall beach, the first one, is constructed along another boardwalk through the swamp to Tribulation Beach, equally as lovely, but busier, with divers and a few visiting yachts.

From October for a few months you cannot swim in these waters, due to stingers (jellyfish) along the coast. A large plastic bottle of vinegar is left in an old bamboo pipe at the entrance to the beach to use in case of stings. One day I walked into the hills with Rob and Wendy, a young couple from Leicester in their twenties, who had flown in on my plane from Bali to Cairns. We saw butterflies that made me gasp, magnificent, iridescent, sapphire-blue Ulysses butterflies, shimmering against the fresh green of the palms, and we heard all manner of bird-calls from high in the rainforest canopy.

Another day, with Rob and Wendy sitting in the back of the 'ute', Russell, Liz and I drove north, with bare feet and wearing swimmys, towards Cooktown. Russell and his vehicle were ideal for that terrain. As soon as we'd gone a hundred yards or so, the tarmac ended and from then on we bounced, rocked and slid over and up long, wide rough tracks, through the rainforest. Occasionally, as we reached a crest, a breathtaking, panoramic view would be laid before us: distant curved beaches, turquoise sandy water, long white rollers, and always the lush green rainforest reaching to the very edge of the ocean. We stopped at small creeks across which our track ran, in between boulders and overhanging trees. In one tall eucalyptus tree we spied a lace monitor, a rather odd name for a very large, beautifully marked lizard, rather like an iguana, making his way vertically and very sedately up the tree.

We were like children. 'Russell, Russell! Can we stop here?' and we'd don sandals and scamper off to look at the view or climb over the rocks to swim in a cold, deep, mountain water-hole, when we were quite sure (we met a National Park Ranger there) that there were no lurking crocodiles. I saw a kingfisher and a colourful double-eyed fig parrot - identified for me by the useful ranger. Rob and Wendy, riding in the tray at the back of the ute, disappeared in thick clouds of red dust every time another hefty vehicle overtook or passed us. We saw small turtles paddling for dear life through mountain streams and Russell identified a stinging tree, a really serious plant that can kill you. If you merely brush against it, tiny filaments stick to you for months and can only be removed with liberal applications of wax while the toxins do their work. We reached a waterfall and after marvelling at the cascading water, sparkling in the searing heat, we cut up a luscious pineapple with a hacksaw, and shared it between us before turning for home. Another very interesting and happy day.

We made great suppers in the communal kitchen at PK's. Real student food consisting of two-minute noodles (Russell reckoned noodles should be issued with our passports) lots of toast and marmite, mayonnaise, and tomato sauce with everything, and wonderful little plump, locally grown sugar bananas. I loved sleeping in the tent without a flysheet, as I could watch the brightest stars through the thin material and also the tracery of palm leaves in the light of a distant beam.

The night noises of the rainforest were reminiscent of Chitwan - deep, throaty calls, answering whistles, inexplicable patterings and the magical rustling of leaves all around us. The others spent time in the bar and one night it was particularly rowdy, with games and much hilarity, though our tent was in a quiet area. Later that evening, with absolutely no warning, it suddenly teemed with rain and the disco and kitchen emptied in a flash, as drying clothes, tents, shoes and other gear was rescued. After half an hour's rain I got up and located Russell and he spread a huge farm tarpaulin over our tent, pinning my drying clothes underneath it. There was now a cat's cradle of guy ropes over which I tripped and crawled back to bed. Once in my excellent sleeping bag cover I was quite snug and it was wonderful listening to the rain.

Thursday 19th September

After last night's rain, I saw no reason to rise early and sauntered into the open kitchen en route to the shower about eight thirty, straight from my bed. Rob and Wendy were there and we discussed the continuing rain. A French couple called to us that they had won a single trip out to the reef in a dive boat for that day, and couldn't use it; the trip was leaving in ten minutes - did anyone want to go? My friends egged me on and I tore back to the tent for hat, swimmy (sopping on the tent roof) sunscreen, etc. and a sarong as a towel, as mine was dripping on the line.

So, I had an extra day on the reef at no minute's notice. As I jumped into the bus someone said 'Oh, you're Cynny, there's a message at reception for you'. And so there was, as I found out later. Gemma had rung twice to say hello. (Russell and I avoided reception like the plague, as we were hoping for a few free nights' camping - eight dollars per person per night was steep and no one was exactly chasing us for it.) Sixteen of us were then transferred by rubber dinghy from the beach to a large motorboat named 'H2O', and sped from the damp and dripping rainforest to the open ocean and the glorious reef for more diving and snorkelling: magical.

That evening, our last, Russell made us all toasted sandwiches, filled with baked beans and cheese and then I caught up with my journal before we head back to Cairns tomorrow. I find it almost impossible to write about a place once I have left and moved on to a totally different environment. I spent a damp but happy last night in the little tent.

Friday 20th September

At last I managed to capture on film, the large rat that visited the kitchen every evening. Eighteen inches nose to tail, he was apparently a potteroo, and wandered into the kitchen at PK's every evening at ten o'clock on the dot. Those of us who'd been there a few days made sure we didn't warn new arrivals and loved seeing the girls shrieking and removing ankles and rucksacks up to table level. Great little guy! That morning a couple who'd been on the dive boat with me couldn't bear the idea that I'd have to spend yet another night amongst the damp trees, and offered me a spare bed in their room, which I declined. I like the sounds of the rustling trees, and I have quite surprised myself at how much fun the camping has been. I realise the weather has been warm, but being very cramped and rather wet and trying not to look at the fearsome sight of hairy old Russell, sleeping next to me nude except for an apology for a tatty old sleeping-bag draped strategically, was very funny.

We packed up and drove south again, towards Cairns. It was the most beautiful morning imaginable and as we wound slowly and happily round the coast road, the scent of the eucalyptus mingled with the shore breeze, warm and heady. The tide was out, and bay after rocky bay sparkled with sun pennies in the hot air as the long foaming breakers swirled on the sand. What a magnificent coast this is. Birds of prey hung and dived above the cane-fields as we left the majestic rainforest for open country.

Back in Cairns, Russell was adamant that five dollars was enough for the entire journey, which was fantastic and Liz and I bade him a fond farewell. He asked for our addresses and, thinking quickly, I gave him my brother Hugh's. Liz and I are in a six-berth dorm room back in the International Hotel and oh joy, I collected eight letters from the huge Australian Post Office. I stopped at the juice bar for a delicious banana smoothie (banana, honey, yoghurt and ice) and a rye sandwich, where I read them all. Oh, wonderful friends and family!

Today I had an unpleasant experience. I rang a man called George who had advertised on the hostel board for travel companions on a trip to Brisbane next week, which is exactly where I plan to go. We met for a drink, and he offered to buy me dinner but I said no, as I didn't want to feel beholden to him. He was a very touchy-feely kind of man about my age, who kept holding my shoulder and nudging me and was very chatty about the route. As soon as we got down to details, he said we would share the cost of a room -'Much more economical'. I said no I wasn't sharing a bedroom thanks, that that wasn't my style at all. He became instantly unpleasant, uncommunicative and surly, finished his drink in two gulps and marched out of the bar. I followed and he hardly spoke. I said I'd come if there was at least one other girl as well, and he said he'd let me know. I reckon he just wanted sex all the way to Brisbane. I might well accept a lift with someone, but not on my own, and would get the record straight from the outset. Otherwise I'll go by coach, though at about eighty-one pounds, rather an expense for me. I intend to return to England happily, and in one piece.

THE MUNG BEANS

<u>Sunday 22nd September</u>
The last twenty-four hours have been really hectic, and someone out there seems intent on proving to me that my adventures are far from over. Yesterday, Liz answered an ad for crew to sail a thirty-six foot yacht down to Brisbane from Cairns, past the beautiful Whitsunday Islands. Oh, I wish I had the time to go too! Brisbane is thirty-six hours from Cairns by train, involving a sleeper or several nights, if driving. At seven o'clock last night, I was called to the reception desk and two friendly young bearded Englishmen, who'd seen Liz's and my advertisement requesting a lift south, said they were driving directly to Brisbane early tomorrow. I had wanted to stop in a few places en route, but if I'm really honest, I've done lots since arriving here just eleven days ago and the thought of reaching my wonderful friends in Brisbane is very appealing. So I agreed to join them.

I had spent time yesterday writing home, and found someone to take a redirection form to the Post Restante office for me and post my letters, all things I was going to do on Monday. I then dashed up to my room to sort out my life. Liz chatted to the two guys, my drivers, Tim and Simon who were travelling down to Byron Beach near Brisbane, for a music festival. They were planning to drive each day until darkness fell, find campsites, and leg it before dawn to avoid paying. Oh, the things I have to turn a blind eye to here! It got worse . . . Liz eventually came up to my room, laughing, saying the guys were really nice, had a small tent that I could use and that they'd probably be rolling marijuana all the way down. I almost had a fit and asked if they'd be capable of driving so Liz put me right and thought it killingly funny when I said I'd sit quietly in the back with my marmalade sandwiches in my1960s sunspecs (I do wind her up and she gives me such a hard time over my non-U sunnies).

I went to bed in great anticipation of another adventurous few days. I borrowed an alarm clock in order to wake in the early hours and ring England, where good friends of mine in London would be in the middle of their wedding party, and where lots of my friends would be getting slowly sloshed. I have thrown economy to the winds on a few important occasions and rung friends; one good friend was devastated by a crisis and I rang her immediately, then Jasper, just before his play opened on The Fringe, and now the newly married chums.

As I lay on my sagging bottom bunk, I mused on the energetic and relentless nocturnal exercises my bunk had obviously been subjected to, by hoards of happy backpackers. The wooden frame above my head was covered in graffiti, explicitly explaining exactly what had gone on there, when and with whom, all of it of course, completely unrepeatable! I ate delicious champagne melon for breakfast, golden yellow and similar to watermelon but with far fewer seeds, wonderfully crisp and succulent. I then walked for one last time along the Esplanade and the seashore. The tide was far out, pelicans were still asleep in the morning sun, cosily fluffed out on the mud flats, joggers jogged and boats set sail for far horizons. Happy day and on with my Adventure!

Monday 23rd September

Simon and Tim collected me at eleven-thirty and off we set in their ancient, roomy Toyota for the Bruce Highway South. As we left Cairns at speed, it seemed that everyone had wings, including us, birds, butterflies, sails and planes, all enjoying the morning breeze. We were soon speeding south on good roads between cane-fields and brilliantly colourful flame trees. We passed Corduroy Creek, many camper vans and a poor dead kangaroo with the most beautiful oyster-coloured coat. The in-flight music hotted up, with sound tracks from Pulp Fiction and Reservoir Dogs and I chatted to the boys. Simon, thirty-two, had lived in England when small, and his parents had then emigrated to Australia where Tim, now twenty-eight, was born. They were both charming and very good looking, although long hair, ponytails and goatee beards don't madly attract me. Both were without jobs at that moment. Tim was a computer buff and Simon had been in PR and latterly a postman. They travelled together through New South Wales and Queensland, following the music festival trail and occasionally working.

It was very heady stuff, cruising fast along the wide, sun-baked highway in the old car, with its thick sheepskin covered seats and piles of junk on the floors, the beat of the music somehow well suited to the glorious open landscape. We stopped in Townsville, a rather dull-looking place, but with pretty city gardens including a memorial to 'Australian and American Sailors who died in the Battle of the Coral Sea' in 1942, Townsville being the closest port. The plaques were surrounded by gardenia bushes, laden with wonderfully fragrant, creamy flowers, which I knelt on the grass to enjoy. On again, after buying rolls and fruit. Later we had to give up our few remaining pieces of fruit at a police post, to stop the spread of fruit flies, as we left the fruit-growing area and entered the sugar cane region.

We passed many creeks and swamps - Sullivan's Swamp, Marta's Creek - and during the afternoon we stopped at a roadside café signed 'Free Driver Reviver'. This excellent scheme, run by the Lions Club in Queensland, offers free cups of tea, coffee, soft drinks or Milo, and a small Kit-Kat, to every driver who calls in. Sponsored by Nestlé Australia since 1990, they supply the sugar, milk and stirring sticks, encouraging drivers to take a break during excessively long journeys, whilst passengers had to pay. There are forty-six such kiosks in the State of Queensland. What a terrific idea. We all took advantage of it (I am ashamed to say we parked the car out of sight, and went up one by one, claiming to be drivers) and sat on a bench by the single gauge cane railway, in the shade of some gum trees. The boys filled their own capsules with guarana powder (a harmless Amazonian herbal extract), shared a roll-your-own cigarette and we were off again.

The cane fields were being burnt off, and in the thick black smoke rising above the licking flames we saw the most extraordinary sight. I counted over forty hawks, buzzards, kites and other birds of prey, circling and wheeling through the dense smoke, presumably watching keenly for the many small mice and other rodents fleeing from the fire. It was an amazing sight and they surely risked getting their feathers singed as they dived down into the smouldering fields. Stopping for petrol in a fruit growing area we found loos, the men's signed 'Mangoes' and the ladies signed 'No Mangoes'. A breathtaking deep golden sunset bade us goodbye on our first day, the spiralling smoke from the burning cane-fields rising before it, seeming for all the world as if the horizon itself was aflame.

We reached Bowen, a small fishing hamlet early that evening, pitched the three-man dome tent and ate fried egg, tomato and baked bean sandwiches with mugs of tea, before bed. Not having a sleeping mat, I arranged an array of different garments above and beneath me, as well as my sleeping-bag, fleece and Gortex jacket. It was my suggestion to pitch just the one tent, rather than the three-man and the single one, to save time and conserve heat; it was definitely chilly after the sunset. I slept surprisingly well, and in the morning found flocks of peacocks and large black, bush turkeys, with pretty fanned tails, wandering about the rather scruffy campsite. Comical looking kookaburras, squat and owl-like, with thick, kingfisher bills, sat on telegraph wires and it was another beautiful morning. We speedily showered, drove hurriedly away from the campsite (don't ask me if we paid . . .) and stopped on a hill outside Bowen to take some photos. The sea was as calm as a lily pond and beyond the many yachts moored below us in the small walled harbour were the wooded picturesque Whitsunday Islands, so named by Captain Cook. They stretched out to sea and down the coast, a chain of secret little bays, hills and channels between islands of every shape and size; it was a wonderful sight.

The morning was fresh and beautiful and the sun shone through a froth of delicate pink grasses along the verge as we sped along. Beyond, a field full of small termite hills, lots of them, fascinated me, as I had seen only single ones before. Brahman cattle grazed on the bushland between the cane fields and sadly we saw several more dead kangaroos by the roadside. Later, we made a short detour to Airlie Beach, the smart Whitsundays resort and the jumping off point for the many expensive trips to the islands with names like Hook Island and Daydream Island. We grabbed a quick breakfast of sausage, egg and chips, tomato and 'bottomless coffee' in a small café, and hit the road again, music blaring, heading for Mackay.

I had rung my friends Colleen and Mark Wheatley before accepting my lift. They had said I couldn't arrive fast enough as far as they were concerned, and if I was to be dropped off at any telephone box in or around Brisbane one of them would collect me. After Mackay, I noticed a sign to Eton, and now the sun was high, shining on the fluffy silver sugar cane flowers. Tim and Simon took turns at driving or dozing in the back. I offered to drive, but they were happy to share it. My musical education continued - Spearhead, Music for a Jilted Generation, Brand New Heavy's Mother Earth and Cruel Sea. Stopping for petrol, an extraordinarily colourful bird flew down to our picnic table and took pieces of Anzac biscuit from my hand. He had duck egg blue circles round his eyes and emerald stripes beneath, the rest of him resembling a starling.

As we drove on towards our camping spot on the coast, huge volcanic rocks reared up out of the bush, mini mountains three hundred metres high and quite spectacular. We camped that night in the most idyllic place you could possibly imagine. A small sandy cove with a rocky shoreline, looking out over the last of the Whitsunday Islands, shaded by waving malaluca trees. It was magical. We erected the two little dome tents under a small breadfruit tree, as Simon's cough was worse and he elected to sleep on his own. On a hill overlooking our bay, were two small open sided barbecue shelters in which a pair of large metal hobs with a central hole allowed two separate families to cook from either side of the shelter. By pressing a button beneath the hob, a gas flame would heat the entire hob for nine minutes at a time, before it extinguished, when you would repeat the process. This wonderful service was free, sponsored by the Lionesses, an offshoot of the Lions' Club. Picnic tables and loos completed this excellent barbecue area. We had bought sausages, steak and salad in Yappoon, the town beyond the cove and, as the sun set, we had a splendid barbecue.

The moon rose and the stars glittered in a vast dome over our little cove, as we lay down that night, and again I had to pinch myself. Was I really here, on the Capricorn Coast, beneath the stars in Queensland? I woke at four o'clock, bitterly cold and rearranged my bedding, squirreling deep into my sleeping-bag. The moonlight was brilliant and for a few minutes I watched the waves and the stars both moving in their own way, across and beneath the heavens. Sleep again, and later I opened one eye and saw the very top of my tent lit by a tiny deep golden ray of dawn. I called Simon and Tim, as we had planned to watch the sunrise. It was quite beautiful, beyond the sand and the small distant islands. I walked for a while, finding shells, as the sun rose and warmed me, and shortly we left our cove, very reluctantly, and rejoined the highway.

We refilled with petrol and all showered in the adjoining, spotlessly clean bathrooms, used by truckers and travellers, and continued on our way. We left Livingstone Shire and made for Rockhampton, Brisbane still over six hundred kilometres south. More music, this time 'Buxom Betty's Bust Reduction Mix', as we crossed Raspberry Gully and signs to Calliope. The undulating countryside was real bush now, grasses bleached by the harsh sun, eucalyptus trees and many dry creeks and river beds. A sign warned of koalas, as we crossed Ginger Beer Creek, and another sign advertised a radio station called 'Beef 97' for local farmers - all talking a load of bull, I daresay!

Now and then, amongst the scrubby bushes, we would spy a fresh and beautiful pink or white blossom tree, a reminder that it was only just springtime here, despite the stifling heat. We reached a pretty town called Gin Gin at midday. As we left the car to shop and stretch, a handsome parrot flew up into a tree above us. With a pale yellow head, blue breast and a blue green back, he looked like a mammoth budgie and was awfully vain. We made sandwiches - sardine for me, chicken crinkle-cut chips (crisps) for S and T. I found a small, plastic camera film canister in the car's food box, one of those small black-lidded ones. It turned out not to contain a stray film, but marijuana butter - silly me, I should have known, for making marijuana cookies I was told. You nibble them with tea or coffee and get very slowly stoned.

We sped on once more, through cane fields and a few neat little mandarin orchards. The fragrance from the mandarin blossom as we whizzed by, with windows down, was heady and delicious and I thought of how much you would miss, travelling this route in an air-conditioned bus or train. It also set me thinking about the scents I really love, and here is my list: fresh waffles, eggs and bacon, old roses, newly-baked bread, roast lamb, coffee, mown grass, primroses, the earth after rain, the sea, and mud. We drove over Woco Creek and past Goodnight Scrub and I spied a solar-powered electric fence on a hillside. By this time it was well into the thirties centigrade, dry and extremely hot. In some places, the earth was an amazing deep red colour, even brighter and richer than Devonshire soil, and similar to that found in the heart of Australia, an area known as The Big Red, and where Ayers' Rock is to be found.

For almost our entire journey on No. 1 Highway, which girdles Australia, we travelled on single lane roads with fairly frequent two hundred metre stretches of three lanes, one an overtaking lane. The fact that there wasn't any dual carriageway surprised me a lot. In a small hamlet called Apple Tree Creek, charming wooden houses on stilts, complete with verandahs and shutters, crowded together amongst a jumble of signs nailed to a tree advertising 'Devonshire Teas' and 'Best Scones in Queensland'. We passed through Cooloola Shire, and the beautiful distant mountains rose, cool and blue, far beyond the hot, dry bush country. We made excellent time and reached Gympie in early afternoon.

I now had a headache from the heat and the loud, relentless drumming music, which had hardly ceased for three days. The co-driver slept in the back, so I was in the front passenger seat, a full frontal victim of the large speakers. I bought a Gatorade, one of those electrolyte drinks that help so much, and rang Mark Wheatley, as it was apparent we would reach Brisbane in just a few more hours, for which I was thankful. Simon and Tim were excellent drivers, always obeying the speed limits, but their lack of knowledge and interest in world matters or their own country concerned me. I found I knew far more that they did about their gun law dilemma, and of events in the Middle East - they just weren't interested. They seemed rather like naughty teenagers, cruising round their country, claiming the dole and playing their music, with no intention of working seriously. I found it hard to condone. However, they were kind to me, and the journey had cost me forty pounds, fantastic value, and I was very grateful.

<u>Wednesday 25th September</u>

Tonight I have had two glasses of wine and the effect has been satisfactorily dramatic, so I think I shall sleep well!

Colleen, my Brisbane friend (Mark's wife), collected me from a telephone box outside a Brisbane shopping centre last night, laden with strawberries and pineapples for her. I then bade a fond farewell to my longhaired deliverers (The Mungbeans, as Colleen called them!).

THE WHEATLEYS IN BRISBANE

She gave me such a welcome. Blonde and beautiful, she and Mark had visited me at my home in Stockbridge almost two years ago, and prior to that had been neighbours of ours in Germany, in the 1980s. Mark was in the Australian Army, and they had a very beautiful rented home. I spent my first day getting used to the things I had done without - a washing machine, space, a lovely bed, laying the table, a luxurious shower, a groaning fridge - a civilized home. These things I had not missed at all, but now much appreciated.

I am quite tired, and considering all I had done and seen in just two weeks in Australia, it was no wonder. Elizabeth, who is five, helped me unpack my entire belongings and I then watched her position small chunks of steak along the top of her swing in the garden for the four huge and friendly kookaburras who swoop and hop down for a daily meal. Sarah, who is ten, is away at the Gold Coast with Colleen's parents, who have asked me to stay with them next week. Mark is an extremely smiley, chunky man, warm and casual and I feel I am with real friends once again.

Sunday 29th September

The last few days have been spent writing letters, sorting out my clothes, ringing the family and my girlfriend in Sydney. My brother Hugh and his family flew to India yesterday, for six months of adventure, and my love and good wishes go with them. My children rang me, which was wonderful: Jasper leaves shortly for his university year in France. Letters awaited me once again, from friends reassuring me about my perfect tenants in Goose Cottage, from Gemma, a parcel of welcome goodies - luxurious soap, a Hello magazine, lip balm, a pumice and a new pair of pretty undies - she is a star. From my mother, my bank and phone statements and a warning that she is concerned about the balance of my travel account. I shall be extremely careful until I get a current update and pay for all my calls this end until then. I also had a letter from Paul, my postman at home, who is missing me!

I found it odd at first, being in a house again, and in a rather sterile environment, with bug screens, extractor fans in the bathrooms and showers and every door locked twenty-four hours a day for security. The Wheatleys were kindness personified, helping me with things I needed to buy, listening to me, cooking me delicious meals and including me in their family life. In very many ways I missed the open-air life I had led, especially at Cape Tribulation, being able to feel the air and the ground, smelling the early morning and the scent of the sea. But I realise life cannot be lived constantly like that, in our civilized society.

One afternoon I was invited out with them all, to tea at a friend's house. They do live well here, with pools and luxurious houses. The children picked macadamia nuts for me from their trees and I admired their pet hermit crabs; pretty trouble free pets I must admit. The lengths to which people here go to avoid AIDS seem sad and bizarre. Parents strongly discourage their children from comforting their little friends by blowing their noses for them, wiping their tears or kissing them, to avoid contact with any body fluids ('Just pat them better on the back, but don't hug them'). Mothers won't let children share friends' food or drinks, for the same reason. I heard of a woman who would not pick up a fallen bag from an airport luggage conveyor belt and replace it, in case it contained drugs and she was detained. Oh Lord, this is paranoia isn't it? How sad. Another interesting observation is that Australian children have little necessity to learn another language. However, Elizabeth, at five, is learning Italian, and Sarah, at ten, Japanese - extremely useful I would imagine.

We drove northwest out of Brisbane one day, and up into the Glasshouse Mountains. It was a very beautiful area. Imagine the Lake District, rolling hills and wooded valleys, with brilliant blue morning glory festooning the trees. Vineyards and pineapple plantations hugged the sunny slopes, and wild jacaranda trees heralded the spring, their vivid lilac blossoms breathtaking against the green hillsides. Far away in the distance the blue Pacific Ocean melted into a deep peacock sky on the Sunshine Coast. We drove for miles and stopped to look at shops in the pretty towns, and I longed to walk those hills.

Over the days we swam at the Sunshine Coast, and visited Colleen's parents at the Gold Coast. Both areas boasted stunning beaches, though were uncomfortably over-populated, with high-rise hotels amidst a mass of traffic and billboards. However the attractions were the wonderful surf and squeaky-clean sands. One day we visited The Big Pineapple, a plantation offering train rides round its acres, an information centre, restaurant, and an enormous shopping area with every imaginable item either pineapple-shaped or flavoured. We all agreed it was a ghastly place, and the Macadamia Nut Centre next door was a carbon copy, with fruit and nuts no cheaper than those in the local supermarket.

The South Bank Park in Brisbane was an eye-opener. The most fantastic man-made area in the heart of the city, its acres contained lagoons, beaches, rocky streams, a small river, play parks and grassy lawns. There were puppet shows and story-telling and large mats strewn around on which children could sit and learn simple crafts. Bands in cafés, restaurants overlooking the wide river, the entire park cleverly laid out with palm trees, brilliant flowers, bamboo, ornamental hedges and trailing climbers, made it an enchanting place. Colleen's children adored it, and the many hundreds of families picnicking, swimming and watching the entertainment were obviously having a wonderfully happy time - and all this was free. Brisbane suffers from frequent electrical storms in the wet season and I was interested to spy a very tall mast standing alone in the heart of the city, on top of which was a lightning conductor; whether this served the city or whether there were individual conductors on other buildings I never found out.

There is no postal delivery on a Saturday, in Australia, sellotape is called Durex causing some confusion (as Colleen had found to her horror when enquiring for some at the Church Army Bookshop in Germany!) and political correctness has reached dizzy heights here - I gather dwarfs are 'vertically challenged' individuals. Elizabeth and Sarah were the same as children worldwide – 'Mummy, what does that sign mean?' (Poster advertising 'How to succeed in business without a penis') and 'Cynny, hold your tongue with your fingers and say 'I was born in a pirate ship" so of course I did, and they both fell about in hysterical laughter. I learned about a novel idea. On children's routes to and from school, there will often be a Safety House, clearly signed, where children with any sort of fear or worry can find help and shelter. The volunteers living there are vetted extremely thoroughly of course, and if children hurt themselves (bearing in mind routes are often in very remote areas) or feel unwell or threatened by anyone or anything, they know where they can go - such a good idea, and sponsored by Australian State Government.

At this point, a propos of absolutely nothing at all, may I request a blackberry and apple pie when I return home?

Thursday 3rd October

Last night I travelled the two hours by coach from Brisbane to Burleigh Waters on the Gold Coast, to stay with Colleen's parents. They live in an extremely smart little bungalow, with a palm-fringed pool, manicured lawn and floors off which you could happily eat. My room faced east, overlooking the pool, and dark blinds outside all the windows kept the house shady and cool. On my first morning I swam, before a breakfast of pineapple and several different kinds of melon – what luxury!

We then set forth in their car down the Pacific Highway and up into the hills. I learned that more and more shopping centres are being built along the coast to serve the fourteen thousand people who move up here annually, mainly from Sydney and New Zealand. Attracted by the lowest annual temperature of around twenty-one degrees, twenty miles of beaches and every sport, facility and theme park imaginable (Wet and Wild, Seaworld, Movie World), it is considered heaven by many. The area we were to visit is cleverly called the Green behind the Gold, and it was quite spectacular. Not unlike the Glasshouse Mountains, the road climbed steeply between rocky cliffs, covered with thorny bushes and gum trees. There was much evidence of bush fires, and the tinder-dry land was signed as High on the Fire Risk charts at the roadside. As we climbed, we swerved to avoid a goanna crossing the road - a large lizard, about four to five feet in length; they have extremely tough skin and very beautiful markings.

We entered the Shire of Beaudesert, and passed Wonglepong. The high ground was extremely rocky, wild and beautiful, with stunning distant views between the eucalyptus trees. We descended to the valley below, and drove into the town of Canungra, parking under a beautiful bottlebrush tree. Its tall trunk was rough and black, its delicate leaves dark green. The showy deep red, fluffy bottlebrush flowers, dipped and swung in the breeze - I was very taken with it. We found an information centre and Peter enquired about the route up Tamborine Mountain, spectacular and quite nearby.

Canungra was an enchanting little town, with a tiny, cream-painted wooden church surrounded with more bottlebrush bushes, and towering over it, a very unusual pine tree. Large clumps of needles grew along the dark green branches, magnificent against the deep blue sky, with high white clouds and the little cream-coloured church beneath it. We ate a delicious picnic of buttered French bread and warm roast chicken in the War Memorial Park, near the black and white half-timbered Canungra Hotel, the Australian flag fluttering above it. Kookaburras eyed us from the branches of an overhanging tree, and a blue-eyed bird of the same species as the one I'd seen with the Mungbeans, dipped his beak into coral coloured blossoms nearby to find the nectar. We walked past more pretty wooden shops, painted in gay colours and I posted cards in the jolly, yellow-painted post office. On the way back to the car, Peter took a photo of me posing against the branches of a creamy blossomed tree. I learned it was a Poor Man's Orchid, and exquisite - a marriage of magnolia and apple blossom.

We drove away, found signs to Mount Tamborine and climbed steeply through the bush and rocky outcrops. The road wound round the mountain, with towering cliffs to our right and incredible views, some thirty kilometres northwards, with four or five distant hill and mountain ranges disappearing into each other in the haze. We stopped and got out at a lookout point, and almost immediately a startlingly bright turquoise butterfly fluttering triangular wings, noticed Trish, who was wearing an identical coloured turquoise T-shirt. He fluttered round her for a full ten minutes, nudging her, obviously perplexed by this familiar coloured but very large object, while I danced around with my camera. He was a gorgeous creature, with brown-bordered blue wings and long feelers. Just as we wondered how we could take our leave of him, he suddenly soared away high up, beyond sight into the sky.

We drove on around the mountain, admiring the breathtaking views of hills to the north, folding into each other like a child's picture book and to the south, far, far below, the Gold Coast and Surfer's Paradise with its tall, white hotels on the sands. The many wooden houses perched on the mountainside were equally attractive, raised on stilts, with verandahs and balconies, pools and colourful, lush gardens. In them we saw brilliant azaleas and the white, blue and mauve of the Yesterday, Today and Tomorrow bush, with its round, wonderfully scented flowers.

We drove on reluctantly, to the small village of Eagle Heights, full of craft shops, a German bakery and various Italian and Polish-run galleries. Rapidly, the rocky, open vegetation ended, giving way to dense equatorial rainforest, an amazingly abrupt contrast, on the eastern, coastal side of the mountain. Palms, ferns and creepers crowded together, winding, dense and polished, the sun warm in dappled beams between them. Slowly we descended down a 1:1 road, over Wongawallan Creek and after a while joined the Brisbane to Sydney Pacific Highway, passing signs to Mudgeeraba and the permanently moored hot air balloon in the distance at Robina. I read a copy of the Tamborine Times I had picked up, advertising 'Mobile Dog Wash' at $6 a day and 'A1 Aussie Moo Poo'.

<u>Saturday 5th October</u>

I am delighted! Yesterday I found one of the two old films, on video, that I had promised to try and find for Bala - The Charge of the Light Brigade with Errol Flynn and Olivia de Havilland, filmed in 1936; he will be so pleased. There it was, in a vast department store in a huge shopping mall at the Gold Coast. Beau Geste may be more difficult as I gather it hasn't been recycled yet. It cost me twelve pounds and I'll absorb it somehow. I also bought two huge and beautiful shells as a wedding present for friends - I hope they'll like them.

The Ryans were kindness itself, but have I changed I wonder? Life, the working days and buying basic needs cannot, I realise, be conducted on the top of a mountain, or sailing the ocean, but times of choice, of soul-refreshing and wonder, do not, for me, include concrete jungles, theme parks, grand hotels, shops or traffic. In dreaming times I return to Nepal and Bali, to Ringstead in Dorset, to Scotland or to the island on the Reef . . .

REDUNDANCY

Monday 7th October

Yesterday, on the way back to Brisbane, we passed a sign to Woodridge and Ipswich and I wondered if the first Australians had brought those names phonetically with them in the 1700s, or whether Woodbridge in England had in fact been Woodridge all along and slowly corrupted by Suffolk men.

Elizabeth's sixth birthday party yesterday in McDonalds, for fifteen small people, went well. The other mothers were politely interested in me, though my life in England and recent exploits were a far cry from their lives here. I in my turn felt rather alien as they discussed friends' children who listened and learned with School of the Air, cooking emu sausages or cleaning their swimming pools. Later that evening Mark called me in to watch a Woodchopping Test Match on television. Seventy-year old men, and even an eighty-year old fellow, competing against one another – amazing. With finely honed axes they chopped through short, thick pieces of tree trunk in several hefty swings - quite something to watch.

5pm. A few hours ago I learned that my boss in England has almost definitely given me the heave-ho from my job at the gallery. I am writing my journal now, very deliberately. I feel numb and very worried. To those who may say 'I told you so', I am determined to prove that my decision to travel for a while was the right one. Thank God I am with the Wheatleys. Colleen hugged me, and made me see that this might be a fatalistic push in a quite different and better direction. I HAVE to believe that this might be so. The news came in a fax from a very good friend of mine, who had been to the gallery and talked to my boss and to my successor. Apparently there is a letter awaiting me in Sydney.

Later I rang my daughter Gemma, in London, and she is putting wheels into motion for me; ringing the gallery, friends of mine, and unearthing my CV from my mother's home. Oh wow! You have to be so strong in life. Gemma suggested my excellent tenants might stay on in Goose Cottage for a while after my return. I glance at my cheap little watch, which I love, bought in a Malaysian night market and inscribed 'Don't Worry, Be Happy' on the dial, while a little smiley face ticks the minutes away - to what? My mind is in a whirl tonight, but I must be optimistic.

Wednesday 9th October

Colleen woke me at six o'clock yesterday with the news of a huge explosion in Lisburn, Northern Ireland. Shortly afterwards I rang the same good friend who had rung with my bad news, and who had just arrived home in Lisburn from England. She rang me back for a forty-minute chat and was fantastic; although some of the windows of her house had fallen out, all she could talk about was my job. Then my mother rang and, like Gemma, was absolutely wonderful, saying it may be a blessing in disguise and asking what she could do. Then the British Isles went to bed and our day began.

Colleen treated me to a wonderful hour-long facial. She had found a newspaper advertisement for a free session if you had one yourself. Just what I now needed, and as I stepped through the door of the beauty salon, strains from Enya's Watermark played softly from a distant room. Bliss. For an hour I lay on a couch and completely relaxed. No chance of rolling back the years face-wise, but it was fun. As the day wore on, Colleen signed the lease on a new hiring (a house they were to rent) in the local realtors and we went to visit it. It was enormous, with an intercom radio and a special plug for the hoover in every room (the dust disappears underground to some gobbledy gook), a double garage, laundry room and a huge and beautiful garden. Houses here are often very grand, and also very American, with not a blade of grass out of place, manicured palm trees, identical brick letterboxes on the front lawns and remote controlled garage doors. Give me the dusty, happy bustle of breezy Goose Cottage, with doors and windows flung open, my pretty leafy garden and, when it's cold, a crackly fire and frosty walks by the river. No, I'm not homesick, just appreciating my lifestyle, a far cry from the luxury here.

As we returned from viewing the Wheatleys' new home, I spied a van advertising 'new and pre-loved baby needs' - what on earth were they? Apparently Pre-loved means second-hand here - what a wonderful expression. Dear, Colleen, house-hunting, the girls' school holidays, Elizabeth's sixth birthday - two parties and a cake to bake for school, Mark coming and going (flying up to Cape York this week for five days, and then over to Thursday Island off the very tip of North Queensland) and still she runs me about, to Post Office, photo shop, radio repairers, coach station, etc. What a friend indeed.

<u>Sunday 13th October</u>

It was very sad saying farewell to Colleen at the airport. She took me there before doing the school run, insisting on coming in with the girls, checking me in and settling me in the departure lounge. As they walked away, Lizzie ran back to me to trill 'La-la-la!' in her high, childish voice. We had all watched the film 'Babe' together, and when I used to say, 'Give me a Babe, Lizzie!' she would yodel 'La-la-la!' and make us all laugh.

CURL CURL WITH THE COLONEL

On the Quantas flight I read a beautiful, affectionate card that Colleen had written to me, and which I shall treasure. I decided I would rather like to be up on the flight deck as we landed in Sydney and asked the stewardess to find out if that would be possible. 'I am backpacking round the world' I said 'and I'm having my fiftieth birthday in Sydney' (true). She returned to say she was so sorry, but the cockpit was full of flight safety officials, but she had organised a window seat for me (I was in the very middle of the wide airbus) and here was a bottle of champagne from the crew - for my birthday today! Was I a Libran like her? 'Er, well, yes' I stuttered. Two minutes later I had a superb view of the hills approaching Sydney, and then of Sydney itself. We flew quite low, and there was the famous harbour, abuzz with yachts and speedboats, the huge coathanger bridge spanning the water, and the familiar wedge cones of the Opera House, as clear and colourful as a poster, just beneath me - it was a fine sight.

Jo, my old schoolfriend, and Lucy her daughter, my god-daughter, were there to meet me, and Lucy, at seventeen, drove us back to Jo's office in Chatswood, on the city outskirts. After coffee and a salad lunch with us, Jo went back to work and Lucy drove me the fifty minutes home to Arcadia, outside the city. Once we had left Sydney, we soon negotiated six hairpin bends, deep down into a very steep gorge and then corkscrewing up high again. Typical bushland rose up either side, the sharp rocks a seemingly impossible host to so many eucalyptus trees, pines and bushes. One sharp bend in the road was known as Roosters' Corner, as someone had released a small flock of cockerels there a few years ago. Others had followed suit and gradually the rooster colony had grown and they now had a marvellous time marching up and down the gorge with plenty to eat and in complete freedom.

Jo's house was in a heavenly position. The area was peacefully rural, with horses in the fields, nurseries, an Arab stud close by and small farms. Set in five acres, Jo's house was surrounded on three sides by paddocks, meadows really, and on the fourth by bush. Tall, silver-barked eucalyptus trees, pines, flowering bushes and other lush and leafy trees surrounded the paddocks, beyond the lawns. A raised wooden verandah ran all round the house woven with thick boughs of white wisteria, and delicately-scented jasmine climbed and wound in such profusion round the pillars and up the verandah that leafy windows were formed, giving warm shade in which to write at the wooden table outside, or to laze in a deckchair outside the many french windows.

Beyond the kitchen window, a small orange tree, laden down with shiny fruit and highly perfumed blossom, rambling passion fruit, lemon and tangerine trees, all provided fruit for breakfast. I absolutely loved it, after the very happy but neat and suburban life in Brisbane. I spent happy, magical, sunny hours writing and reading and just dreaming, beside the scented jasmine, with the sunlit meadows beyond, and rainbow lorikeets (bright, multi-coloured parrots) skimming over the garden and up into the high eucalyptus trees. Jo had two horses, a dog and a black cat called Zulu, oh, and several chooks (chickens).

<u>Wednesday 16th October</u>

So much has happened. On Saturday we towed their speedboat down to Berowra Waters, where we sped downstream for a picnic on a tiny beach. The scenery was dramatic, with high rocky cliffs dropping down to the sea along the creeks, and holiday houses, mostly wooden, with verandahs, balconies and boathouses, perched on the rocky outcrops, accessible only by water. Tiny sandy beaches sparkled in the sun, almost hidden by trees, and we tied up to an overhanging gum tree at our beach and paddled ashore.

It was glorious. Sitting under the pines we watched sea eagles circling overhead, a seaplane disappeared to land out of sight in a creek across the water, and Jo plucked oysters off the rocks for lunch. We watched large goanna lizards, four foot long, slide and slither in the steep rocky bush behind us and climb the trees. A pair of pretty ducks swam in to join us for lunch, and we lazed in the sun. Later we whizzed across the water to investigate the seaplane's mission. Around the headland out of sight of our beach, a huge barbecue was in full swing in the grounds of an enormous beach house, with tables set out along a verandah and, moored at a jetty nearby, the various expensive boats used to ferry guests and among them, the seaplane.

Jo rose at six-thirty each morning and, after feeding the horses and chooks, we both went to the National Park nearby, to walk Maggie the dog. Summer is not quite here yet and it is fresh in the mornings with a heavy dew and often wonderfully misty. She told me about a local rodeo we might try and go to, where an infamous bull named 'Chainsaw' unseats everyone who tries to mount him, and we talked of England and Australia and some of the differences. The grass verge along a road is called the public nature strip and is maintained by the Government. In Queensland, small, brightly painted totem poles either side of the entrance to a school road, warn drivers - an excellent idea. I had sent the Wheatleys in Brisbane, a huge basket of native flowers and fruit as a thank you for having me, and we saw some of them growing wild on our early morning walks. It is strange to see agapanthus and amaryllis flowers growing in huge clumps here, and the orange and lemon blossom scents the air everywhere you go.

On Monday I had arranged to meet Xanthe, who lived in Sydney and who had worked in a pub at home in Stockbridge. I had befriended her and her boyfriend Mark. I had only a phone number for her, no address, so she knew nothing of my travels. Suddenly, there I was in Sydney. We were thrilled to meet again and caught a metro train, with an upper deck, down to the harbour area. There we walked by the high and elegant bridge, past gardens, and watched the many yachts, barges and ferries and examined a statue of Captain William Bligh, who was much involved in the birth of the city of Sydney. We had lunch in a café near the ferry, where I was shocked to see Japanese tourists taking photos of a man threatening to jump from the roof of the railway station, on a hill just above our café. He was standing on a narrow ledge, facing outward, and two people were talking to him from the flat roof behind him, while a Police Rescue Squad ambulance stood by in the street below.

Police on motorbikes cleared the area around the ambulance, and a crowd formed either side behind security tape, to watch the drama unfold. Some tourists even videoed him, how could they?

Xanthe and I boarded a local commuter ferry for a short, round trip to the far side of the harbour. It was a glorious day, sunny, breezy and full of colour, and as we passed close to the spectacular opera house, majestically poised on a spur, surrounded on three sides by the harbour waters, I remembered only a short while before, spying it from high up as we flew in. It reminded me of a water lily bud, folding its petals back towards the shining sun and I so want to do a tour inside it. The ferry stopped at only three places, and being a commuter ferry, was the cheapest way to see a bit of Sydney from the harbour. We passed splendid yachts moored at a smart club, and sumptuous houses with gardens overhanging the water, before returning across the harbour again. The poor man was still thinking of ending it all on the roof of the railway station. We walked to where the replica of H.M.S. Bounty is moored, a fine little ship, only marginally larger than T.S. Royalist, the square-rigger in which I have sailed. How brave those first adventurers were.

Jo and I went off to collect Lucy's horse, Lucky. A horse trailer is called a 'float', though no one could tell me why and we towed it behind Jo's large 4 x 4 jeep. We retraced the route we had taken on Sunday with the boat, down through the gorge to Berowra Waters, where we crossed the creek on a small, free, chain car ferry. Driving off, the cliffs rose steeply on the other side, and we negotiated the sharp bends slowly, before joining a main highway. The whole journey took about an hour and we eventually drove up an enchanting valley called Yarramalong Valley, which reminded me of a lush Yorkshire Vale. Towering, wooded, rocky hills rose either side of the road and the gentle pastures undulated ahead. Horses and goats grazed beneath willow trees while ducks floated on ponds. Farms and pretty wooden houses, shaded by palm trees and Christmas bushes, stood in the fields, many with avenues of liquid amber maples winding from the road. It was a lovely place.

We reached Jo's friend Amanda's farm, and as I opened the gate, three bright red parrots with long green tails swooped over my head and up into the gum trees. Fat Boy Farm was at the end of the valley, peacefully nestling among the eucalyptus trees on twenty-five acres of grazing land. Amanda greeted us and later we ate french bread and salad on her verandah, under a canopy of swaying, white wisteria blooms. Beside us orange and grapefruit trees rustled, laden with heavy fruit and creamy blossom. Amanda was a hearty, horsy Englishwoman, fun and lively. Her surname was Woolley and she was married to a mad Irishman some years her junior. She told us of her brother back home, who sailed a yacht in the Solent, called Woolley Knickers, much to the horror of their mother. In the afternoon, we walked across a couple of fields to pick limes, oranges and grapefruit to take home, before catching Lucky. Passing avocado and pecan trees, we crossed a muddy stream and loaded Lucky into the float. There were lots of wombat holes in the fields, looking just like badger setts and again those wonderfully bright King parrots flew above us, among the trees.

On our homeward journey, I noticed golden wattle trees in the bush, rather like broom, cascading down the rocky cliffs with showers of tiny flowers as round as berries, We passed through Kangy Yangy and crossed the Mooney Mooney bridge high up over a river gorge. The scenery was quite spectacular, the road cutting through enormous sandstone mountains towering above us.

Later. I have had great difficulty finding out about the wonderful trees and flowers I have seen since arriving in Australia. The common ones, eucalyptus, jacaranda and so on are easy enough, but I remember Jagdish telling me that of all the people who trek with him in Nepal, the Australians have the least interest in the flora and fauna, and that he could never understand why they go trekking. Ah well...

My girlfriend Susie rang tonight from Ireland, and we talked about jobs for me. I am determined to remain optimistic. I also have a lot of contacts to look up and I have been invited out tomorrow.

Friday 18th October

Yesterday I had a fun day out with Barry Campbell, a retired Aussie colonel. He is a friend of the Dufalls in Bangkok and they told me he was often seeking crew to sail in Sydney harbour with him, so I had eagerly made contact. Kate Dufall also told me that he's looking for a new wife, so I was somewhat wary! We made arrangements to meet in an Italian café opposite Jo's newspaper office, where I'd met Xanthe, and Jo came with me. We spotted him immediately, in jeans, aged fifty-five plus and with a long, grizzled, grey ponytail. Both our hearts sank. His probably did too!

He was great fun, amusing - just this side of being a burk - and though my opinion soared when he carried my heavy bag (camera, binoculars etc.) it wavered a bit later, on discovering the scented loo paper in his house. We majestically toured the city in his huge white Rear Tank Land Cruiser 4 x 4, complete with Recaro designer seats, a CD player and every other gizmo you can imagine. The back was fitted out like a caravan with dinky little curtains and a stove. My front seat swivelled round apparently, for eating. He was very informative and well read, on the past and present history of Australia and, of flowers and trees (at last).

We drove to a high point from which we could see different sides of the spectacular harbour and right out to the Pacific. On this spot a Scottish cairn had been built to commemorate the Bicentennial of the 1788 landing. The stones set into the high pyramid had been gathered by ministers of each parish in Scotland then flown by Royal Mail to be erected here. They included stones from four Scottish cathedrals and the finial stone came from the Island of Ulva, off Mull, which was the birthplace of Lachlan MacQuarie, later the Governor of NSW and known as the Father of Australia. The Duke of Argyll had dedicated the cairn on St. Andrew's Day 1988. The stones were all such wonderful, heathery colours, their resting place gloriously high and windy.

We drove to the place where Barry keeps his boat, moored off the Royal Australian Naval Yacht Club, and watched a naval yacht sail in and moor, the stars of the Southern Cross painted white against her midnight hull. We went everywhere. Through the infamous King's Cross area, where I saw a most lovely fountain, a round ball with delicate metal rods all over it, emitting very fine sprays of water, so that it looked like a huge dandelion clock. Up hills, through imposing Victorian Barracks, past Balmoral Beach, Dee Why Beach (surveyed, way back as DY beach, do you suppose?) and Curl Curl Beach. We drove up to an even higher headland at the entrance to the enormous harbour, where squat 'black boys' or grass trees grew a foot every hundred years. Some were almost two feet high, with sprays of coarse grass, like fireworks exploding out of the top. He showed me pretty white daisy-like flannel flowers and many other Australian bush plants on the top of the cliff. It was wild and wonderful up there with a sheer drop of a hundred feet to the sea while the opposite cliffs were even higher.

He told me of a large ship which had sailed all the way from England, only to crash at night head first into the sheer cliffs opposite us, mistaking the lighthouse on top for the light at the entrance to Sydney's inner harbour, which was actually around the headland and some miles upstream. Only one girl on board survived. He was a kind and thoughtful friend and early in the afternoon we drove to his home, where he told me he had a couple of steaks marinating for lunch. His house was luxurious - leather armchairs, an all-singing kitchen, a wonderful garden of orchids, roses, ancient trees and lilies, built in and around a virtual rock face, with steep steps down to a swimming pool and a fantastic view. What a pity I didn't fancy him!

Lunch was perfect, and we watched Hoppity, a one-legged magpie eating bits of steak on the doorstep, almost inside the dining-room (magpies are huge here, looking like piebald ravens) and three rainbow lorikeets - blue-headed, red, green and yellow parrots, straight out of a pirate story, pecking at his red bottlebrush flowers just outside the window beside us. After a really good pot of loose-leaf Prince of Wales tea (Twinings and it's delicious) he delivered me back to where we'd met, with a loose arrangement to meet again next week. He told me one really funny story, when I was admiring the parrots. He had been picnicking in a park in Sydney with a friend, when a small flock of parrots flew low overhead and as they passed, the tail-end bird was distinctly heard to shriek, 'Hurry up, Charlie!' They do quite often escape from captivity, he told me.

This morning, Friday, dear Angie Hood, with whom I shall be staying in New Zealand, rang to say they would scoop me up from the airport next Friday and whizz up to their house on the Bay of Islands. It was a long holiday weekend and she wondered if I could perhaps come a day early, so that we could then have all of Friday up there. This I have arranged, so I fly to Auckland on Thursday 24th. I told her calls and faxes might arrive in New Zealand regarding a job for me, she said she also knew that it would turn out all right; Colleen had said the same thing.

Sunday, 20th October

I had a lazy day. In the afternoon Steve called me and there, only fifty yards from the house were six or seven magnificent yellow-tailed black cockatoos. They were over two feet long, perched high up in a pine tree, cracking cones with their tough, grey beaks. One pair were silhouetted so clearly against the sky, balanced on a low branch, that I could see their rough little tongues licking out the contents of the pine cones. They sported glossy black feathers with a bright yellow patch on their cheeks and yellow tail feathers - quite beautiful. They looked very comical, holding the pine cones in their large claws and balancing cleverly with their tails.

In the evening we drove an hour away to North Head, where I had stood on the cliffs with Barry. A mile below, on the Bay, stood the old Victorian Quarantine Station into which we were booked for the Night Ghost Tour. A collection of interesting buildings in use from 1832 to 1984, formerly housed the passengers and crew from every ship arriving in Sydney, reporting cases of typhus, influenza, smallpox, bubonic plague or diarrhoea.

The accommodation was strictly divided into First, Second, Third and Steerage classes and the Australian National Parks guide made much of this. The new arrivals were herded into a small room and made to breathe in sulphur fumes for ten minutes (then the only known form of bodily toxification). Then every single soul and item from the ship was bathed, showered or wheeled through a vast steam chamber. The shower water contained fennel, a natural antiseptic. Life there for some was like being on holiday, with bars, beach games and grand living. For others, in the earlier years, living in tents, cooking for themselves in a strange land surrounded by several cemeteries, and witnessing deaths from smallpox every day, must have been quite horrific.

There were incredible views over Sydney Harbour from the winding paths and the verandahs as we descended the hill. The many tales of ghosts – including that of a tiny boy with smallpox, and a Chinese sailor in blue uniform - made it an interesting tour. Down by the beach, carved inscriptions on the rock gave a clue to the names of the ships and their passengers, including S.S.Lusitania (sunk off Ireland in 1915 with the loss of 1,195 lives) and a ship carrying British evacuee children in 1940. What a way to be welcomed to a new life in a new land, a necessary precaution though, in days gone by.

THE BOWERBIRD

<u>Wednesday 23rd October</u>
Well, I've had an interesting few days. On Monday I took a train into the city. The local trains are superb, silver, sleek and modern, they are double-decker monsters and extremely efficient. A decent run of ten stops will cost about a pound. The views from the top deck over the harbour and the opera house are excellent, before the train glides over the huge harbour bridge. I got off before that, found the Qantas and Air New Zealand offices, confirmed my altered ticket, then wound my way down George, Pitt and Phillip Streets to the Museum of Sydney.

A fascinating couple of hours passed. The museum was very contemporary with thoughts, poems and writings musing on the past, present and future of the city of Sydney. Many artefacts dug from the foundations of the first Governor's mansion on which the museum was built, gave you a detailed insight into colonial life in the late sixteenth and seventeenth centuries. Interestingly, nothing really caught my imagination or thrilled me, and this was not a reflection of a traveller's jaded interest but, I think, of the fact that we are lucky enough to see so many old items in England, older than anything here.

On my way home in the train, I reflected on this country. I find the lack of permanence disquieting. By this I mean ancient places, old brick and stone cottages, houses and churches. I have only seen a minute part of this enormous continent I realise, and for the most part the climate dictates that dwellings are made of wood, with balconies on stilts, and often looking fragile and birdcage-like. Churches are often very modern. As an Australian girl remarked to me, 'Australia is so strange, it is such an old country but with nothing old in it'. There are Aboriginal cave paintings and tools and weapons to be seen, but they were not builders and, much to the present generation's amusement, Aboriginal 'middens' are now revered and visited, although they are nothing but mounds of old seashells on a beach - an Aboriginal rubbish tip, many crushed by the colonial settlers to make lime. I miss our cottages and cathedrals, our country churches and ancient farms, and yet the countryside I have seen on this eastern seaboard is quite spectacular.

Jo travelled to interview a maker of unusual musical instruments this week, as part of her job, and I accompanied her up into the foothills of the Blue Mountains to find him. It was a very pretty area, with undulating valleys, fertile land and fresh mountain air. As she asked him about the exquisite wooden xylophones, marimbas and lyres he lovingly made, I listened to the bellbirds high in the gum trees, their call clear as an anvil strike, echoing over the valley. A delicate little welcome swallow brought insects for her wobbling babies, balanced along the telegraph wires. On another walk, Jo and I had seen scribbler gums - eucalyptus trees with childlike scribbles up and down the trunk, made by a species of moth.

I have had another outing with 'Colonel Ponytail', but before meeting him, I had had an interesting visit to the local Medicare Office. Having had to consult a doctor over a minor matter, I filled in an application form for Medicare, which has a reciprocal arrangement with our N.H.S. After queuing for half an hour, it should have been a simple matter of having the fourteen pounds refunded. However, after the administrator had punched in my details and Australian address into her computer, she said, 'Are you staying with a close friend? You and Joanna share a birthday?' 'Yes' I said. 'We are having our fiftieth birthday together'. She then excused herself and disappeared into a back office. After five minutes she re-appeared and, most apologetically, said the computer would not sanction a payment, as we shared a birthday and I would have to make a further visit although I had shown my passport and International Driving Licence. I couldn't believe it.

Colonel Barry was great company and, as before, whisked me up and down the hills, beaches, headlands, coves and residential areas of this wonderful city. We finally parked on Dee Why beach road, where I sat at a picnic table after he had filled two pewter wine glasses, and then sprinted off to 'The Best Fish And Chip Shop In Australia' - what a star he was. We ate the tastiest, lightest, crispest fish, scallops and chips that I have definitely ever enjoyed, watching the blue Pacific surf rolling into the curved bay, while amazingly agile wet-suited surfers twisted and crouched on their boards, riding the crests of the high, wind-whipped waves. What a marvellous sight it was.

Flocks of gulls jetted in from the whole of NSW it seemed, while Barry was definitely showing an interest in me. I pondered on how to let him down gently, if I was reading his intentions correctly. Then an opportunity arose. As I took the rubber band off my small address book to read him a quote, I dropped the band. We looked under the table and he jokingly pulled my skirt hem up a little way. 'Barry, I'm afraid you'll get nowhere if you try and lift my skirts' I said smilingly, and in an instant the message was conveyed. I felt much more comfortable after that. He was such an interesting man, and when we arrived back at his house, he made me tea and found brandy snaps. He then fed steak to his tame garden magpie while I read his Great Explorations of the World book on Cook, Tasman and the other great sailors who first navigated round Australasia. He paid me a lovely compliment as he dropped me near Jo's office, and I kissed him on the cheek, asked him for a sail next time and hopped out.

The centres of Sydney and Brisbane, much larger cities than Cairns, are very odd places, and it took me a little while to work out where the difference lay. People do not shop there. With so many shopping malls in the suburbs only office workers frequent the city centres, and yet even at lunch time I found the windy streets, winding between tall, tall chrome and glass-pillared offices, empty and lifeless. None of the bustling, jostling, frustration and excitement of London and other European cities, though I suppose if I worked in Sydney I would find that suited me well. I am generalising, but much of the area of Sydney frequented by visitors is like the Square Mile in London on a Sunday.

Thursday 24th October

Yesterday Jo and I drove up to the Watagan Mountains to visit Carol, a delightful friend of hers. To reach the area, north of Sydney, meant crossing the Hawkesbury river bridge and then taking the Berowra Waters Creek ferry, which was fun and rather like a Devon chain ferry. Trees grew down the rocky hills right up to the waterline, and many boats were moored in the creek. Carol lived in a haphazard collection of huts with king parrots and galahs (the prettiest pale grey and pink cockatoos) flying in for birdseed, and kangaroos hopping about her paddocks in the evenings. We collected her and the second half of our picnic, and made for the mountain trails, attempting to find a large stand of huge, red waratah flowers, one of the most spectacular of Australian blooms, that Carol had spied a week earlier. As we drove off her land, we stopped briefly to say hello to her four horses, one a very pretty little foal, and as we did so, I noticed a large bird of paradise plant, a mass of dancing flowers, growing virtually wild on the grass verge. As we climbed up into the forest behind her house, the tarmac petered out, and the wide track of amber soil threw up clouds of dust behind our vehicle as we passed.

The mountains were absolutely glorious - rocky outcrops soared into the blue sky above us and the new fresh red leaves on the gum trees glowed warmly in the sun. In the end, Carol couldn't remember where she had seen the waratah stand, but we did spy one specimen. It was magnificent, an explosion of layer upon layer of red petals like an open thistle, deep in the bush. We found wild mint, and the delicate fronds of tea tree bushes, some over six feet tall, ready to burst into a froth of tiny white flowers; ironically I had a stick of Body Shop Tea Tree lip salve in my jacket pocket. We found a picnic spot under tall pine trees and drank Earl Grey tea with warm scones and before you could say 'currawong' a squawking band of those raven-like, black and white birds had come a-begging. High overhead we saw, and heard, a squadron of twenty or thirty gang-gang parrots, as noisy as a classroom of schoolboys let out early.

It was easy to imagine how wild and wonderful the first settlers had found this new land. The forest was in the main still untouched but well managed, with cleared, well-marked trails, covered rubbish bins and chopped wood provided in great quantities for the picnic-site barbecues. We drove on, walking to sunny lookout points, from where we could see for miles over the gorges and valleys below and up to the mountains above. I learned there are many kinds of eucalyptus trees, all very beautiful. Their rough brown bark, shed once a year, reveals smooth bare limbs in shades of ivory or grey. Their curved, scented leaves, grey blue and delicate, give great character to the land, whether standing sentinel-like on a patch of lush meadow or crowded splendidly together on a mountainside. Carol and Jo are both endurance riders, and as we went, Carol recorded the mileage between various points on a map, in preparation for the next event. The riders would begin the day negotiating their horses through the forest at four o'clock, with torches on their helmets - no mean feat on the unlit tracks.

We had lunch by a narrow creek, and there I saw one of the most extraordinary sights of my travels so far. Carol led us a little way into the undergrowth, thick with tree creepers and ferns, and there, on a bed of twigs and grass, lay an amazing collection of blue plastic objects. Strips of blue tape, a blue metallic crushed can, even a broken container for holding Bloo Loo disinfectant blocks. This colourful cache was the work of the satin bowerbird, a shy creature seldom seen. He would assemble all these goodies, almost always blue in colour, to attract a mate, often building an intricate tunnel through the walls around them. It was such a thrill to see.

As we feasted on fireman's bread, Camembert, salad and smoked salmon, Carol and Jo drank Bucks Fizz - I enjoyed fresh orange juice. More currawongs cruised in, and as Jo threw bread to them, they were joined, quite suddenly, by both the male and female bowerbirds. The male was superb - a deep rich blue, his body shining like moonlight on rich satin, as he hopped into the sun. His mate was green and brown, pretty, but quite different; we were all agog as we watched them.

As we finished our lunch, a forester named Garnett, whom Carol knew, drove up in a large 'ute' with another following, and she walked across to greet him. He had with him five Aboriginal chain-saw students, and they explained the project they were working on. They looked around the forest clearing for a while, and then left. It was after their departure that Carol and Jo displayed a certain animosity towards the students. I hadn't even noticed they were different, quite deeply tanned, that's all. Garnett had apparently introduced them to Carol rather mockingly as 'The rightful owners of the land' and there is not much love lost between the two races. As we left I suggested we leave an offering for our beautiful bowerbird, and this we did - two blue biro tops, carefully placed on our picnic table.

As we drove back down the mountain the sun disappeared, and it became quite chilly. We stopped once again, for a quick mug of tea in the forest where the distinctive black boy trees grew in great profusion, some up to twelve feet tall. As they only grow a foot every hundred years I was somewhat in awe of these tall fellows. We descended and dusk fell. I remarked that I hadn't yet seen a live kangaroo. Within five minutes we had seen five of them in five separate sightings; bush wallabies and small kangaroos, hopping away from the roadside as we approached. Dark and furry, this was obviously their feeding time and I was thrilled to see them. We later saw a male lyrebird crossing the road, his long, beautiful tail sweeping the ground behind him, rather like a peacock and once again I was enchanted. So ended a wonderful day with a lot of driving, but a day experiencing the mountainous forest with someone who knew about it and cared for it.

(Sign seen in the grounds of a keen gardener near Jo's - 'All trespassers will be composted')

BAY OF ISLANDS, NEW ZEALAND

At midday on 24th October I was airborne again, heading for New Zealand. I had noticed all sorts of aeroplanes at Sydney Airport, among them an American airline called Polar Air, and a Qantas jumbo jet decorated all over with Aboriginal art, explosions of wheels and dots and kangaroos against the wonderfully bright red fuselage - a jolly sight. A Maori dance team was on my flight, a group of chunky, smiling people with thick black hair and colourful jewellery. We flew out over the Tasman Sea, and I was excited at the prospect of further adventures in a land I knew to be extremely beautiful. The head cabin steward's name was Mr. Sharp and I spoke to him, spinning the usual story (my big birthday soon) and found myself climbing upstairs to the cockpit. Once the two pilots, Mark and his second pilot Ross, had chatted to me for a while (I piled on the charm, of course), they asked if I'd like to stay in the cockpit for the landing.

The first sight I had of landfall, was the top of a spectacular mountain called Mount Taranaki (formerly Mount Egmont, named by Captain Cook after Lord Egmont) its graceful curved slopes rising to a pointed, snow capped peak. It shone in pink sunlight far away to our right, with small clouds drifting beneath the snowline. I almost expected to see angels there. It was too far away to photograph with my simple camera, but I shall always remember that sight. As we approached Auckland, down through the clouds, I could see many green and rocky islands, moored yachts, and water everywhere, sea, sounds, inlets. What a sight!

The sun shone rather coldly onto the sea in front of us, so that the far distant islands were darkly silhouetted as we descended, and the water gleamed like pewter. The runway jutted out into the sea, a smooth hardly discernible landing and we were there. At times of take-off and landing I feel very emotional and tearful, but gratefully and happily so. I never seem to become weary in spirit; I thirst for new places, new friends and experiences, and to be lifted gently into the sky, to new adventures in new countries, is a magical feeling - thanks be, again, to God.

Auckland, NEW ZEALAND

My friend Angie was there to meet me, but there was a short delay while the quarantine people cleaned my walking boots. Filling in the Customs and Quarantine forms on the plane, there was a question on whether we were carrying foodstuffs (yes, chocolate-covered macadamias for Angie) or any items made from wood, leather, feathers etc. (yes, my walking boots and straw hat) and whether we'd been to a forest or farm in the last thirty days, yes I had. So I had to unpack my walking boots which in my haste I hadn't cleaned very well, just brushed. The chocs and straw hat were fine and the boots were then cleaned to perfection.

Dear Angie, how wonderful to see her again after ten years. We drove home in her large jeep and I was given a pretty double bed in the basement of her house, next to the piano and pool table room. The house was light and modern, with lots of attractive pine furniture, a heavenly kitchen and a swimming pool – gorgeous. The girls, Lydia ten and Jessica fourteen, were delightful - chatty, fun, undemanding and mature. Lydia and I weeded the garden one morning and did various other chores for Angie, and we got on famously together.

Shortly after I arrived in the house, I was called up to the sitting room where friends of theirs had congregated for a drink. It was so nice to see Rob, Angie's husband again. We had all met in Germany, while living there with the army. He and Angie, who is a New Zealander, had moved back here after Rob, who is English, had left the British Army. This is now firmly their home. Twice a week, Rob goes on a ten-kilometre Splash and Dash - five kilometres kayaking and five kilometres running, and their visiting friends were the chums who joined him in this, plus their wives. They were all extremely nice, well travelled, interesting and relaxed, and made me feel very welcome.

<u>Monday 28th October</u>

Well, the days have flown by, full of interest and kindness and I have learnt much. We set off on Friday in Rob's Range Rover for their other home on the Bay of Islands, north east of Auckland. The countryside was utterly different from anything I had seen in Australia, and this fascinated me. Gentle, rolling grassy hills and valleys reminded me of Wales, and many sheep and cows grazed in the lush pastures. In Auckland gardens, I had seen lavender and roses, and so many reminders of an English summer, and then in the midst of these, the intense perfume of a lemon tree or a huge jasmine bower would remind you of where you were. So it was on these lovely hills. Oak, and tea trees now in bloom and very like may blossom, grew near mangrove swamps or next to huge and beautiful bushes of arum lilies, or small avocado and citrus orchards. I asked the names of many glorious trees – amongst them pohutekawa, the New Zealand Christmas tree, which sports pretty red flowers and glossy leaves in December. Tall stands of toi-toi grasses, rather like our pampas grass, and huge tree-like ferns as tall as palm trees, added an exotic touch to the gentle landscape. As we reached the coast again, we crossed on a small ferry to the other side of the bay and were almost there.

Auckland has the largest number of yachts per capita in the world, and I noticed some vast marinas as we left the city. Up here too, were many sleek and beautiful craft at anchor along the coast. There are twenty-three ports of call on this east shore, and between Whangarei and Whangaroa, many safe and commodious harbours - a sailor's paradise. We reached Manawaora Bay, and the pretty, winding, flower-lined drive to the house. Wow! I was to stay for the weekend in one of the most beautiful houses I had ever seen.

Set on the side of a steep hillside, just above its own beach on Jack's Bay, the house was a perfect family retreat. The gardens, landscaped down and along the hill round the house, were full of colour and interest. Olive, macadamia, lemon, lime, grapefruit and orange trees, king proteas with giant pale pink flowers, agapanthus, palms, hibiscus, bougainvillea and fantastic red passion flowers grew in the lee of palm and pine trees. The tall avocado tree was so prolific, that it yielded three large boxes of pears over one weekend the previous summer. The house itself was on two levels, with a huge thirty-foot square sitting and dining room, the length of which ran glass doors to a wide deck overlooking the bay and an incredible view. The forested headland curled round and out to sea and many small islands lay offshore, paradises of tiny silver sand beaches and lagoons. What a place!

The weather tried, but didn't succeed, to dampen our spirits. It poured and poured with rain all weekend. We - Rob, Angie and I - drove to several towns nearby, KeriKeri, Russell and Waitangi where, in 1840 the Treaty of Waitangi was signed between England and forty-six Maori chiefs, effectively heralding the beginning of New Zealand as a British colony. Both the Germans and Russians were sailing around the area at that time, and the chiefs, admiring British justice, decided to accept British protection as the lesser of three evils. The wonderful grass headland on which the famous, tall white flagpole stands, commands a view across river and islands and out to sea. Behind it nestles the Treaty House, built in 1834 to house the first British Resident, installed to protect British commerce and to put an end to the outrages perpetrated against the Maoris by British settlers. It is an historic and magnificent place and even in the teeming rain I was much moved. In an open boathouse to one side was a Maori war canoe - the largest in the world, thirty-five metres long and built to carry eighty warriors. Richly carved from three massive Kauri pine trees, it is launched once a year to commemorate the Treaty signing.

Russell was a most attractive little town, and was the first capital of New Zealand. Weatherboard houses painted in pale sugar almond colours stood prettily among cottage gardens, and those along the foreshore were particularly lovely. The Coastal Classic yacht race from Auckland to Russell had taken place the previous day and a large fleet of craft rocked at anchor and filled the trots off the pretty, bustling town, their crews milling about in the bars and narrow streets. The leading boat, a catamaran, had taken seven hours to complete the trip reaching speeds of up to twenty-six knots. Even in the steady drizzle, I loved the town and should like to return there one day.

The next day the three of us set off in the rain, bundled up in jackets and walking boots, and drove a short way to begin a cliff walk. It was spectacular. We parked the car by a field of shorn sheep, the rolling green hills and streams, the turf and the meadows of cow parsley all so reminiscent of Dorset or Wales. We climbed a steep hill and as we did so, the winding path took us past flowering tea tree bushes, toitoi grasses and palm-like tree ferns, their thick spiral coils unfurling from the crown like giant wood ferns. It rained. Well, drizzled incessantly, but we didn't mind, though we had to watch our footing on the brick red, muddy soil. Up we climbed, and the thick forest on the ridge slopes was fragrant in the damp air, full of strange and interesting tropical plants.

We came out into a high clearing and laid before us were a series of beautiful rocky bays, surrounded with cliffs and wooded headlands. We descended through a field of tall grasses and here the rain was needle-sharp, as I remembered it had once been on the Brecon Beacons, stinging my face and eyes, but so invigorating. A stream flowed down through the fields to the sea, and in the boggy ground at its mouth, grew large stands of wild arum lilies, their beautiful white cornets catching the rain, tall and lush below the palm trees - what a picture! We clambered over rocks, up and down a path and into another bay. This remote and windy beach had once been a thriving whaling station and a board of old photographs depicted the horror, both to man and beast, of days gone by.

The men would row out beyond the headland, having set huge nets across the known sea passage of these magnificent mammals. Once netted, the whale would thrash until exhausted, when the hand, and later mechanical harpoon was employed, and the creature then tied to the boat and towed to shore. A slipway with small rails leading up the beach marked the track of open containers in which parts of the whale were trundled, and large vats and tanks held flesh and oil. From the mid 1800s until the 1930s the terrible slaughter continued, with loss of life on both sides. 1924 was hailed as the most successful year, with seventy-four whales killed. Somewhat sobered we retraced our steps up the hill and so, through this fascinating countryside, to home.

Below us, beyond the gardens, gannets wheeled and dipped and dived for fish, and we had hot showers and tea in our house on the hill. Later that evening we went for drinks in another stunning house by the shore. A huge log fire greeted us, high beams, Persian rugs, piles of cushions and views of the windswept beach beyond the blue agapanthus and palm trees, filled every window. We ate large and luscious Orongo Bay oysters, arranged on glossy leaves, with lemon and ice on an enormous platter, and listened to the owner's tale of piling up his helicopter with oodles of food for the weekend, without letting my jaw drop. That magnificent, warm, light and lovely house beat anything I have ever seen in Homes and Gardens.

Rob whizzed out round the headland in the dinghy before nightfall, to put down a net for fish - and so to bed.

Next day, as the rain persisted, Jessie helped Rob recover his net in the bay. The rest of us sat quietly and wrote or read round the fire, before us the fabulous view of the islands, clouded by the squalling rain. Suddenly the front door burst open and a breathless Jessie told of a large shark in the net, of having to cut some of the net away, and of bringing home snapper, sole and two baby sand sharks. We all donned macs and dashed barefooted to the boathouse. Rob had indeed had to cut the net; something very large had gnawed through one of the net anchors and had been thrashing about in the net; despite all his strength he could not tow it in. However, we all admired the three plump little snapper, the sole and the two perfectly formed baby sharks.

Later - The journey home to Auckland was interesting. The rain had caused many landslips down the tall cliffs round which our narrow road wound and the unsealed surface caused the tyres to slip a bit, even on Rob's Range Rover. Small bridges just skimmed the rushing water over the swollen rivers, and many fields were flooded. Over nine inches of rain had fallen that weekend. I sat with the wriggling children in the back, enchanted as ever with this beautiful land, an orchard of apple blossom amidst waving palm trees, said it all.

The next few days flew past. As I write, Nikki Anderson is also staying here - a pretty eighteen-year old on her gap year, travelling with a beautiful leather carpetbag and a cashmere coat. Her father is Military Attaché in Morocco, and together we went to investigate the Auckland Backpackers' Travel Centre. Trains are practically non-existent in New Zealand, and buses not cheap, so I left a message on the notice board requesting a lift south, and hoped for the best. I changed my flight, which was expensive but still cheaper than returning to Auckland after time in the South Island. I now fly back to Sydney from Christchurch on December 18th. Fate will decide what I do on my birthday.

I rang Gemma with all my news, and my mother faxed me, whilst letters arrived from family and friends - how good to hear news from home. I rang (wait for it) my best-man's-stepfather's-eldest-son's-ex-wife who lived in Auckland and who turned out to be a very charming seventy-year old Danish woman. We had lunch and a very happy few hours in her pretty home overlooking Auckland Bay.

Today, Sibilla Giardet, a young zoologist friend of Nikki's popped in, with bird and seashore books and a map of Tiritiri Island, which we may visit next week - a protected bird sanctuary and a thrilling prospect for me. I have a bad sore throat, which I must kick before the weekend when I am invited up to Taupo to a fishing batch, or holiday cottage.

I am fascinated by the different attitudes to the mother country, in both Australia and New Zealand. There is a definite undercurrent of anti British feeling in Australia. Only one in sixty-four Australians was actually born in that country and many are from countries other than Britain. So, the sovereignty issue seems pointless to them. The word 'invaders' is much used in Australia, even in official pamphlets and lectures. This saddened me rather, although the Aborigines were there hundreds of years before us, and it is still apparent that much of the prevailing attitude stems from the penal colonial beginnings in the 1700s. It seems quite extraordinary to me that people can still harbour this animosity, but two hundred years it was pointed out to me, is only just over two generations and not that far back. It is generally accepted, even in New Zealand, where I have noticed a far more ambivalent attitude, that Australia will have broken away from the United Kingdom within ten years from now, and that New Zealand, for socio-economic reasons, will probably join her.

LILIAS

<u>Saturday 2nd November</u>

Last night I arrived by this large and peaceful lake. I was given a lift with Angie's sister Diana and her husband Mark Newcombe, who, coincidentally, owned a batch in exactly the same small settlement as my friends. I had piled into yet another capacious, all electronic 4 x 4 jeep, joining Murphy, a long and lanky red setter with mournful eyes. New Zealand drivers I have known seem to delight in making and receiving endless calls on the car phone. Four came in or out - one from Canada, as we bowled along a New Zealand road.

Yet again, the country enchanted me. We wound south between grassy hills, where sheep and cattle grazed in the sun, and small weatherboard farmhouses nestled in deep valleys, or perched on windy hilltops, often quite a distance from each other. Occasionally we would notice a particularly high hill, with old, dug out fortifications still visible. These were Maori 'Pa's'. With their farms in the lowlands, the Maoris would retire to their high 'pa's' when under threat, and trenches would be dug, marked out with tall, sharpened stakes. A central wooden meeting house or 'whare', and surrounding sheds, would be erected off the ground. A storage pit was dug and an armoury built, for their clubs and spears. Many kumara (sweet potatoes) were stored in the pits in case of need. Much of the fighting, when it occurred, was hand-to-hand; the Maoris were fearless warriors.

As we drove on, the almost mogul-like hillocky pastures gave way to an enormously wide valley, rich dairy lands where huge herds of sleek cows ambled in for milking. We passed through Matamata, a renowned bloodstock centre with pretty, neat stud farms and a splendid racecourse. As we drove on, our conversation turned to fishing and shooting and I learnt an interesting fact. Every river in New Zealand over ten feet wide has what is called the Queen's Chain, a strip a chain's width (22 yards) from the water's edge owned by the Crown or local authority. The riverbank is (usually) publicly accessible, and as long as you hold a current licence anyone can fish the river. Thus, on any stretch of any river, an executive and a manual worker may fish side by side. In the case of land of course, it is often owned freehold, but a polite request to shoot pheasant or duck over a farmer's land will rarely be denied. When the first settlers arrived from England, they elected to break away from the feudal system of manor house and estate worker's cottages. Farms and houses were deliberately built in the same fashion, thus an egalitarian society was formed, with the farm owner's or manager's house being no different from the rest. The Queen's Chain was also instituted, to give public access to rivers and land that in the British Isles would often be privately owned.

As we drove south, we saw various gorgeous flowering shrubs. Masses of sun-worshipping flame-coloured azaleas and sugar pink rhododendrons, the flowers completely smothering their leaves so that bushes and trees hardly looked real from a distance, but more like clouds of candyfloss. We passed the world's largest cheese factory, very modern and owned by Anchor. Quite suddenly and dramatically the geography and flora changed. Towering, rocky, pine covered hills heralded the area of volcanic eruption, rivers cut deep through small gorges and, a joy to behold, brilliant golden bushes of broom, often six to ten feet high, grew between blue gums and dark pines. It was breathtaking. Mile upon mile of shining broom carpeted the hills, bordered the rivers and lined the roads.

We descended towards Lake Taupo and stopped to look at a fast-flowing river far below us, the shallow water a pale and impossible turquoise, before the river tumbled, white and foaming, over giant rocks. Lake Taupo was formed over two thousand years ago, and is the largest crater in the world. Forty kilometres long, it is twenty-seven kilometres at its widest point, more or less the size of Singapore. It is one hundred and sixty metres at its deepest. The first white man, or pakeha, to set eyes on the lake in 1831, was a prisoner of the Maoris, and several years later the first white settlers arrived. It offers superb fishing; the largest rainbow trout caught here was almost three feet long, weighing nearly twenty-three pounds.

Many New Zealanders, both from the north and south of North Island, have holiday homes or 'batches' here, and you can ski just forty-five minutes away. We passed small heads of white steam, seemingly coming directly out of the ground, as indeed they were. Geothermal steam bores were used for driving electricity. We reached the town of Taupo and the lake. It was enormous and entirely surrounded by blue, hazy mountains. Weatherboard houses lined the shores, and I learnt that on a certain part of the beach, the sand was too hot to walk on, even on a cold day, due to underground thermal activity. On we drove, round the eastern shore of the lake, past small Maori farmsteads, orange trees and pine forests, over the River Waitahanui and down to the lakeside at Hatepe, some twenty minutes from Taupo.

Johnny and Lilias Bell, with whom I was to stay, had already arrived from the city, and invited us all in for a drink. Their small 'batch' was delightful. It had been in Johnny's family for over twenty years and stood beneath a group of tall, fresh green poplar trees. Totally unpretentious, with an open fire and old, comfortable furniture, it was a perfect holiday home for a young family. On the mantelpiece, large white trumpets of 'Fragrantissima' rhododendron flowers arranged in a vase perfumed the cosy sitting room. Lilias was the cousin of a good friend of mine in Scotland. She was a tall, slim woman, extremely good looking, who had been brought up for much of her life in Zimbabwe. She had only lived in New Zealand for two years, after starting married life in England with Johnny, her New Zealander husband, who was charming. Dressed very much in the English style, with brogues and a big jumper, he had a mass of curly hair and an impish smile. When with English friends, Lilias delighted in calling him her 'dustman' - he was actually a civil engineer specialising in waste disposal! Their children, Charlie, three, and Eleanor, two, were the most delightful calm, undemanding children I had met so far. They never whined or complained, had wonderful English diction and smiled a lot. The Hinemaiaia River flowed into the lake between pines and poplar trees, just beyond the sitting-room window, whilst the far distant hills rose up across the lake – heaven. There was often both a large grey wading heron and a wader-clad fisherman casting, in thigh deep water off the beach just beyond the window - a tranquil and pleasing scene.

We enjoyed a delicious chicken supper, followed by my gift of plump strawberries and very thick cream. Soon afterwards the children went to bed, Johnny went out fishing, and Lilias and I sat curled up by the fire, talking of England, life out here, children and city (London) life. I found her a stimulating and amusing new friend, and in some ways we were able to compare notes. I had, albeit temporarily, stepped outside my conventional life whilst travelling, and she had come to live amongst very different people over here. We discussed my redundant state and she showed me the smart company brochures of the headhunting firm she had worked with in London. She asked me if I was any good on the telephone ('Brilliant' I replied 'most woman are!') wondering if I might make a good researcher for Saxton Bampfylde Hever in Westminster. It all seemed a bit impossible to me, kind though she was. We both laughed about the cluttered diaries, formal entertaining and exaggerated pomposity of some we knew at home in England. She missed her girlfriends, but had obviously made many new and refreshingly casual friends, got on well with her in-laws, and was enjoying life in New Zealand. She also told me how honest and down-to-earth people here are. A friend of hers who had fallen on hard times, gardened for her, and neither felt awkward about payment. This girl had a large house full of beautiful antiques, and when Lilias's mother (who happens to be a Duchess) came to stay, she was intrigued at being asked to dinner by the gardener!

After breakfast the next morning, we all walked the few yards down to the beach. It was the first time I had thrown stones into water and watched them actually float away. The beach was made up of all kinds of volcanic stones and pebbles, much of it pumice. We had a very happy couple of days. We walked on the beach and beside the river, ate freshly caught, hot smoked trout and other delicious meals, in the garden, with the scorching sun shining through the wonderful pink and red maple leaves waving over the lawn. On November 2 we joined another family for a firework party on the beach. The tiny children, wide-eyed with their sparklers, stood on the pebbles in woolly hats, and we crowded round the driftwood fire and drank whisky and wine. A man known as 'Father Tim' by Charlie his godson, arrived for the night. Tim was charming and a true godfather, mischievous and caring.

The fireworks over, the children were taken home to bed and we joined Diana and Mark in their very beautiful beach house for coffee and chocolate cake. I bowed out early with rather a nasty cold and walked back along the beach in the dark. The heavens seemed to arch into infinity, over the beach, the lake and the mountains. Thousands of stars shone brilliantly down through the velvet night, and there among them on the far horizon, I saw the Southern Cross.

I learned from Lilias that eighty per cent of New Zealanders are non-believers in the church and of the remaining twenty per cent, ten per cent are not churchgoers. No religious education is taught in government schools - not even assembly, with hymns or prayers. Some of her friends had never entered a church or sung a hymn in their lives. She also announced that 'People are my petrol' - a sentiment I thoroughly agreed with.

The day I left, Sunday, I took the children off to the beach while Lilias cleared up the batch. Johnny was fishing. We made 'sea puddings' (my name for sand castles) and I marvelled once again at the breathtaking view. The deep blue lake gently lapped at our feet, while in the distance the mountain range, the ancient crater rim, stretched all round us, and to the south, the snow-capped volcano peak of Mt. Ngaruhoe gleamed in the sun. After lunch we drove south from Hatepe, crossing the Tongariro River, arguably the best trout river in the world, Johnny had told me. The Bells dropped me at Turangi from where I caught a bus north to Taupo, Cambridge, Auckland and home. I remember seeing pretty wild white hollyhocks covering a hillside, shaded by palm trees - such a lovely and yet incongruous sight.

Facts: there are three million people in New Zealand and yet, fifty million Bic pens are imported every year. Only ten per cent of the population of New Zealand are Maori.

TIRITIRI MATANGI

<u>Tuesday 5th November</u>

Today I had such a happy day with Thomasina Stacey one of Emma, my sister-in-law's three sisters. I have only met her once or twice before, fleetingly in London, and here, far from home we so enjoyed each other's company. She is a midwife here in Auckland and her boy friend Morgan is involved in films and lives in Sydney. She moves there in January and will gain Australian residency from that date. We whizzed off in her little old car, up into the hills west of Auckland from where we had a fantastic view back over the sea towards the city. Beneath us, a vast tapestry of greens - oaks, tree ferns, palms and a marvellous variety of trees and bushes with exotic names – unfolded right down to the sea. On we went, over the top and down to a lookout point.

Laid before us was a beautiful bay - Piha Bay - with a huge expanse of black sand, dominated by the Lion Rock, a two hundred foot high crag at one end, cut off by the waves at high tide. We drove down the steep hill road and parked by the sand. It was almost deserted. A few surfers bobbed like seals in their black wetsuits out in the breakers, but the beach was ours. We climbed first to the top of the Lion Rock and what a view we had. The next bay along had been the scene of filming for 'The Piano'. I had watched it in Bangkok, never dreaming I would stand here one day, with a delightful member of my extended family - how very strange life is.

New Zealanders are very involved with the sea and the rivers. It is geographically a narrow country and people I've met seem to dash off on sailing courses or to go sea fishing, river fishing or kayaking off every coastline. The climate has a lot to do with this.

Facts: there are only three million people in this country and, for what it's worth, health visitors are known here as Plunket nurses. The Plunket Movement was born in Dunedin in May 1907 to 'help the mothers and save the babies'. An offer of patronage from the influential Lady Victoria Plunket, wife of the then Governor General and mother of eight children, gave rise to its name.

<u>Thursday 7th November</u>

Yesterday, Nikki and I set off in a large, gleaming inter-island catamaran for the open sanctuary of Tiritiri Matangi. We sailed out of Auckland harbour and sped past beaches and headlands to pick up further passengers from a smart marina called Gulf Harbour. There were only four of us on board to begin with and we were congratulating ourselves on the prospect of a peaceful day. At Gulf Harbour we took on twenty-five doddery OAPs and about twenty serious looking trampers (hikers). After the usual 'Oh, are you from England? I was there in Coronation year . . .' we settled down to enjoy the trip.

We passed a wonderfully sleek navy-hulled seventy-foot ketch, called Sassafras as we left the harbour. She hailed from Guernsey, and looked brand new with gorgeous wooden decks, dinghy and masts. What a passage that must have been - or perhaps she had been built here and was about to be sailed home. We approached the island of Tiritiri slowly, through a rocky bay, with Little Barrier and Great Barrier Islands visible through the haze on the horizon. The perfect volcanic peak of Rangitoto Island lay to the south and behind us and opposite it lay the entrance to Auckland harbour.

Tiritiri Matangi is a world-renowned conservation project and a scientific reserve, which has been and continues to be immensely successful. Centuries of Maori occupation followed by European farming had transformed the landscape from dense forest into an island of rolling grassy hills. Only a few pockets of forest remained. In the early 1970s it was decided to remove the stock and begin an ambitious programme of natural regeneration. Bracken, ferns and rats had to be cleared and routed out, the latter finally by means of a 1993 aerial bait drop. As. many birds as possible were put in aviaries, and within four days the island was rodent free and has remained so. The rats had eaten birds' eggs and chicks, and practised ring-barking, destroying much of the vegetation. Overnight, thirty or more rats could almost completely destroy a tree.

In 1983 Sir Peter Scott was taken to the island on behalf of the World Wildlife Fund; he was asked if he thought the idea of setting up an open sanctuary, introducing local seed from native trees, and endangered species of birds, was a viable one. He was so impressed and excited by the venture that forty thousand dollars was gifted to begin the scheme. Over twenty thousand trees have been planted there since 1984 by thousands of volunteers, many from local schools, clubs and tramping associations. And now those former nine and ten year olds are returning to work as conservation students, ten years on.

Various birds were introduced. Eighteen rare stitch birds, the tui or parson bird (a 'dog-collar' of curly white feathers under the chin of this otherwise blue-black bird, gives him this name), a pair of small brown teal (the fourth rarest duck in the world) and a pair of large takehe birds, looking like enormous blue and green moorhens, and thought to be extinct until 1948. The pair of takehes, known to be homosexual, started building a nest. Two dummy eggs were brought in, on which they began to sit. Then one of two precious, fertile eggs was flown by plane and helicopter in an incubator, from the only other known place where a pair had bred, and our boys successfully hatched it three days later - this chick was a female. Saddleback, whitehead, and little spotted kiwis have also successfully bred here. Never before had such a venture been undertaken.

Volunteers still help maintain the habitat and breeding programmes at weekends. They pay for boat and bunkhouse, bringing their own food with them, and these sought-after days are booked up to two years in advance. It was a magical island. We began with a guided walk up the wattle path, accompanied by a ranger, and Nikki and I were very happy to stroll slowly in the hot sun with our aged companions, as the ranger was most interesting and informative. The serious-looking trampers took another route. Many of the nectar-loving birds we saw had vivid orange heads, perplexing the ornithologists amongst us, but this proved to be merely flax pollen collected as they dipped for nectar. 'And there you see', said the guide 'a saddleback fossicking for insects'. This word, meaning rootling, panning (as in the case of gold) or searching, is widely used in Australasia and much amused me.

Quite soon we could identify many of the birdcalls and songs, and the beautiful trees and bush vegetation. We walked on into the open, up a hill to the sixty-foot lighthouse. There, a free cup of tea or coffee was on offer in the tiny shed that doubled as the postcard and gift shop - and the only place of its kind on the island. As we walked up, the views over the sea to the far distant volcano and down into rocky bays through the cabbage and cork trees, were breathtaking. Nikki and I bought cards, studied the fascinating project information board and then, passing the trampers as they came in, we shouldered our rucksacks once more and made for the ridge, knowing we had the whole of this beautiful island to ourselves. White fronted terns flew overhead, an Australasian harrier circled in a small valley, and the bush smelt glorious in the hot sun.

We ate our picnic lunch in a small Maori pa, a grassy indentation in a clearing, high above the rocky shore. There, Maoris would have conducted important meetings in years gone by. Tuis and bellbirds flew to and fro over us and it was very peaceful. Later on we descended to a tiny cove along a fantastic boardwalk through the bush, which had taken four years for volunteers to construct. As the tree canopy was relatively low, we saw the almost tame birds at very close quarters - remembering there were no predators here, besides the bigger birds of course - I loved it all.

Vast, dead tree branches, hundreds of years old, were left for birds and insects to live in, and secret gullies gave cover for shy birds like the little kiwis. Down on the beach, we marvelled at the tiny, exquisitely delicate shells and searched for the cleverly designed stone nesting boxes. School children and others could view Little Blue penguin chicks through the boxes' glass lids, happily nestling against their furry brothers, quite undisturbed. We had had a good walk by the time we boarded the boat in mid-afternoon, though I should have loved to have stayed a lot longer. It was thrilling to see so many rare birds, breeding and flying happily around, adding so much to a world from which we take so much, and to know that their numbers would increase, on this very special island in the sun.

ROTTENRUA

On 7th November, a Thursday, I caught the bus to Rotorua, which was en route to Napier, on the east coast, where I hoped to stay with friends of my mother's. Rotorua is roughly in the middle of North Island, and a famed centre of volcanic and geothermal activity. I shall investigate the bubbling mud pools, geysers and hot springs in this strange area. As we approached Rotorua in the bus, the wonderful velvety green hills, on which the sheep and horses grazed or dozed, under large oak or chestnut trees, gave way to a land punctuated by extraordinary hillocks and pinnacles. Grass covered their steep little slopes, giving way to explosions of dark stone pointing skywards, and in the distance I saw Lake Rotorua, lying in a crater below us. Quite suddenly the grass gave way to bushland around the city and then we were there. Clouds of steam rose from a hot spring pool in a city park and floated across the road. I found a cheap dorm room in the town; three German girls share my room and I am back with the eyebrow-pierced and dreadlocks brigade.

<u>Friday 8th November</u>

I slept well in my dorm room with the three girls - and two boys. We think we have waterbed mattresses. They were very odd, very warm and very comfortable, but none of us was sure. This morning I chose a thirty-dollar (fourteen pound) bus trip out to see the extraordinary thermal fields for which Rotorua is famous. Most of the trips were seventy dollars plus, and I picked a real winner.

Tourists began coming here from all over the world in the 1800s. Once here, they travelled by horse and carriage, mainly to see the eighth wonder of the world, wide pink and white terraces of sinter (silicate of lime), hard deposits of thermal rock 'flowing' like a delicately tinted glacier, over the land. They also came to take the spa waters. Rotorua is in the Bay of Plenty area, named by Captain Cook when he revictualled his ships from this part.

The valley in which Rotorua lies is known as the valley of a thousand hills, and indeed it was incredible to see how the farmers managed their sheep in the gorges, gullies and cuttings scarring their pastures so deeply. Sheep graze all around this city on the lush hillsides . . . at the last count there were 48.6 million sheep in New Zealand ('automatic lawn mowers'). Rotorua is nicknamed Rottenrua, for the pervading smell of sulphur, which is pretty awful but soon got used to. Twenty-nine crater lakes surround the city, positioned in what is known as Earthquake Valley, where three of the earth's plates meet. There are around twelve thousand earth shakes and two hundred mini earthquakes each year in New Zealand, reaching 3.6 to 3.9 on the Richter scale. The South Pacific Rim of Fire, which circles the world, passes through this area.

Our bus travelled through wonderful forests of Douglas fir, Californian pine, larch, black poplar, redwoods and Mexican pines with droopy needles, making them look very funny and almost huggable. Golden broom, grasses and foxgloves grew amongst them, and we saw many huge log lorries coming from the wood mills. The contrast of the fifty or so different shades of green, and leaf textures, was a marvellous sight. Farming was not possible in this area as the pumice and porous ground would not hold water, but neither was there any flooding. Two large volcanoes loomed ahead of us, still extremely active. Though grass and forest covered, they could apparently blow at any moment. A small lake was pointed out to us - at the last eruption its depth fell from seven metres to over seventy. We passed tree-covered Rainbow Mountain, with wisps and spurts of steam rising here and there from between the dark trees - an eerie sight. Next we alighted to view a hot crater lake, steaming at the foot of the hill. Once in every ten days or so it apparently boils. This was 'eggshell' country, the steam often causing the land to collapse before it found another outlet.

We drove on, and I saw sheep grazing peacefully in fields from which, again, little wisps and spurts of steam were erupting - most alarming. Rhododendrons bloomed a wonderful deep pink and broom and tea trees grew beside a hot, steaming stream. We drove on to see the Lady Constance Knox geyser. In 1896 prison labourers planting the original pine forest, came upon a clearing and finding a hot chloride spring, decided to camp and wash their clothes in it. They were astounded to find that after soaping their clothes, the spring erupted violently, high into the air, no doubt scattering their washing!

In 1903, Lady Knox, daughter of the then Governor General of New Zealand, 'soaped' the geyser, christening it and lending her name to this extraordinary phenomenon. Until 1931 it erupted of its own accord, approximately every one to two days and would still do so today, but to accommodate visitors, a ranger now 'soaps' it each morning. Beneath the geyser cone is a natural reservoir of up to twenty-seven thousand litres of water, and the soap disperses an upper layer of water, allowing the super heated steam and water from far below to release its pressure. Our ranger tipped in one and a half kilos of ordinary soap and, with much anticipatory frothing, up she blew, twenty metres high in the air, as cameras clicked and many of us got soaked. It was indeed a spectacular sight.

On again to Wai-o-tapu, meaning sacred waters in Maori, and what an awe-inspiring insight into the power and instability of the earth we stand on. Really quite frightening. Paths and boardwalks led through an area literally covered with collapsed craters, boiling pools of mud and water, and steaming fumeroles. Craters up to twenty metres in diameter and twelve deep, contained boiling springs, and most smelt acridly sulphurous, with many-hued deposits around their rims and sides - yellow sulphur, orange antimony, black carbon, purple manganese, red iron oxide and green arsenic deposits were all there, resulting in pools, streams and craters appropriately named. Rainbow Crater, Devil's Inkpots (boiling mud pools, smelling just like stink-bombs), Artists' Palette with constantly changing colours in the hissing water, the Champagne Pool, sixty metres wide and the same deep. At 74 degrees centigrade it bubbles with carbon dioxide, a beautiful steamy green with a red, crusty rim, hot mud blopping and globbing as it boiled violently. Inferno Crater incubated the eggs of birds nesting in holes along the crater wall.

Walks along the sides of streams and mineral (once water) falls wound beside tiny steaming holes, and the noises from small craters reminded me of coffee in a percolator; it was an amazing sight. The wind blew great clouds of steam over the pools - magnificent and awesome. Later, on our way back to the city, we stopped at a mud lake, where boiling whirls and spurts of mud erupted all over the surface; I had never seen anything like it. On again, past hedgerows bordered with wonderful thick carpets of forget-me-nots and a golf course where players calmly aimed their shots between spirals of steam escaping in bursts from the turf - an extraordinary sight. Long, long ago, the South Island of New Zealand was part of Australia, and later, when it broke away, the North Island was born out of the sea during an eruption. What a place this is!

In the afternoon I dealt with post office, bank, photocopying and lunch. I can manage on cereal, a light lunch and a snack in the evening. New Zealand is very expensive for the average backpacker, especially where transport is concerned.

Saturday 9th November

This morning I left Rotorua, but not before a few hours wandering around the town. I visited the Museum, housed in a splendid boathouse built at the beginning of the century, complete with leaded windows and a clock tower. It was hoped that Rotorua would become a famous spa town, but that never really happened. On the immaculate lawns at the front, several croquet matches were being played by the townspeople of Rotorua, resplendent in white trousers and cherry red blazers. The museum was rather a muddly place, but the staff were very pleasant. There was much information about the Maoris. They had originally come to New Zealand from Polynesia, sometime prior to 800 AD and colonisation continued until the fourteenth century, when the settlers no longer felt the need to be tied to Polynesia. It was not until the first white men arrived in the early 1800s that they named the many tribes 'The Maori People'. I walked beside Lake Rotorua where families rowed old-fashioned wooden boats and a large flock of beautiful black swans milled around with their fluffy brown cygnets in search of food - a peaceful scene. A helicopter and a seaplane stood by the small jetty, ready to whisk those who wished, up over the volcanoes and bubbling craters.

I walked round the lake to the tiny Maori Anglican church of St. Faith's. Christianity was first preached in this area by a British missionary in 1831, and the original church was built in 1885. In 1910 it was shifted forward towards the lake and turned round to face west. In 1918 the present church was consecrated but collapsed in a storm in 1936, and was once again rebuilt. It was a small white building, with brick-red half timbers and pretty windows, giving it a Tudor appearance. Many Maoris are buried around it, in raised graves, the ground being too unstable to dig up. Wonderful Maori carvings adorn the woodwork inside, symbolic creatures with pearly pau (abalone) shells for their shining eyes. The main window above the altar depicts 'Christ knocking at the door', in beautiful pastel-coloured stained glass. Another window, above a simple altar in a side chapel was one of the most beautiful I had ever seen.

Through the window Lake Rotorua lay blue and calm beyond the grasses fringing its shore. The deeper blue of the distant hills rose, far away. Etched in clear glass on the window, was the figure of Jesus, barefoot, wearing a Maori cape of kiwi feathers, with one hand outstretched, and seemingly walking into the little church, across the water. It was a simple picture and very moving.

MILK FROM BULLS

My bus journey to Napier was marvellous, with spectacular scenery at every turn of the twisting road. Though I borrow books from fellow travellers, to look up particular places, this is the only country for which I have not bought a Lonely Planet or Rough Guide. The advantage of not reading up too much beforehand is that every new place is a surprise and often a revelation - Rotorua was such a place. I had been totally dumbfounded by what I'd seen there and now this journey to Napier was yet another incredible trip. The landscape was extraordinary, with huge hills plunging to rocky gorges and valleys, up and down which our creaking bus laboured. It was like an exaggerated lunar landscape, the whole covered with thick, green velvety pasture. Rivers wound far below, tumbling and rushing, and sheep with their lambs grazed high above us on the skyline. In two hours we reached the Bay of Plenty and Napier.

The whole town was destroyed in an earthquake in the 1930s and then entirely rebuilt in Art Deco style, in varying shades of ice cream colour. Star Absolom, with whom I was to stay, was there to meet me, so I didn't see much of the town. She and her husband John, farm a three thousand acre cattle station at Rissington, up in the hills behind Napier. Once again we drove up and over the land, reminiscent of the Scottish Borders, and turned down a drive lined with huge, old, pointed cypress trees. A most beautiful house and garden came into view - my home for a couple of days. Star and John, friends of friends, deal in bull semen, a huge concern, involving cattle breeders in New Zealand, Queensland and the USA. Their wonderful house, built in 1906, was cool and grand, with a heavenly garden. A maze of rose arches, lawns, wisteria climbing high into the cypress trees, herbaceous borders, a wood, a pretty wild pond, a swimming pool hidden between philadelphus, jasmine and scented roses, an old wooden verandah covered in more climbers, a dovecote by the grapefruit tree, a tulip tree in flower . . . oh!

<u>Sunday 10th November</u>
After breakfast I took myself off for a long walk. It was lovely to stretch my legs after pounding the Rotorua tourist trail and after my bus journeys. I crossed a field of inquisitive bullocks just beyond the Absolom's garden, and found a path down a steep cliff with old tyres set into the earth as descending steps - how clever. Below me, a long swing bridge straddled the river; it swayed as I crossed - really fun doing this completely on my own. Then I set off upstream for a mile or so, watching darting brown and white dotterels, pied pigeons, and beside me the shallow river tumbling over small stones. The cliffs rose up from the water on the far side and sheep grazed high above. I ran and sang in the sun and sat in the shade with my binoculars – bliss.

That afternoon Daniel, who was delightful and so good looking (Star and John have four sons; all of whom have attended Whanganui School here) dropped me off at the top of McNeil Hill, a thousand feet high and overlooking almost the entire Absolom estate. The views were incredible, up towards the hills and gorges I had passed in the bus, and in the distance I could see Hawke Bay and Napier town and the Sacred Hill Winery, far below me. It was very cold on the hilltop - too cold, sadly, to hang around or walk on the ridge for long, so I set off for home the way we had driven, with Lettie, a small Cairn terrier. An hour later I was back at base, not a long walk, but a happy day in fantastic country.

The next day, Monday 11th November I caught the bus from Napier to Palmerston North. Before that, I had helped Star by following her in Daniel's car, which had to go into the garage. It was an absolutely GLORIOUS morning and the first song that played on the tape deck as I got into the driving seat was 'Morning has broken'. To that lovely tune, I followed Star up the steep hill roads, with a far distant view of the sea, sparkling in the morning, with the wildly undulating hills spread out below me, covered with fresh green velvety grass. Sheep dotted the pasture like stars, and neat lush hedges wound over and around the hills like woolly green caterpillars.

The bus journey took just a couple of hours, with the magnificent Tararud Mountains in the distance, their summits streaked with snow. We passed an ostrich farm and many orchards - this area is known as the fruit bowl of New Zealand, and vineyards whose signs I recognised from the liquor stores - Sacred Hill, Hawke's Bay and others. At eleven o'clock I kept a private, two-minute, eyes-shut silence, remembering so well the war graves I had seen at Kanchanaburi on the River Kwai in Thailand.

New Zealanders often drive wonderful old 1960s and '70s cars and I have seen many Austin vans, Minis, Morris Minors, Triumph Heralds and so on. It is such a beautiful country (and I haven't begun in the South Island yet, which apparently surpasses anything I have seen here) and yet I have heard murmurings that it is rather dull and comfortable living. Certainly the standard of living is very high, but some feel there is no 'edge' to life here - no challenges, deprivation or real hardship - amongst those whom I have met, that is. I state this merely as an observation and from what I have gleaned from conversations - I could not argue it.

My bus passed an 'Opossum Centre' where you could stroke, feed and watch the creatures, then buy the T-shirts, chocolate opossums and goodness knows what - probably opossum flavoured ice cream! Next came fields of cows, many with their tails cut off to just a few inches, a practice that is dying out, I gather. It is done for hygienic reasons to prevent their dirty tails from getting scrambled up in the milking machines. One thing I haven't written about much recently, is the weather. I have been cold at some time every day since I arrived in Sydney from Brisbane. Australia (NSW) was occasionally hot by day but quite cold at night, and now here in New Zealand I am regretting sending home my big jumper, polo tops and leggings. Difficult, as I did not want to carry them from Nepal to Sydney for a few brief weeks of use. However, as I had hoped, fate has helped me yet again. I had told my mother on the phone on Sunday that I would have to go out and buy a jumper. Lo and behold, Lilias was about to take some to a charity, so instead I became her charity. I now have two lovely wool cardigans (one belonged to her father, and she wore it when pregnant) and an old cashmere jumper with holey arms and patches on the elbows – bliss. Lilias had met me at the bus station with Charlie and Eleanor (three and two).

They are a delightful family and live in a typical, large, comfortable New Zealand house, with a spacious playroom and lovely garden. There are lots of beautiful paintings, and porcelain and pieces of furniture reminding me of England and Scotland, and photographs of Lilias's illustrious ancestors. Lilias tells me travellers tend to merely pass through by bus en route to Wellington. I shall help her look after the children and with the ironing etc. which she said she'd love in lieu of housekeeping pennies.

<u>Tuesday 12th November</u>

Today I hung out, folded and ironed washing, made biscuits with Charlie and took Eleanor shopping - not a chore for me at all, but a help I think to Lilias. They are sweet children with such a charming turn of phrase and very polite. I also managed to write lots of letters and my diary, did some mending and read my book - a good administrative day. Tomorrow I shall go further afield. It is as cold as Auckland here at night and a fan heater is needed in the drawing-room. Houses in this country are not at all geared up for cold weather. None seem to be centrally heated; the odd night storage or portable radiator heaters are used - so much for hitting Hampshire with my tan on my return! I hope Sydney will be warmer at Christmas time, after all, we're only just coming into summer here.

The fact that some of the families I have stayed with have been part British (Rob Hood, Jo, Steve, and Lilias) and are bringing up their children as Australians/New Zealanders, has made me view my own children in an entirely new light, as young Englishmen. Yes, we all hope they will be a credit to their families, but I had not thought of them in that way before, as the inheritors of our loved and lovely land, hopefully proud to be English (or British) and to carry the best values and aspirations of our society with them into future years. I am so proud of them both - that would embarrass them - and grateful for the enthusiastic, affectionate, enterprising man and woman they have become. I only hope our country encourages and rewards them fittingly.

On another topic: obviously when travelling, you listen carefully to advice on where to go and what to see, from other adventurers. However, I have gained just as much pleasure from the places I have been warned against. Kuala Lumpur ('just another moderate city'), Bali ('awful, no decent beaches"), Sydney ('nothing much to do, just concrete") were typical examples. You must of course, look at your own situation. If lucky enough to stay with friends, you obviously see the very best of any place, in being taken around by people proud to show it all to you (as Kuala Lumpur and Sydney - both wonderful cities) and Bali, if you travel away from the tourist hordes and befriend the Balinese, is a magical place! In only one case have I been encouraged and in fact persuaded, to travel a distance to a place I did not want to visit - Chiang Mai in Thailand, and I did not enjoy it. Difficult though, when your hosts insist it is wonderful, and so you go. The standard of living between a half-decent hotel and a backpackers' hostel in Chiang Mai were worlds apart, and of course most of my friends would have stayed in the good hotels there.

<u>Wednesday 13th November</u>

Today I borrowed Lilias' car and visited the excellent little museum in Palmerston North. The exhibits were beautifully and simply displayed and the staff so helpful and nice. I spent four hours there. Rain lashed outside, and as little Charlie was under the weather at home, it was a day well spent. I learnt that the first settlers arriving here from Europe were mainly working-class, escaping unemployment, poor housing and squalid working conditions. There were two seasons, named mud and mosquitoes, and it was a terribly hard life - the men would leave their young wives alone for weeks on end in remote homesteads while they worked at a distance on the land. The women were dreadfully lonely, and one I had read about, used to climb a nearby hill every three or four days just to look for the column of smoke miles away, rising up into the sky from where her husband was working. Thus comforted, she would return home.

<u>Thursday 14th November</u>

Johnny Bell is wearing a splendid waistcoat in his wedding photos, hand painted silk and made by - my brother - how's that for a coincidence?

Lilias has been a most marvellous friend. Despite being tied by small children, we have talked at length about our two countries and our different lives. She was a very successful headhunter in London, and has again floated the idea with me, of my being a researcher for her old company in St. James's. I will contact them in the New Year, as I am now definitely interested.

On my last day with the Bells, we drove through beautiful countryside to see friends of hers. Cecelia (English) and Hew (New Zealander) Dalrymple, who own a large farm near the sea. Their several thousand acres of beef and forestry surround their lovely house, which is perched high on a knoll with superb views in every direction, over hills to the distant mountains. On the way, we passed through the town of Bulls and Lilias remarked that Palmerston North is the only town in the world that gets its milk from Bulls!

Cecelia was paralysed in a riding accident after just four months of marriage and whizzes round their land on a kind of open buggy with her year-old son Benjamin in a car seat behind her. Their beautiful house is adapted for her needs, and from her wheelchair she served us a delicious lunch of homemade soup, corned silverside and chunky bread. They were a delightful couple. We later drove to see yet another friend of Lilias', Sally Marshall, who had a happy, chaotic house, a smiley baby and a most heavenly garden. A virtual New Zealand Wisley, it was a profusion of foliage, a rainbow of colour, a dream of scents – oh, it was glorious! Pale yellow foxgloves, white forget-me-nots and a quite stunning pink calico bush called Kalmia - I should love to grow one - were particularly memorable. Then back home, over the green, green, lamb-strewn hills, with avenues of elegant poplar trees planted to bind the sandy soil and views of distant hills from every road - a happy day.

THE BACKBENCHER HOUSE WITH NO PEERS

<u>Saturday 17th November</u>

Yesterday I caught the bus down here to Wellington. Before I left, young Charlie and Eleanor Bell had called me excitedly to breakfast and to open a present from them all - a pair of warm socks for my South Island adventures - how welcome! It was sad bidding farewell to Lilias; I had become very fond of the family and they were incredibly kind to me. I helped where I could, clearing up after the children, playing with them and doing a bit of shopping. Nevertheless, the chance of spending five days with new friends was a great kindness to me; luckily it has been a very happy time.

The trip to Wellington was, as always, interesting. We passed many pretty wooden farmhouses with lush gardens; wood is used a great deal for building in New Zealand, as it gives and sways during earthquakes. I learnt that the gargoyles, cherubs and other embellishments were removed from many colonial brick-built buildings in Wellington, as they tended to fall off during big earthquakes.

Old friends of mine from my Washington DC days, Jo and Piers Reid, met me off the bus - it was wonderful to see them again. I wore my 'new' maroon cardigan, which is very flattering, and felt good. Jo teaches part time, Piers is head of the New Zealand army, and they live in Paramata in their own house high on a hill overlooking Pauatahanui inlet. The inlet was Wellington's original harbour in the 1800s, and the first hostile engagement between the Maoris in a war canoe, and a merchant ship, was fought right opposite my bedroom window.

In 1855 an earthquake raised the level of the seabed and it could no longer be used for trading. As I entered the house I gasped in amazement. Almost every room had one hundred and eighty degree views over the inlet, hills and further distant inlets from high above the water, some two hundred feet or so. My bedroom was a bedsitting-room, with a sunny, glass-sided conservatory attached, rush mats on the floor and a view almost beyond belief.

In the afternoon we went out for a drink in a large yacht club bar with all round views of Mana Island, and the rough wind-tossed sea, breaking on the rocks beneath us. At supper, Piers talked of two rude letters he had had from a member of the royal family, of his visit to Iraq, of the problems over Maori land claims dating back to 1840, and of the present government's problems, or the fact that they cannot seem to form one after the recent election.

Their son James, who is eighteen, is a very nice young man and exceptionally well informed. I do find the conversations I have had with men, such as Sadip Shah and Piers absolutely fascinating and illuminating. I seem to know a lot more than I realise, of world events and personalities, and also find such conversations a source of stimulation and compliment. My views are however, sometimes ill informed or simply mistaken, which I willingly admit to, and am happily put right. Later in the evening, Jo and I watched the video of 'Once Were Warriors', a very violent film, but brilliantly depicting Maori values and problems as an urban sub-culture. I was hocked, but it was sadly all too true; domestic violence is much the same in many other countries.

<u>Tuesday 19th November</u>

On Sunday, Jo and a friend Margaret, and I, went off for the day visiting various craft shops, a farm and a rather run-down bird sanctuary. At the latter, I declared I wanted to find a cockerel's feather and I ventured into an enclosure with llamas, turkeys and cockerels in it. A boy of about twelve was attempting to feed the rooster, and I asked him if he'd try and get me a feather. I didn't realise quite what I'd requested, and he chased the poor bird round, grabbed it and pulled out a long, curved, greenish black tail feather. The various bystanders were both horrified and amused, as he proudly handed it to me. Jo and Margaret had walked quickly off, disowning me. I thanked him and fled. (Margaret had recognised him as Keith, a very disturbed boy whom she had once taught. He had a mean streak in him poor lad, and she was convinced he would kill someone or something one day - he almost did, poor rooster).

On we went, along a bush-walk in the bird sanctuary. I learnt that the Maoris used to bend back the leaves of the silver fern along trails and pathways, to mark the route. The upper side of the fern was bright green, the underside a silver grey. The almost metallic colour would gleam in the sun, at dusk or in the moonlight, against the dark bush foliage - an excellent and very simple sign. We drove on up a steep winding hill road to a lookout point, and watched paragliders circling beneath us, their colourful floating chutes far below, sailing down to a tiny grass clearing above the thundering sea. Further on, descending the hill to a pretty lush valley, we followed the riverbank for a while, and I was enchanted to see great clumps of tall, creamy, arum lilies growing on both sides of the river - it was magical, with sheep and lambs grazing beside them.

On Monday, Jo dropped me in Wellington city, where I had arranged to meet Christian, a young school friend of my son's working there for Mobil for a few months. He was delighted to see me, and bought me lunch and a drink in a fashionable bar called Paris. We talked about home, our families, and our travels. We couldn't believe we had met up again so far away across the world. Piers joined us for coffee, and after Christian had returned to work, Piers invited me up to see his office.

Well, we swept into Army Headquarters, and with a wave of his pass he shepherded me through security checks, into a lift and out into a very smart deeply carpeted corridor, and along to his office. The view over the city buildings was spectacular, including a good view of the largest wooden building in the southern hemisphere, the Law Faculty, an attractive cream coloured building, elegant in the colonial style. I saw many interesting presents given to Piers by foreign dignitaries, and he chatted to me for a few minutes. He was such a nice, considerate and interested man.

Once out in the street again, I walked some distance in the rain to the Tourist Information Office, hoping to catch a bus tour of the city. It had already gone, so I caught a local bus up to an old church, which I'd hoped to visit. Outside the church sat a small, rather smart tour bus; I had caught it up. Up by the altar stood a bus driver-cum-guide, two American girls and their New Zealand girlfriend. I asked if I could join them and they readily agreed. I had apparently only missed seeing Katherine Mansfield's house, and anyway it was closed.

Wellington is a most unusual capital city. It is built along and into the hills surrounding a harbour and a series of inlet, and was once a thriving port. Thousands of homes, grand and modest, perch several hundred feet above the city centre and around bays and parks. It is all very higgledy-piggledy and most attractive. In the 1855 earthquake, the quayside ended up in the middle of the city, as the ground rose, and there are now shops and offices galore on reclaimed land. So the street named Lambton Quay is in the middle of an office and shopping complex.

The beautiful church, St. Paul's Cathedral, was built by boat builders in 1864 without a single nail - tongue and groove throughout, with a ceiling identical to a bottom of a boat if you inverted it. It had a lovely airy feeling about it, despite the conker-brown polished wood from floor to ceiling. We visited the National Archives and saw the original Treaty of Waitaingi, signed in 1840 between Queen Victoria's representatives and the Maori chiefs. It is kept in a huge sealed room with a bank safe door, along with other historical documents and treaties.

We passed the Beehive, the seat of government, designed by Sir Basil Spence and completed in 1980. I couldn't make up my mind if I liked it - a cross between a round beehive and a spacecraft; it was certainly impressive. From between the shops on Lambton Quay we ascended one of the hills overlooking Wellington, in a shiny red cable car. Stops on the way were named Talavera and Salamanca. We scooted through the rain on to the bus again and wound our way back down the hill via a most beautiful rose garden and a huge Begonia House - part of the Botanical Gardens.

Round bays we drove, marvelling at the smart houses; many quite old, and literally perched some distance above the road and the sea on rocky cliffs. Owning a garage at the bottom, by the roadside, these intrepid residents had their own small, private cable cars, the rail rising vertically and most alarmingly from inside or beside their garages to their front doors. Heaven knows how they carried building materials up there to construct their houses - downwards from helicopters I believe. Until 1962 there was no airport here and the only aerial connection with the outside world was by flying boat to Sydney. New Zealand has more boats of all descriptions per capita than any other country in the world, and this was very apparent in all the coastal cities and villages I had visited.

We drove on up to Mount Victoria and an incredible view over the harbour and the city from an open grassy lookout point. It is not a very beautiful city in itself, but its proximity to forested hills, rocky cliffs, and the fingers, inlets and bays of the sea, give it a fascinating feel. My tour cost just ten dollars, much cheaper than the original one would have been, so I did well. (I clinched the deal in hushed tones with our driver, away from the others - pure jam in his pocket, of course).

Afterwards I met Christian again for hot chocolate, and later an early supper in a splendid pub opposite the Parliament buildings called The Backbencher House with